The Impact of ICT on Literacy Education

D0224563

What is the impact of ICT on literacy learning in English?

This authoritative, landmark text examines the topical and important issue of ICT in literacy learning. Its distinctive focus on providing a systematic review of research in the field gives the reader an essential, comprehensive overview. As governments worldwide continue to invest heavily in ICT provisions in educational institutions, this book addresses the need to gather and synthesise evidence about the impact of ICT on literacy learning.

A vastly experienced team of writers draws upon an international range of research literature across a wide age range, to take a discursive and expansive look at the subject. Within its wide range and scope are chapters on:

- evidence for the effectiveness of ICT on literacy learning;
- the impact of networked ICT on literacy learning;
- the impact of ICT on moving image literacies;
- the impact of ICT on learning English as an additional language;
- ICT's impact on reading literature;
- the methodology behind the systematic reviews of research literature.

This book will be an invaluable and informative read with international resonance for student teachers, teachers, academics and researchers worldwide.

Richard Andrews is Professor of Education at the University of York, UK.

The Impact of ICT on Literacy Education

Edited by
Richard Andrews

RoutledgeFalmer
Taylor & Francis Group

LONDON AND NEW YORK

First published 2004
by RoutledgeFalmer
11 New Fetter Lane, London EC4P 4EE

Simultaneously published in the USA and Canada
by RoutledgeFalmer
29 West 35th Street, New York, NY 10001

RoutledgeFalmer is an imprint of the Taylor & Francis Group

Typeset in Sabon by
HWA Text and Data Management Ltd, Tunbridge Wells
Printed and bound in Great Britain by
TJ International Ltd, Padstow, Cornwall

British Library Cataloguing in Publication Data
A catalogue record for this book is available from the
British Library

Library of Congress Cataloging in Publication Data
The impact of ICT on literacy education / edited by
Richard Andrews.
    p. cm.
Includes bibliographical references and index
1. English language–study and teaching–Computer-assisted
instruction. 2. Language arts–Computer-assisted
instruction. 3. Computers and literacy.
    I. Andrews, Richard (Richard J.), 1953–

    LB1576.7.166 2004
    428'. 0078'5 – dc22   2003016883

ISBN 0–415–28695–6 (hbk)
ISBN 0–415–28696–4 (pbk)

Contents

7 Methodological issues 180
REBECCA REES AND DIANA ELBOURNE

8 Conclusion 202
RICHARD ANDREWS

Figures

Tables

Contributors

Richard Andrews is Professor of Education at the University of York and co-coordinator of the English Review Group. He is author of *The Problem with Poetry*, *Teaching and Learning Argument* and co-author of *Essays in Argument*; and associate editor of the journal *Education, Communication and Information*. He is on the editorial boards of *Informal Logic* and *English in Australia*.

Sue Beverton is Convenor of Primary Initial Teacher Training programmes in the School of Education at the University of Durham. She is also leader of the BA (Ed) course. She is a member of the Editorial Advisory Group for the *Journal of Research in Reading*, a role she has fulfilled for the last eight years. During this period, she also spent two years as Book Reviews Editor for *JRR*. She has completed a case study research project for QCA into the impact of the primary National Literacy Strategy in Secondary Schools. She was also involved with a TTA-funded school-based research project into a Key Stage 3 Writing Across the Curriculum staff development initiative.

Andrew Burn is Lecturer in Media Education at the Institute of Education, London, and conducts research in the Centre for the Study of Children, Youth and Media. He was formerly Assistant Head at Parkside Community College, Cambridge where he had responsibility for the college's specialist Media Arts programme. He is associate editor of *Education, Communication and Information*, and has researched and published in the field of moving image and language education, most recently in collaboration with the British Film Institute and the English and Media Centre, London.

Diana Elbourne has a background in social sciences and in statistics. As such, she currently holds two half-time posts: as Professor of Health Care Evaluation in the Medical Statistics Unit at the London School of Hygiene and Tropical Medicine; and as Professor of Evidence-Informed Policy and Practice at the EPPI-Centre in the Social Science Research Unit at the Institute of Education, London. Her main interests are in randomised controlled trials and systematic reviews. She works in both applied and methodological areas, with a particular interest in methods for including trials of alternative designs (such as cluster randomised and cross-overs) in systematic reviews. She is involved in qualitative studies of the views of participants in trials, and is also active in moves to involve consumers in reviews (having long done so in individual trials). A major challenge of her work in the EPPI-Centre is the inclusion of studies with qualitative and/or non-randomised designs in systematic reviews. She has published widely in peer-reviewed journals in health, social sciences and statistics.

Jenny Leach is Director of the Open University's TeachandLearn Programme (http://www.teachandlearn.net), and coordinator of the Department of International Development (DFID)-funded Digital Education Enhancement Project (http://www.open.ac.uk/deep). Much of her research and many of her publications have focused on the use of ICT to support the professional development of (English) teachers. She is co-editor of *Learners and Pedagogy* (Chapman, 1999), and the international journal *Education, Communication and Information*.

Terry Locke is Senior Lecturer in English Education at Waikato University, Hamilton, New Zealand – a partner institution of the University of York. He is the author of several books on poetry and argumentation in the secondary school curriculum and is also a published poet. He has been instrumental in coordinating the website, Critical English Online, for English teachers worldwide. He is coordinating editor of the online journal *English Teaching: Practice and Critique*. His research interests include the application of ICT in English teaching, curriculum and assessment reform, and issues of teacher professionalism. He is a member of the Australian Association for the Teaching of English (AATE). He was Visiting Research Fellow at the University of York in 2001.

Graham Low is Senior Lecturer in Second Language Education and formerly Director of the English as a Foreign Language Unit in the Language Teaching Centre at the University of York. His research interests include figurative language and he has co-authored with Lynne Cameron the highly acclaimed *Researching and Applying Metaphor* (Cambridge University Press).

Rebecca Rees has a background in research methods for the social sciences. Her role as research officer at the EPPI-Centre includes the production of systematic reviews in health promotion and the development of systematic review methods and quality assurance systems. Research interests include methodological reporting and data quality in non-trial research, methods for involving a range of research users in the production of research and the use of complementary medicine. Recent publications include a systematic review of the barriers and facilitators to physical activity in young people, a population-based survey of complementary therapy use by women with a diagnosis of breast cancer and an overview of the research-base for complementary therapies in cancer care.

Alison Robinson is an experienced administrator who has worked in a variety of environments in the private, voluntary and public sectors. Her focus within the English Review Group is to manage the bibliographic database and provide general administrative support for the Review Team. Immediately prior to joining the Review Group, she was employed by Tees and North-East Yorkshire NHS Trust as administrator to the Ryedale Community Mental Health Team. She previously worked at project, and then divisional level for the children's charity, Barnardo's.

Carole Torgerson has a background in English teaching and research, having taught English in secondary schools in England and Scotland for ten years. She has also undertaken research into the development of children's writing abilities. She is currently Research Fellow in the Department of Educational Studies at the University of York, where she is involved in systematic reviews in English teaching (as co-coordinator of the EPPI English Review Group), and in the Outcomes of Volunteering (with NHS Centre for Reviews and Dissemination and the Centre for Criminal Justice, Economics and Psychology at the University of York). She has a methodological interest in the design and reporting of randomised controlled trials in educational research.

Die Zhu is a research student in the Department of Educational Studies, University of York. Her interests include aspects of effective teaching, especially in the environment of L2 teaching and learning. Her Masters dissertation in Shanghai, China suggested the use of discourse strategies in helping adult EFL learners achieve a higher level of listening comprehension. Her Masters dissertation in York looked at the perceptions of the idea of 'the hidden curriculum' among the teachers and students in a local case study school. Her current research focuses on the levels and types of motivation to learn English as a foreign language among senior middle school students in China and the role the significant others (teachers, parents and peers) play on influencing their motivation. Her involvement with systematic reviews began when she prepared for one of her Masters essays on the impact of information and communications technologies (ICT) on literacy learning in the field of dyslexia (specific learning difficulties), under the co-supervision of Richard Andrews and Carole Torgerson.

Preface

This book is based on a number of reports written as part of the Evidence-Informed Policy and Practice Initiative (EPPI) between 2001 and 2003. The EPPI project is funded by England and Wales' Department for Education and Skills and hosted at the EPPI-Centre (the Evidence for Policy and Practice Information and Coordinating Centre) in the Social Science Research Unit of the Institute of Education, University of London.

The work has been undertaken by the English Review Group, one of the first wave of review groups set up by the EPPI-Centre. The English Review Group is based at the University of York in the Department of Educational Studies; its members also come from the Department of Psychology at York, as well as from the Open University, the University of Durham, the Institute of Education, City of Kingston-upon-Hull Education Services and Parkside Community College in Cambridge; Waikato University in New Zealand; Queensland University of Technology, Brisbane; Harvard Graduate School of Education; and the National Health Service Centre for Reviews and Dissemination, based at the University of York.

I have attempted to bring together the results of a number of reports in this book. Andrews *et al.* (2002) is the report of the first year of systematic reviewing in the field, which resulted in an initial map of the field plus an in-depth review into the impact of *networked* ICT on literacy learning. The in-depth review on networked ICT was updated in 2003 and forms the basis of the chapter on networked ICT included in this book (Andrews *et al.* 2003). The reports of the second year of the project are Burn and Leach (2003), Locke and Andrews (2003), Low and Beverton (2003), Torgerson and Die (2003). These focus on different aspects of the overarching question:

'What is the impact of ICT on literacy learning in English, 5–16?' The focus of our research has been on the compulsory school years, and does not necessarily apply to pre-school or adult learners.

I hope this book (and the full technical reports on which it is built, which are available on the Research Evidence in Education Library: http://eppi.ioe.ac.uk/reel) will provide clarification and impetus for further research at the interface of ICT and literacy education.

Richard Andrews
York, 2003

Acknowledgements

The EPPI English Review Group is part of the initiative on evidence-informed policy and practice at the EPPI-Centre, Social Science Research Unit, Institute of Education, University of London, funded by England and Wales' Department for Education and Skills (DfES). Particular thanks go to Diana Elbourne, Jo Garcia, David Gough, Rebecca Rees, Katy Sutcliffe and all members of the EPPI-Centre team.

The Review Group acknowledges financial support from the DfES via the EPPI-Centre and via core institutional research funding from the Higher Education Funding Council for England; from the University of York's Innovation and Research Pump-priming Fund and from the Department of Educational Studies at the university. It is working within a University of York context where the National Health Service Centre for Reviews and Dissemination, the Department of Health Sciences, the Social Policy Research Unit and the Centre for Criminal Justice, Economics and Psychology are major players in evidence-informed research.

Thanks are also due to Sir John Daniel at UNESCO; Julie Glanville at the NHS Centre for Reviews and Dissemination at The University of York; Ann Oakley at the Social Science Research Unit for her advice and guidance; and Judy Sebba, who in her capacity as Senior Research Adviser at the Department for Education and Skills, was a major influence and support on the project. We would also like to thank the anonymous reviewers who have made many contributions during the course of the reviews and who, though they remain nameless, have helped to ensure the quality and rigour of the research. Thanks are also due to Scott Windeatt, of The University of Newcastle, for helpful discussions on several background issues.

The Review Group's steering committee deserves particular thanks: Judith Bennett, James Durran, Peter Hatcher, Nick McGuinn, Gloria Reid, Nancy Rowland, Maggie Snowling.

Alison Robinson's administrative and information management expertise has been instrumental in enabling the review team – the contributors to this book – to complete the work on time.

Finally, on behalf of the review team, I would like to thank all those researchers whose work we have reviewed over the past two or three years. If your work was not included in our reviews, there is no implication that it was not quality work in its own right. We have set out to ask an overall question and a number of more specific sub-questions, and sought out research that helps us answer those questions. We would like to hear from anyone with an interest in the field and intend to update the reviews in due course.

Abbreviations

BECTa	British Educational Communications and Technology Agency
BEI	British Education Index
BFI	British Film Institute
BPRS	Best Practice Research Scholarships (England and Wales)
CAI/CAL	computer-assisted instruction/computer-assisted learning
CALL	computer-assisted language learning
CD-ROM	compact disc, read-only memory
CPD	continuing professional development
CT	controlled trial
DfES	Department for Education and Skills (previously DfEE Department for Education and Employment) (England and Wales)
EAL	English as an Additional Language
EFL	English as a Foreign Language
EPPI	Evidence-Informed Policy and Practice Initiative
EPPI-Centre	Evidence for Policy and Practice Information and Coordinating Centre
ERIC	Educational Resources Information Center
ESL	English as a Second Language
ESOL	English for Speakers of Other Languages
GCSE	General Certificate of Secondary Education (England and Wales)
HDT	hypertext discussion tool
ICT	information and communication technologies
ITT	initial teacher training
L1	first/mother language
L2	second/later acquired language

NHS CRD	National Health Service Centre for Reviews and Dissemination (UK)
OECD	Organization for Economic Cooperation and Development
OFSTED	Office for Standards in Education (UK)
PC	personal computer
PPI	paper and pencil instruction
QCA	Qualifications and Curriculum Authority (England and Wales)
RCT	randomised controlled trial
REEL	Research Evidence in Education Library
SEN	special educational needs
SIGLE	System for Information on Grey Literature in Europe
SSCI	Social Science Citation Index
TESOL	teaching English to speakers of other languages
TTA	Teacher Training Agency (England and Wales)
VCE	Victoria Certificate of Education (Australia)

Chapter 1

Introduction

Richard Andrews, Alison Robinson and Carole Torgerson

The impact of ICT on literacy learning in English is a topical and important issue. There is a need for an authoritative review of research in this field, not least because governments worldwide are investing heavily in the provision of hardware and software to educational institutions as well as in the training of teachers and students of all ages in the application of ICT in literacy learning. To date there has been no such review. We need to gather and synthesize evidence about the impact of ICT on literacy learning.

Between March 2001 and June 2003, the English Review Group, based at the University of York, carried out a two-part systematic review in attempting to answer the overall question 'What is the impact of ICT on literacy learning in English, 5–16?' The first year consisted of the development of a map of the field, followed by an in-depth review on the impact of *networked* ICT (i.e. email and the Internet).[1] The second year looked at a number of aspects of the impact of ICT on literacy learning: effectiveness (by identifying and synthesizing all the randomized experimental research); moving image; literature-related literacies; and software packages for teaching language and/or literature in English as a first and/or additional language. These separate in-depth reviews form the basis of the chapters in this book, with the addition of a chapter on the methodology used to undertake the systematic review.

The overall aim of the project has been to determine the impact of ICT on literacy learning for 5–16-year-olds.

Definitional and conceptual issues

Literacy can be defined narrowly, as the ability to understand and create written language. It is, however, frequently defined in two broader senses, and both are included in the present study. First, the scope can be expanded so that written language becomes written language and graphical or pictorial representation. Second, the skill can be treated as social, rather than psychological; in this view, literacy is the ability to operate a series of social or cultural representations. We have chosen 'literacy' for a number of reasons: first, to delimit the field of enquiry to reading and writing; second, to distinguish the learning of literacy from the subject English as taught in the National Curriculum for England and as a school subject in other countries; third, because as a term (especially in its pluralistic sense of 'literacies') it is both narrowly definable and open to wider interpretation; and fourth, because it allows us to review research that takes place outside formal education, e.g. in homes and other communities in which young people operate. In the studies that follow, we focus on reading and writing (in the broadest senses of those terms). Such delimiting of the focus of our project does not mean that the results will not be relevant to the teaching of literacy in other countries; nor that we will limit ourselves to research undertaken in England. On the contrary, our net is spread wide.

ICT stands for 'information and communication technologies'. In the present project, we limited ourselves to stand-alone and networked technologies with a multimodal interface, i.e. networked and stand-alone computers, mobile phones with the capacity for a range of types of communication, and other technologies which allow multimodal and interactive communication.

By 'English' we mean, for the purposes of this study, English as a first or second (or additional) language learnt as a medium of instruction in school or spoken and written at home (and, for example, encountered on the Internet) – not as a 'foreign' language in, for example, a modern foreign languages department. In terms of commonly used abbreviations, we include ESL and EAL, but exclude EFL.

There remains controversy about the term 'impact'. We have chosen the term for the present project in order to stand between the precision of the term 'effect' (which would require randomized controlled trials and/or controlled trials to determine such outcomes) and the broad (and vague) generality of the term 'influence'. A recent publication from the Qualifications and Curriculum Authority (Coles 2002) explores the meaning of the term 'impact' by defining a number of receivers of impact: individuals, groups, institutions and curricula or regulations/procedures. Because our focus is on literacy *learning*, we have concentrated on the impact on individuals and groups of young people rather than on institutions or curricula.

One final but important conceptual issue has emerged during the course of the research. By assuming the impact of *x* on *y* (of *ICT* on *literacy learning*) we have assumed a causal one-way connection and have thus operated within a broad scientific paradigm. Although such an approach has many virtues and has shed light on such a connection, we acknowledge that the broader relationship between ICT and literacy learning is probably symbiotic. A symbiotic relationship would have implications for the design of research studies that attempted to explore further the connection between ICT and literacy.

Impact or symbiosis?

The question of whether to approach the relationship between ICT and literacy from a causal, scientific perspective or via an assumption of the symbiotic relationship between the two has many implications. To date, we have attempted to investigate the relationship within a causal paradigm. We have taken this approach because it is a question – 'What is the impact of ICT on literacy learning?' – that teachers and policy-makers have asked us to try to answer. We have also been interested in the answer ourselves.

Part of the problem with such a question is that, as some of the chapters acknowledge, literacy and ICT are moving targets. Put scientifically, it is hard to control the variables that are at play in each area. It is not only the case that the targets have moved during the course of our project; they have been moving for over ten years – and, indeed, for thousands of years. Technology has an intimate relationship with literacy: the ability to make marks on rock; the invention of the stylus and of parchment; the printing revolution; the more recent ICT revolution. All these stages in the development of what it means to be literate (and, by implication, illiterate) are tied up with the means by which literacy is expressed.

The relationship between ICT and literacy is therefore two-way: new technologies are conceived by new literacies as much as the other way round. It is possible to focus on the impact of ICT on literacy learning, as we have done, but the larger picture must be acknowledged. As each of these agents affects, impacts and influences the other, so they both change. At the very least, what we have tried to do in the current project is to see how clear an answer we can get to the question, 'What is the impact of ICT on literacy learning?' In answering that question, we hope to have contributed to the wider debate.

For a further discussion of the problem, see Andrews (2003a, 2003b).

Policy and practice background

There has been much literature on the topic that is exciting and speculative. Much of this literature emerged in the early 1990s as the Internet began to become more widely used, especially in schools. The UK government, for instance, has invested a large amount of money over a number of years in the provision of computers to schools. Equally, many (not all) families use computers at home and young people are increasingly using them to research, word-process, compose and present homework – and for a number of other functions. Questions remain, however, on what impact ICT has on schooling and in particular on literacy learning.

In addition, many of the same complementary projects, reports and publications still apply. For example, the New Opportunities Fund ICT training for teachers programme, which has been training all primary and secondary teachers in schools in the UK since 1999, was completed in the summer of 2003. The ImpaCT2 project, which concentrated on the impact of ICT at Key Stages 2 and 3 in the core subjects of English, Maths and Science, published its final report in 2002 (BECTa/DfES 2002) and is discussed in the following section. Various other initiatives, at international (OECD), national, regional and local levels, continue to take place.

Ofsted, the UK's Office for Standards in Education (2001, 2002) has published reviews on the impact of government initiatives on standards and on literacy. It concludes (2001: 2) that there is 'emerging evidence of a link between high standards across the curriculum and good ICT provision' but that the 'contribution of ICT to the raising of standards in individual subjects remains variable' – a finding confirmed in the ImpaCT2 study. Specifically, the 2001 report on the impact of ICT in schools notes that:

> in English, for example, CD-ROMs of Internet searches are sometimes used well to support the development of reading skills. Pupils make good progress where they have the skills to

select relevant information, frame research questions...take concise notes and recast information in their own words.

(Ofsted 2001: 9)

Furthermore,

Pupils' standard of written composition is raised where they use wordprocessing to help them draft, review and edit imaginatively, and exploit the provisional status of the word-processed text to full effect.

(Ibid.)

The 2002 (Ofsted 2002) review of the impact of the National Literacy Strategy on practice and attainment notes the following with regard to ICT:

- the use of ICT in the teaching of literacy continues to improve steadily, but remains limited in around one in four schools
- there is still a big gap 'between the schools where ICT is used effectively and those where its contribution to pupils' learning is very limited' (p.23)
- where ICT work is related to literacy, it is generally concerned with research and non-chronological report-writing
- the use of computers for literacy by pupils in classrooms is mostly confined to individual work on phonics and spelling programs, and for composing and editing text on the computer. The copying of handwritten text onto a computer, which was common in the early days of the National Literacy Strategy, is now rare.

A summary paper on developing effective practice with ICT has been published by BECTa (BECTa nd).

In New Zealand, one of the most telling recent studies has been by Parr (2002). The study, entitled *A Review of the Literature on Computer-Assisted Learning, particularly Integrated Learning Systems, and Outcomes with Respect to Literacy and Numeracy*, concludes that 'the effectiveness of computer-assisted learning has not been conclusively demonstrated' (p.2). Whereas the best results appear to be in improvements in basic mathematics skills, those for reading are negligible. The Integrated Learning System approach with its 'current form of neo-behaviourist, mastery learning' tends to support the gaining of basic procedural skills but does not assist in the acquisition of higher level literacy skills like composition, comprehension and textual analysis. There is a gap between the mastery of basic skills and the transformation and application of that knowledge into language in use. The pedagogical model underpinning much of this 'independent' literacy learning via computer is therefore primitive.

The more important questions in the New Zealand context are those framed by Locke (2003):

- How can we utilize ICT to achieve our current teaching/learning objectives?
- If the rapidly changing nature of ICT is changing the nature of literacy, how are these changes reflected in our learning objectives, our pedagogy and our envisionments of the future of classroom programmes?

These are the questions that are more likely to drive new practice, and which policy-makers would do well to consider.

Research background

The in-depth study from the first year of the current project (Andrews *et al.* 2002) – a mapping exercise on the impact of ICT on literacy learning and an in-depth review of the impact of *networked* ICT on literacy for 5–16-year-olds – identified 188 papers published since 1990 that examined the impact of ICT. Most of these originated from the USA, though a significant minority arose from research in the UK, Canada, Australia and New Zealand. Of the total, 67 per cent were set in primary/elementary schools (especially in the 7–11 age range), with about 44 per cent set in secondary/high schools (some studies were conducted in both types of setting). About two-thirds of the studies assumed a psychological representation of literacy: that is, they assumed that literacy development was an individual matter concerned with writing and reading processes. One-third adopted a more sociological conception of the practice: that is, one that assumes that literacy development is a matter of the academic and social communities in which you learn. Of the 188 studies, 57 per cent were focused on writing, graphical or pictorial production, whereas 46 per cent had an interest in reading.

As far as the in-depth study on *networked* ICT goes, results were inconclusive. Many of the studies focused on the primary/elementary school sector, with at least four concentrating on fourth/fifth graders (i.e. 9–10-year-olds). Three of the studies looked at out-of-school activities, and only two (and both indirectly) turned their attention to the impact of ICT on literacy at secondary or high school level. The principal areas of interest for the studies were reading and writing, but those twin aspects of literacy were often narrowly conceived, so that they looked at the impact of new technologies on old practices rather than at the symbiosis between new technologies and new forms of literacy. Four of the studies looked at word-processing; two at new conceptions of literacy; and one each on speaking and listening, and on special educational needs.

Few of the studies in that particular in-depth review provided a firm basis for accepting their findings. Of the remainder, two provided theoretical and practical insights into widening conceptions of literacy; five suggested increased motivation and/or confidence in pupils as a result of ICT use with regard to literacy development; and one saw empowerment and ownership as an important factor to bear in mind in an increasingly diverse and divided digital world. In general, these studies assumed that a positive impact was made on literacy development by networked ICT, and explored *how* that impact was made; in most of the studies, the conception of literacy was narrow, based on pre-digital notions of reading and writing. The results were therefore suggestive rather than conclusive.

Much of the research on the impact of ICT on literacy in the 1990s was in the form of evaluations of curricular or governmental initiatives. A study by McFarlane *et al.* (1995), though focused on science teaching, noted better data handling and transfer, and increased ability to read, interpret and sketch line graphs with ICT. Lewin *et al.* (2000) identified gains in understanding and analytical skills, including improvements in reading comprehension. They also observed the development of writing skills (including spelling, grammar, punctuation, editing and re-drafting), particularly in fluency, originality and elaboration. Harrison *et al.* (1998) in an evaluation of the use of multimedia portable PCs by teachers, concluded that gains for teachers in ICT literacy skills, as well as increased confidence and enthusiasm, were a result of the use of ICT. These and other benefits of the use of ICT are summarised in BECTa (2003).

The ImpaCT2 project (BECTa/DfES 2002: 3) was carried out

between 1999 and 2002, involving sixty schools in England. Its aim was to contribute to the evaluation of the ICT in Schools programme for the training of all teachers in the UK in the skills needed for the application of ICT in their teaching of 7–16-year-old children and young people. The project was designed to 'identify the impact of networked technologies on the school and out of school environment' and to 'find out the degree to which these networked technologies affect the educational attainments of pupils at Key Stages 2, 3 and 4 [i.e. ages 7–16]'. There are general findings on the relationship between ICT use and attainment – for example in every case except one, the study found evidence of a positive relationship. As far as the interests of the current report are concerned, the following findings pertained to attainment in English and therefore to literacy development:

- a statistically significant positive association between ICT and National Tests for English was found at Key Stage 2 (7–11-year-olds)
- the acceleration in progress in English at this stage was 16 per cent over two years' education (measured in terms of progress against the National Curriculum 'levels' of attainment), compared with conventional learning
- the general level of ICT use in Key Stage 2 English was the highest reported for any subject at any key stage in 2001: 61 per cent of the pupils reported using ICT in their English lessons at least some weeks (with 41 per cent reporting using ICT at home some weeks)
- positive associations were not found in English at Key Stage 3 (11–14) or Key Stage 4 (14–16), though there was positive association in Science
- usage at Key Stage 4 in English was 29 per cent, with over 50 per cent reporting use at home some weeks.

Specifically, teachers in schools where pupils used ICT in English and achieved higher mean gain scores identified the following factors in relation to the use of ICT in English at Key Stage 2: increased motivation and greater involvement in learning; higher quality outcomes encouraging greater commitment to writing tasks; relevant software making the learning of key skills fun; increased time for reflection; use of ICT to support research skills; and use of ICT to develop materials incorporating text and graphics (BECTa/DfES 2002: 16).

The ImpaCT2 report, however, is at pains to point out the following:

- the proportion of lessons involving ICT was generally low over the period 1999–2002, though likely to rise as more teachers gained more confidence in its use
- there was no consistent relationship between the average amount of ICT use reported for any subject at any key stage and its apparent effectiveness in raising standards. *It therefore seems likely that the type of use is all important*
- the schools used in the study do not necessarily form a representative sample of schools in England (Ibid.: 4).

In another BECTa publication (BECTa 2001: 20), an agenda for further research on the general impact of ICT on practice in education was set out, involving more managed longitudinal studies, adding value to secondary sources, improved data analysis, the use of focus groups and online forums, and the setting up of a number of planned interventions.

A map of the field

As Rees and Elbourne explain in their chapter in this book, the mapping stage of a systematic review is an important step in surveying the research literature in a field before any in-depth reviews can be undertaken. A map consists of a record of the number of studies found in relation to a particular research question. These studies are identified by the development of a protocol or plan, a keywording strategy that derives from the research question, and a search strategy that usually includes electronic searches and hand searches of specified journals. The map is basically quantitative, but it also allows the researchers to take stock of the field and to decide where it is desirable and feasible to take the next step: that of the in-depth review. A number of in-depth reviews can derive from a map.

Table 1.1 illustrates the process of identifying, obtaining and describing reports for the two-year systematic review. Unless otherwise stated, each report contains only one study.

A revised version of the mapping study retrieval process reported in Andrews *et al.* (2002) is shown in column one. The revisions were the result of further de-duplication of the database (four papers deleted), annotation of reports received outside of the review's original timeframe (n = 8), and re-keywording of included reports

Table 1.1 The process of retrieval of the reports in the mapping study

	Andrews et al., 2002 (revised)	Review update	Current review
Total number of 'hits'	1,867	452	2,319
Met mapping study inclusion criteria on the basis of the title or abstract	358	70	428
Not received or unavailable	22	12	34
Full reports available	336	58	394
Full reports that did not meet mapping study inclusion criteria	159	23	182
Met mapping study inclusion criteria and keyworded	177	35	212

in accordance with EPPI's revised guidelines (EPPI-Centre 2002),[2] which led to further exclusions (n = 8). In addition, five papers originally excluded at the second stage were included in the current review following re-keywording. Column two shows the mapping study retrieval process for those additional reports identified by an update of the electronic and hand searches. The final column merges the original mapping study retrieval process with the update to show the process of retrieval of the reports in the mapping study for the current review.

A total of 2,319 potentially relevant reports were identified for the current project. Just over 81 per cent (1,891) of these 2,319 reports were excluded by screening titles and/or abstracts and 428 were sent for. Fewer than 8 per cent of these (34) were not received within the timeframe of the review or were unavailable. A reading of the full paper resulted in the exclusion of a further 182 studies, leaving a total of 212 that met the criteria for inclusion in the mapping study. The columns in Table 1.1 refer to the reports identified in the 2002 review, the new reports identified in the updating process, and the total number of reports by 2003, respectively.

Table 1.2 presents the origin, by database or other method of retrieval, of all the 212 reports included in the mapping study. It also shows the process of retrieval for each database.

The great majority of the reports found to meet the mapping study's inclusion criteria (185: 87 per cent) were found with the database searches. Hand searching found an additional 22 (10 per

Table 1.2 Origin of reports in the mapping study

	Found	Included
PsycINFO	849	97
ERIC	880	62
BEI	295	20
SSCI	59	2
Cochrane	26	0
SIGLE	48	2
C2–SPECTR	49	0
DisAbs	56	2
Hand search	43	22
Citation	8	4
Website	3	0
Contact	3	1
TOTAL	2,319	212

Note: Reports could originally have more than one origin but a hierarchy of databases and other sources was created resulting in each category being made mutually exclusive.

cent). The checking of citations (systematic review bibliographies and citations in the text of full reports) and reviewers' searches of their own shelves identified a further 4 and 1 relevant reports respectively. No reports were identified solely through Cochrane, C2–SPECTR or webpage searches.

The remaining tables in this section present analyses of the included and keyworded studies contained in the 212 reports.

Table 1.3 shows the number of studies according to the country in which they were conducted. Most (63 per cent) were conducted in the US. A total of 39 (18 per cent) were from the UK. In 3 cases (2 per cent) it was not possible to determine where a study had taken place. These figures may reflect bias within the bibliographic sources searched towards reports published within North America, Australasia and the UK.

Table 1.4 describes the educational setting for the studies. A study could be conducted in more than one setting. Primary education was the most frequently studied (66 per cent of reports look at this kind of setting, compared with 34 per cent that look at secondary settings). A total of 32 studies were conducted in both primary and secondary settings. Thirty studies were conducted in other settings, including independent schools, special schools and the home.

Table 1.5 presents the number of studies that conceptualised literacy in psychological and/or social/cultural/critical terms and the number that focused on reading and/or writing. Of the studies identified, about two-thirds (62 per cent) assume a psychological

Table 1.3 Study country

	Number
USA	134
UK	39
Australia	17
Canada	15
New Zealand	2
Sweden	1
Netherlands	1
Not stated	3

Note: All studies were conducted in one country only.

Table 1.4 Educational setting

	Number
Primary education	140
Secondary education	74
Other	30

Note: A single study could be conducted in more than one type of educational setting.

Table 1.5 Principal aspect(s) of literacy

	Number
Conceptualisation of literacy	
Psychological aspects or representations	131
Social representations and/or cultural/critical representations	73
Unclear	21
Reading/writing	
Writing print and graphical or pictorial representation	131
Reading print and graphical or pictorial representation	106
Unclear	5

representation of literacy. A third (34 per cent) adopt a more sociological conception of the practice. Two-thirds (62 per cent) focus on writing, graphical or pictorial production, whereas half (50 per cent) have an interest in reading. Studies could have more than one focus with respect to both of these dimensions of literacy. For both dimensions there was a number of studies where reviewers were unable to categorise the aspect of literacy under study.

Table 1.6 shows the overall distribution of reports according to study type. Most (179) of the 212 reports meeting the inclusion criteria for the mapping study evaluated outcomes; 169 of these were researcher-manipulated and 10 were naturally occurring. Of the 169 researcher-manipulated evaluations, 45 were RCTs, 84 were trials and 41 were other types of evaluation. One report contained both an RCT and a trial.

The type of ICT focused on by the identified studies is illustrated by Table 1.7. This shows the relative popularity of 'stand-alone' ICT as a topic of study in comparison with networked ICT systems. The use of email was studied more frequently than internet use.

Table 1.8 illustrates the process of identification by keyword of reports for inclusion in the four specific in-depth reviews. Each report was subject to the inclusion/exclusion criteria of the specific in-depth review for which they were identified. This process is described in the individual review reports.

The significance of the mapping stage is that it provides an overall picture of the field of research literature in the particular area of

Table 1.6 Study type

	Number
Evaluation: researcher-manipulated	169
RCT	45
Trial	84
Other	41
Evaluation: naturally occurring	10
Exploration of relationships	29
Description	3
Review	6
Systematic review	5
Other review	1

Note: Studies could be defined as more than one type.

Table 1.7 Type of ICT

	Number
Computer – stand alone (software)	191
Computer – networked (email and internet)	24
Computer – networked (email)	20
Computer – networked (internet)	11

Note: Studies could focus on more than one aspect of ICT.

Table 1.8 Identification of reports for inclusion in the specific in-depth reviews

Keyword	Total reports
RCT	45
Moving image	12
Literature	12
ESL/EAL	10

Note: Reports could be included in more than one in-depth review.

enquiry. The chapters that follow investigate in more depth five aspects of the impact of ICT on literacy education; and the methodology used to review the research.

Carole Torgerson and Die Zhu's chapter focuses on the *effectiveness* of ICT on literacy learning in English. In order to review the effects, it has looked exclusively at randomized controlled trials in the field, dealing with ICT as an *intervention* in literacy teaching and learning. The assumption behind this approach is that all other factors or variables are controlled or assumed to be stable so that the effect of an intervention into this state of affairs can be measured. Even if the state of affairs is not stable, the factor of change can be taken into account as the attempt to measure the effect of the intervention is measured. It is certainly true that the computer has been introduced into primary/elementary and secondary/high school literacy classrooms as an intervention, though this has been a gradual and fitful process. The review which is the basis of Torgerson and Die's chapter takes 1990 as its starting point, as is the case with all the reviews that underpin this book. While this is an arbitrary date in many ways, it did mark a watershed between initial experiments with computers in classrooms in the 1980s, and a more widespread use of ICT (including the Internet) in the 1990s and the first years of the twenty-first century. It should be noted that Torgerson and Die's chapter is different from the others in this book in that it concentrates on research in one particular study type – the RCT – whereas the other chapters and the English Review Group's approach as a whole is to review a range of study types. The authors' conclusion, after reviewing a number of RCTs in the field, is that the evidence so far is equivocal and that a large-scale study is required to gauge the effectiveness or otherwise of ICT in literacy learning.

Chapter 3 is an account of the revised and updated review by the whole team of research on the impact of *networked* ICT on literacy learning.

The next chapter concentrates on the impact, rather than the effectiveness, of ICT on literacy learning for learners for whom English is a second or additional language. Graham Low and Sue Beverton find that the research in this area in the last fifteen years or so can only be rated as having 'medium' weight of evidence, but they do look at the impact on the educational system and on learners, with respect to gender, ethnicity, student attitude and staff attitude or behaviour. Results show that collaborative work is an unanticipated benefit of the advent of computers in ESL/EAL classrooms, but that overall, there is as yet insufficient research of high quality to answer questions about the impact of ICT on ESL/EAL learning. Implications for policy, practice and further research are drawn out: two implications for practice are that teachers and learners seem to use ICT 'more readily for basic work, such as word-level operations and proof-reading' rather than for higher level text processing; and that teachers' roles are changing in the presence of computers in the language classroom.

The principal focus of Terry Locke's and Richard Andrews' chapter is on literature, or, as we have specified it, literature-based literacies. We have made that shift not just to accommodate the review within the framework of the research that underpins this book, but because the category of 'literature' itself is problematic. Given the three moving targets of ICT, literacy and literature, we have wanted to explore some of the conceptual issues before reviewing existing research in the field (such discussion begs the question about another key concept in the research – learning – which needs to be addressed but which has not been the subject of in-depth investigation in the reviews to date). Although, like Low and Beverton, we found that the quality of the research in the field overall was not high, there are tentative conclusions to be drawn from a review of the available research. One of these is that technologised practices are mediated by discourse; and another, related, finding is that 'impact' is mediated more by the ways the teachers themselves construct 'literature' than by the technology *per se*. The clear implication is that it is teachers who are at the heart of the question about the impact of ICT on literature-based literacy learning, and teachers who need investment rather than ICT infrastructure, hardware or software.

Andrew Burn and Jenny Leach look at another of the literacies – in the broader sense of literacy as a set of social semiotic practices. In their particular case, it is the moving image that is the focus of their attention. The chapter contains much necessary definitional discussion, part of it with regard to the curricular position of moving image work and its political significance in twenty-first century conceptions of what it means to be literate. Most of the studies reviewed are small-scale, but the range of studies in this field was found to contain some high quality research combining quantitative findings with observation and interview data, as well as work with conceptual and theoretical significance. One of the key findings of the research review is that there has been, to date, insufficient emphasis on making (or, to use a term borrowed from the narrower conception of literacy, on 'writing') in moving image work; most of the conceptions and practice in moving image work have been and still are based on a critical 'reading' of the medium.

It is important, in a book like this, to give a full account of the methodology employed in arriving at our conclusions. The full technical in-depth reviews that underpin each chapter are available on the Research Evidence in Education Library (see below) and a chapter on methodological issues is included in this book. Rebecca Rees and Diana Elbourne set out clearly the parameters within which the methods developed by the Evidence for Policy and Practice Information and Coordinating Centre have been produced (and continue to be developed). One consistent criticism of systematic review methodology in educational research is that education has adopted an inappropriate methodology from another field (medical and health education). Rees and Elbourne show how the methodology has been adapted to deal with a range of research study types. One of the challenging and engaging aspects of the systematic review work in education has been the new methods that have been required to account for a wide range of quantitative and qualitative studies. In particular, synthesis of research findings is an area for continued work.

The book ends with a summary and conclusion, with implications explored for future research, policy and practice. The appendices contain information of a supportive or technical nature.

Anyone wishing to see the full in-depth reviews, which include detailed accounts of the methodology used in each review as well as other information as to how the results and conclusions were drawn in each case, is referred to Andrews *et al.* (2002, 2003), Burn and Leach (2003), Locke and Andrews (2003), Low and Beverton (2003), Torgerson and Die (2003). These reviews are available online at http://eppi.ioe.ac.uk/reel, the address of the Research Evidence in Education Library.

Notes

1 The networked ICT review, which was originally undertaken in 2002, was updated in 2003. The updated version forms the basis of the chapter in the present book.
2 See the Rees and Elbourne chapter.

The 212 studies included in the research project

Abbott, C. (2001) 'Some young male web site owners: the technological aesthete, the community builder and the professional activist', *Education, Communication and Information*, 1: 197–212.

Adam, N. and Wild, M. (1997) 'Applying CD-ROM interactive storybooks to learning to read', *Journal of Computer Assisted Learning*, 13: 119–32.

Allen, G. and Thompson, A. (1995) 'Analysis of the effect of networking on computer-assisted collaborative writing in a fifth grade classroom', *Journal of Educational Computing Research*, 12: 65–75.

Allred, R.A. (1993) 'Integrating proven spelling content and methods with emerging literacy programs', *Reading Psychology*, 14: 15–31.

Angeli, C. and Cunningham, D.J. (1998) 'Bubble dialogue: tools for supporting literacy and mind', in C.J. Bonk and K.S. King (eds) *Electronic Collaborators: Learner Centered Technologies for Literacy, Apprenticeship, and Discourse*, Mahwah, NJ: Lawrence Erlbaum Associates Inc.

Anon. (1999) *Idaho Statewide Implementation of Reading Renaissance: Summary of First Year's Results Monograph*, Wisconsin: The Institute for Academic Excellence Inc.

Bahr, C.M., Nelson, N.W. and Van Meter, A.M. (1996) 'The effects of text-based and graphics-based software tools on planning and organizing of stories', *Journal of Learning Disabilities*, 29: 355–70.

Baker, E.A. (2001) 'The nature of literacy in a technology-rich, fourth-grade classroom', *Reading Research and Instruction*, 40: 159–84.

Bangert Drowns, R.L. (1993) 'The word processor as an instructional tool: a meta-analysis of word processing in writing instruction', *Review of Educational Research*, 63: 69–93.

Barker, T.A. (1994) *An Evaluation of Computer-assisted Instruction in Phonological Awareness with Below Average Readers*, Florida: Florida State University.

Barrera, M.T., III, Rule, A.C. and Diemart, A. (2001) 'The effect of writing with computers versus handwriting on the writing achievement of first-graders', *Information Technology in Childhood Education Annual*, 13: 215–28.

Barron, R.W., Golden, J.O., Seldon, D.M., Tait, C. ., Marmurek, H.H.C. and Haines, L.P. (1992) 'Teaching prereading skills with a talking computer: letter-sound knowledge and print feedback facilitate non-readers' phonological awareness training', *Reading and Writing: An Interdisciplinary Journal*, 4: 179–204.

Bentivolio, K. (2001) *Improving a Student's Reading Comprehension Skills by Teaching Computer Aided Design*, Notre Dame Preparatory, Michigan, USA.

Berninger, V., Abbott, R., Rogan, L., Reed, E., Abbott, S., Brooks, A., Vaughan, K. and Graham, S. (1998) 'Teaching spelling to children with specific learning disabilities: the mind's ear and eye beat the computer or pencil', *Learning Disability Quarterly*, 21: 106–22.

Bigum, C., Durrant, C., Green, B., Honan, E., Lankshear, C., Morgan, W., Murray, J., Snyder, I. and Wild, M. (1997) *Digital Rhetorics: Literacies and Technologies in Education – Current Practices and Future Directions* (Executive Summary and Volumes 1, 2 and 3), Canberra: Department of Employment, Education, Training and Youth Affairs.

Blasewitz, M.R. and Taylor, R.T. (1999) 'Attacking literacy with technology in an urban setting', *Middle School Journal*, 30: 33–9.

Blok, H. (2001) 'Using computers to learn words in the elementary grades: an evaluation framework and a review of effect studies', *Computer Assisted Language Learning*, 14: 99–128.

Bonk, C.J. and Reynolds, T.H. (1992) 'Early adolescent composing within a generative-evaluative computerized prompting framework', *Computers in Human Behavior*, 8: 39–62.

Boone, R. and Higgins, K. (1993) 'Hypermedia basal readers: three years of school-based research', *Journal of Special Education Technology*, 12: 86–106.

Boone, R., Higgins, K., Notari, A. and Stump, C.S. (1996) 'Hypermedia pre-reading lessons: learner-centered software for kindergarten', *Journal of Computing in Childhood Education*, 7: 39–70.

Borgh, K. and Dickson, W.P. (1992) 'The effects on children's writing of adding speech synthesis to a word processor', *Journal of Research in Computing in Education*, 24: 533–44.

Braden, J. P., Shaw, S. R. and Grecko, L. (1991) 'An evaluation of a computer-assisted instructional program for elementary hearing-impaired students', *Volta Review*, 93: 247–52.

Breese, C., Jackson, A. and Prince, T. (1995) 'Promise in impermanence: children writing with unlimited access to word processors', *Early Child Development and Care*, 118: 67–91.

Brush, T.A., Armstrong, J., Barbrow, D. and Ulintz, L. (1999) 'Design and delivery of integrated learning systems: their impact on student achievement and attitudes', *Journal of Educational Computing Research*, 21: 475–86.

Burn, A. (2000) 'Repackaging the slasher movie: digital unwriting of film in the classroom', *English in Australia*, 127–8: 24–34.

Burn, A., Brindley, S., Durran, J., Kelsall, C. and Sweetlove, J. (2001) ' "The rush of images": a research report into digital editing and the moving image', *English in Education*, 35: 34–47.

Burn, A. and Parker, D. (2001) 'Making your mark: digital inscription, animation, and a new visual semiotic', *Education, Communication and Information*, 1: 155–79.

Burn, A. and Reed, K. (1999) 'Digi-teens: media literacies and digital technologies in the secondary classroom', *English in Education*, 33:5–20.

Butzin, S. M. (2001) 'Using instructional technology in transformed learning environments: an evaluation of Project CHILD', *Journal of Research on Technology in Education*, 33: 367–73.

Calvert, S.L., Watson, J.A., Brinkley, V. and Penny, J. (1990) 'Computer presentational features for poor readers' recall of information', *Journal of Educational Computing Research*, 6: 287–98.

Cardinale, P. and Fish, J.M. (1994) 'Treating children's writing apprehension with word processing', *Journal of Personality and Clinical Studies*, 10: 1–15.

Carlson, P.A. and Miller, T. (1996) *Beyond Word Processing: Using an Interactive Learning Environment to Teach Writing*, Texas: Brooks Airforce Base.

Casey, J.M. (2001) *A Path to Literacy: Empowering Students in Your Classroom*, California State University, California, USA.

Cato, V., English, F. and Trushell, J. (1994) 'Reading screens: mapping the labyrinth', in D. Wray (ed.) *Literacy and Computers: Insights from Research*, Royston: United Kingdom Reading Association.

Chambers, B., Abrami, P.C., McWhaw, K. and Therrien, M.C. (2001) 'Developing a computer-assisted tutoring program to help children at risk to learn to read', *Educational Research and Evaluation*, 7: 223–39.

Chambless, J.R. and Chambless, M.S. (1994) 'The impact of instructional technology on reading/writing skills of second grade students', *Reading Improvement*, 31: 151–5.

Chang, L.L. and Osguthorpe, R.T. (1990) 'The effects of computerized picture-word processing on kindergarteners' language development', *Journal of Research in Childhood Education*, 5: 73–84.

Chu, M.-L.L. (1995) 'Reader response to interactive computer books: examining literary responses in a non-traditional reading setting', *Reading Research and Instruction*, 34: 352–66.

Clouse, R.W. (1992) 'Teaching and learning with computers: a classroom analysis', *Journal of Educational Technology Systems*, 20: 281–302.

Collins, J. (1993) 'Beyond the word processor: computer-mediated communication with pupils and teachers', *Computer Education*, 73: 13–17.

Cramer, S. and Smith, A. (2002) 'Technology's impact on student writing at the middle school level', *Journal of Instructional Psychology*, 29: 3–14.

Cunningham, A.E. and Stanovich, K.E. (1990) 'Early spelling acquisition: writing beats the computer', *Journal of Educational Psychology*, 82: 159–62.

Daiute, C. and Morse, F. (1994) 'Access to knowledge and expression: multimedia writing tools for students with diverse needs and strengths', *Journal of Special Education Technology*, 12: 221–56.

Davidson, J., Elcock, J. and Noyes, P. (1996) 'A preliminary study of the effect of computer-assisted practice on reading attainment', *Journal of Research in Reading*, 19: 102–10.

Dawson, L., Venn, M.L. and Gunter, P.L. (2000) 'The effects of teacher versus computer reading models', *Behavioral Disorders*, 25: 105–13.

Deadman, G. (1997) 'An analysis of pupils' reflective writing within a hyper-media framework', *Journal of Computer Assisted Learning*, 13: 16–25.

DeCosta, S.B. (1992) 'Sociological findings in young children's word-processed writings', *Computers in Human Behavior*, 8: 17–25.

Divine, K.P. and Whanger, R.E. (1990) 'Use of a computer learning laboratory with at-risk high school students', *Educational Technology*, 30: 46–8.

Douglas, G. (2001) 'A comparison between reading from paper and computer screen by children with a visual impairment', *British Journal of Visual Impairment*, 19: 29–34.

Dwyer, H.J. and Sullivan, H.J. (1993) 'Student preferences for teacher and computer composition marking', *Journal of Educational Research*, 86: 137–41.

Dybdahl, C.S., Shaw, D.G. and Blahous, E. (1997) 'The impact of the computer on writing: no simple answers', *Computers in the Schools*, 13: 41–53.

Elkind, J., Cohen, K. and Murray, C. (1993) 'Using computer-based readers to improve reading comprehension of students with dyslexia', *Annals of Dyslexia*, 43: 238–59.

Erdner, R.A., Guy, R.F. and Bush, A. (1998) 'The impact of a year of computer assisted instruction on the development of first grade learning skills', *Journal of Educational Computing Research*, 18: 369–86.

Erickson, B., Allen, A. and Mountain, L. (1992) 'Telecommunications promotes summer reading and writing: a pilot project report', *Journal of Computing in Childhood Education*, 3: 295–302.

Erickson, K.A., Koppenhaver, D.A., Yoder, D.E. and Nance, J. (1997) 'Integrated communication and literacy instruction for a child with multiple disabilities', *Focus on Autism and Other Developmental Disabilities*, 12: 142–50.

Ewing, J. (2000) 'Enhancement of online and offline student learning', *Education Media International*, 37: 205–17.

Farmer, M.E., Klein, R. and Bryson, S.E. (1992) 'Computer-assisted reading; effects of whole-word feedback on fluency and comprehension in readers with severe disabilities', *Remedial and Special Education*, 13: 50–60.

Fawcett, A.J., Nicolson, R.I. and Morris, S. (1993) 'Computer-based spelling remediation for dyslexic children', *Journal of Computer Assisted Learning*, 9: 171–83.

Feldmann, S.C. and Fish, M.C. (1991) 'Use of computer-mediated reading supports to enhance reading comprehension of high school students', *Journal of Educational Computing Research*, 7: 25–36.

Fletcher, D.C. (2001) 'Second graders decide when to use electronic editing tools', *Information Technology in Childhood Education Annual*, 74: 155.

Foster, K.C., Erickson, G.C., Foster, D.F., Brinkman, D. and Torgersen, J.K. (1994) 'Computer administered instruction in phonological awareness: evaluation of the DaisyQuest Program', *Journal of Research and Development in Education*, 27: 126–37.

Fuchs, L.S., Fuchs, D., Hamlett, C.L. and Allinder, R.M. (1991) 'Effects of expert system advice within curriculum-based measurement in teacher planning and student achievement in spelling', *School Psychology Review*, 20: 49–66.

Fulk, B.M. and Stormont-Spurgin, M. (1995) 'Spelling interventions for students with disabilities: a review', *Journal of Special Education*, 28: 488–513.

Garner, R., Tan, S. and Zhao, Y. (2000) 'Why write?', *Computers in Human Behavior*, 16: 339–47.

Golden, N., Gersten, R. and Woodward, J. (1990) 'Effectiveness of guided practice during remedial reading instruction: an application of computer-managed instruction', *Elementary School Journal*, 90: 291–304.

Greenleaf, C. (1994) 'Technological indeterminacy: the role of classroom writing practices and pedagogy in shaping student use of the computer', *Written Communication*, 11: 85–130.

Greenlee Moore, M.E. and Smith, L.L. (1996) 'Interactive computer software: the effects on young children's reading achievement', *Reading Psychology*, 17: 43–64.

Grejda, G.F. and Hannafin, M.J. (1992) 'Effects of word processing on sixth graders' holistic writing and revisions', *Journal of Educational Research*, 85: 144–9.

Harris, E.A. and Bond, C.L. (1992) 'A holistic approach to guided writing: using the WICAT program supplemented with peer critique', *Journal of Computing in Childhood Education*, 3: 193–201.

Harris, L., Doyle, E.S. and Haaf, R. (1996) 'Language treatment approach for users of AAC: experimental single-subject investigation', *AAC: Augmentative and Alternative Communication*, 12: 230–43.

Hartas, C. and Moseley, D. (1993) '"Say that again, please": a scheme to boost reading skills using a computer with digitised speech', *Support for Learning*, 8: 16–21.

Hasselbring, T.S., Goin, L., Taylor, R., Bottge, B. and Daley, P. (1997) 'The computer doesn't embarrass me', *Educational Leadership*, 55: 30–3.

Heise, B.L., Papalewis, R. and Tanner, D.E. (1991) 'Building base vocabulary with computer-assisted instruction', *Teacher Education Quarterly*, 18: 55–63.

Higgins, C. (2002) 'Using film text to support reluctant writers', *English in Education*, 36: 25–37.

Hine, M.S., Goldman, S.R. and Cosden, M.A. (1990) 'Error monitoring by learning: handicapped students engaged in collaborative microcomputer-based writing', *Journal of Special Education*, 23: 407–22.

Horney, M.A. and Anderson Inman, L. (1994) 'Students and hypertext: developing a new literacy for a new reading context', in D. Wray (ed.) *Literacy and Computers: Insights from Research*, Royston: United Kingdom Reading Association.

Horney, M.A. and Anderson Inman, L. (1999) 'Supported text in electronic reading environments', *Reading and Writing Quarterly: Overcoming Learning Difficulties*, 15: 127–68.

Howell, R.D., Erickson, K., Stanger, C. and Wheaton, J.E. (2000) 'Evaluation of a computer-based program on the reading performance of first grade students with potential for reading failure', *Journal of Special Education Technology*, 15: 5–14.

Ignatz, M. (2000) *The Effectiveness of the Read, Write & Type! Program in Increasing the Phonological Awareness of First Grade Students*, Florida: Florida A. & M. University.

Jinkerson, L. and Baggett, P. (1993) 'Spell checkers: aids in identifying and correcting spelling errors', *Journal of Computing in Childhood Education*, 4: 291–306.

Johnston, C.B. (1996) 'Interactive storybook software: effects on verbal development in kindergarten children', *Early Child Development and Care*, 132: 33–44.

Jones, I. (1994) 'The effect of a word processor on the written composition of pupils', *Computers in the Schools*, 11: 43–54.

Jones, I. (1998) 'The effect of computer-generated spoken feedback on kindergarten students' written narratives', *Journal of Computing in Childhood Education*, 9: 43–56.

Jones, I. and Pellegrini, A. D. (1996) 'The effects of social relationships, writing media, and microgenetic development on first-grade students' written narratives', *American Educational Research Journal*, 33: 691–718.

Joram, E., Woodruff, E., Bryson, M. and Lindsay, P. (1992) 'The effects of revising with a word processor on written composition', *Research in the Teaching of English*, 26: 167–93.

Labbo, L.D. (1996) 'A semiotic analysis of young children's symbol making in a classroom computer center', *Reading Research Quarterly*, 31:356–85.

Laframboise, K.L. (1991) 'The facilitative effects of word processing on sentence-combining tasks with at-risk fourth graders', *Journal of Research and Development in Education*, 24: 1–8.

Laine, C.J. and Follansbee, R. (1994) 'Using word-prediction technology to improve the writing of low-functioning hearing-impaired students', *Child Language Teaching and Therapy*, 10: 283–97.

Leahy, P. (1991) 'A multi-year formative evaluation of IBM's "Writing to Read" program', *Reading Improvement*, 28: 257–64.

Leong, C.K. (1992) 'Enhancing reading comprehension with text-to-speech (DECtalk) computer system', *Reading and Writing*, 4: 205–17.

Leong, C.K. (1995) 'Effects of on-line reading and simultaneous DECtalk auding in helping below-average and poor readers comprehend and summarize text', *Learning Disability Quarterly*, 18: 101–16.

Leong, C.K. (1996) 'Using microcomputer technology to promote students' "higher-order" reading', in B. Gorayska and J.L. Mey (eds) *Cognitive Technology: In Search of a Humane Interface. Advances in Psychology, Vol. 113*, New York: Elsevier Science.

Levary, E.F. (1992) 'Starting out: computer activities and the development of transitions in student writing', *Educational Computing and Technology*, 13: 73–4.

Lewin, C. (1997) ' "Test driving" CARS: addressing the issues in the evaluation of computer-assisted reading software', *Journal of Computing in Childhood Education*, 8: 111–32.

Lewin, C. (2000) 'Exploring the effects of talking book software in UK primary classrooms', *Journal of Research in Reading*, 23: 149–57.

Lewis, R.B., Graves, A.W., Ashton, T.M. and Kieley, C.L. (1998) 'Word processing tools for students with learning disabilities: a comparison of strategies to increase text entry speed', *Learning Disabilities Research and Practice*, 13: 95–108.

Lin, A., Podell, D.M. and Rein, N. (1991) 'The effects of CAI on word recognition in mildly mentally handicapped and nonhandicapped learners', *Journal of Special Education Technology*, 11: 16–25.

Love, K. (1998) 'Old cyborgs, young cyborgs (and those in between)', *English in Australia*, 121: 63–75.

MacArthur, C.A. (1998a) 'From illegible to understandable: how word prediction and speech synthesis can help', *Teaching Exceptional Children*, 30: 66–71.

MacArthur, C.A. (1998b) 'Word processing with speech synthesis and word prediction: effects on the dialogue journal writing of students with learning disabilities', *Learning Disability Quarterly*, 21: 151–66.

MacArthur, C.A. (1999) 'Word prediction for students with severe spelling problems', *Learning Disability Quarterly*, 22: 158–72.

MacArthur, C.A., Ferretti, R.K., Okolo, C.M. and Cavalier, A.R. (2001) 'Technology applications for students with literacy problems: a critical review', *Elementary School Journal*, 101: 273–301.

MacArthur, C.A., Graham, S., Haynes, J.B. and DeLaPaz, S. (1996) 'Spelling checkers and students with learning disabilities: performance comparisons and impact on spelling', *Journal of Special Education*, 30: 35–57.

MacArthur, C.A., Graham, S., Schwartz, S.S. and Shafer, W.D. (1995) 'Evaluation of a writing instruction model that integrated a process approach, strategy instruction, and word processing', *Learning Disability Quarterly*, 18: 278–91.

MacArthur, C.A., Haynes, J.A., Malouf, D.B., Harris, K.R. and Owings, M. (1990) 'Computer assisted instruction with learning disabled students: achievement, engagement, and other factors that influence achievement', *Journal of Educational Computing Research*, 6: 311–28.

Mackereth, M. and Anderson, J. (2000) 'Computers, video games, and literacy: what do girls think?', *The Australian Journal of Language and Literacy*, 23: 184–95.

Mander, R., Wilton, K.M., Townsend, M.A.R. and Thomson, P. (1995) 'Personal computers and process writing: a written language intervention for deaf children', *British Journal of Educational Psychology*, 65: 441–53.

Marston, D., Deno, S.L., Kim, D., Diment, K. and Rogers, D. (1995) 'Comparison of reading intervention approaches for students with mild disabilities', *Exceptional Children*, 62: 20–37.

Matthew, K. (1997) 'A comparison of the influence of interactive CD-ROM storybooks and traditional print storybooks on reading comprehension', *Journal of Research in Computing in Education*, 29: 263–75.

Matthew, K.I. (1996) 'The impact of CD-ROM storybooks on children's reading comprehension and reading attitude', *Journal of Educational Multimedia and Hypermedia*, 5: 379–94.

McAteer, E. and Demissie, A. (1992) 'Schoolchildren's revision tactics', *Instructional Science*, 21: 109–24.

McClay, J.K. (2002) 'Hidden "treasure": new genres, new media and the teaching of writing', *English in Education*, 36: 46–55.

McKeon, C.A. and Burkey, L.C. (1998) 'A literature based e-mail collaborative', in E. G. Sturtevant and J. Dugan (eds) *Literacy and Community: the Twentieth Yearbook*, Carrollton, GA: College Reading Association.

McKeon, C.A., Sage, M.C.G. and Gardiner, H.W. (2001) 'E-mail as a motivating literacy event for one struggling reader: Donna's case', *Reading Research and Instruction*, 40: 185–202.

McNamee, G.D. (1995) 'A Vygotskian perspective on literacy development', *School Psychology International*, 16: 185–98.

McNaughton, D., Hughes, C. and Ofiesh, N. (1997) 'Proofreading for students with learning disabilities: integrating computer and strategy use', *Learning Disabilities Research and Practice*, 12: 16–28.

Merchant, G. (2001) 'Teenagers in cyberspace: an investigation of language use and language change in internet chatrooms', *Journal of Research in Reading*, 24: 293–306.

Meskill, C. and Swan, K. (1996) 'Roles for multimedia in the response-based literature classroom', *Journal of Educational Computing Research*, 15: 217–39.

Meskill, C. and Swan, K. (1998) 'Response-based multimedia and the culture of the classroom: a pilot study of Kid's Space in four elementary classrooms', *Educational Computing Research*, 18: 339–67.

Meyers, L.F. (1992) 'Teach me my language: teaching children with learning disabilities to link meaning with speech and text', *Writing Notebook: Creative Word Processing in the Classroom*, 9: 44–6.

Miller, L., DeJean, J. and Miller, R. (2000) 'The literacy curriculum and use of an integrated learning system', *Journal of Research in Reading*, 23: 123–35.

Mitchell, M.J. and Fox, B.J. (2001) 'The effects of computer software for developing phonological awareness in low-progress readers', *Reading Research and Instruction*, 40: 315–32.

Moore Hart, M.A. (1995) 'The effects of multicultural links on reading and writing performance and cultural awareness of fourth and fifth graders', *Computers in Human Behavior*, 11: 391–410.

Moore, M.A. and Karabenick, S.A. (1992) 'The effects of computer communications on the reading and writing performance of fifth-grade students', *Computers in Human Behavior*, 8: 27–38.

Morgan, W. (1995) 'Safe harbours or open seas: English classrooms in an age of electronic text', *English in Australia*, 111: 9–16.

Morgan, W. (1997) 'From the margins to the centre: schools online', *English in Aotearoa*, 32, 3–11.

Morgan, W. (2001) 'Computers for literacy: making the difference?', *Asia Pacific Journal of Teacher Education*, 29: 31–47.

Morocco, C.C., Dalton, B. and Tivnan, T. (1992) 'The impact of computer-supported writing instruction on fourth-grade students with and without learning disabilities', *Reading and Writing Quarterly: Overcoming Learning Difficulties*, 8: 87–113.

Moseley, D. (1999) *Ways Forward with ICT: Effective Pedagogy Using Information and Communications Technology for Literacy and Numeracy in Primary Schools*, Newcastle: University of Newcastle.

Nelson, M.H. (1994) 'Processing poetry to develop literacy', *Computing Teacher*, 22: 39–41.

Nettelbeck, D. (2000) 'Using information technology to enrich the learning experiences of secondary English students', *Literacy Learning: the Middle Years*, 8: 40–9.

Newell, A.F. (1992) 'Increasing literacy levels by the use of linguistic prediction', *Child Language Teaching and Therapy*, 8: 138–87.

Nichols, L.M. (1996) 'Pencil and paper versus word processing: a comparative study of creative writing in the elementary school', *Journal of Research in Computing in Education*, 29: 159–66.

Nicolson, R.I., Fawcett, A.J. and Nicolson, M.K. (2000) 'Evaluation of a computer-based reading intervention in infant and junior schools', *Journal of Research in Reading*, 23: 194–209.

Nicolson, R.I., Fawcett, A.J. and Pickering, S. (1991) 'A hypercard spelling support environment for dyslexic children', *Computers and Education*, 16: 203–9.

Nwogu, K. and Nwogu, E. (1992) 'Computers and ESL in the West Midlands', *Language Learning Journal*, 6: 74–6.

O'Brien, D.G., Springs, R. and Stith, D. (2001) 'Engaging at-risk high school students: literacy learning in a high school literacy lab', in E.B. Moje and D.G. O'Brien (eds) *Constructions of Literacy: Studies of Teaching and Learning in and out of Secondary Schools*, Mahwah, NJ: Lawrence Erlbaum Associates Inc.

Olson, R.K. and Wise, B.W. (1992) 'Reading on the computer with orthographic and speech feedback: an overview of the Colorado remediation project', *Reading and Writing*, 4: 107–44.

Olson, R.K., Wise, B., Ring, J. and Johnson, M. (1997) 'Computer-based remedial training in phoneme awareness and phonological decoding: effects on the post-training development of word recognition', *Scientific Studies of Reading*, 1: 235–53.

Owston, R.D., Murphy, S. and Wideman, H.H. (1991) 'On and off computer writing of eighth grade students experienced in word processing', *Computers in the Schools*, 8: 67–87.

Owston, R.D., Murphy, S. and Wideman, H.H. (1992) 'The effects of word-processing on students writing quality and revision strategies', *Research in the Teaching of English*, 26: 249–76.

Owston, R.D. and Wideman, H.H. (1997) 'Word processors and children's writing in a high-computer-access setting', *Journal of Research in Computing in Education*, 30: 202–20.

Palumbo, D.B. and Prater, D.L. (1992) 'A comparison of computer-based prewriting strategies for basic ninth-grade writers', *Computers in Human Behavior*, 8: 63–70.

Parker, D. (1999) 'You've read the book, now make the film: moving image media, print literacy and narrative', *English in Education*, 33: 24–35.

Parker, D. (2002) 'Show us a story: an overview of recent research and resource development work at the British Film Institute', *English in Education*, 36: 38–45.

Parr, J.M. (1997) 'Computer assisted learning with an integrated learning system: another front for raising literacy and numeracy amongst secondary students?', *New Zealand Journal of Educational Studies*, 32: 37–51.

Peterson, S.E. (1993) 'A comparison of student revisions when composing with pen and paper versus word-processing', *Computers in the Schools*, 9: 55–69.

Peyton, J.K. (1991) 'Electronic communication for developing the literacy skills of elementary school students: the case of ENFI', *Teaching English to Deaf and Second Language Students*, 9: 4–9.

Pinkard, N. (1999) *Learning to Read in Culturally Responsive Computer Environments CIERA Report*, Michigan: Center for the Improvement of Early Reading Achievement.

Pinkard, N. (2001) '"Rappin' Reader" and "Say Say Oh Playmate": using children's childhood songs as literacy scaffolds in computer-based learning environments', *Journal of Educational Computing Research*, 25: 17–34.

Potter, L. and Small, J. (1998) 'Utilizing computers for reading improvement in a junior high: a case study', *International Journal of Instructional Media*, 25: 383–7.

Pritchard, A. (1997) 'The refinement of an "ideas map" as a means of assessment and of enhancing children's understanding of texts', *Reading*, 31: 55–9.

Pullen, M.C. (1993) *A Comparison of Writing Performance Using Conventional and Computer-based Writing Techniques*, Memphis: Memphis State University.

Reinking, D. and Rickman, S.S. (1990) 'The effects of computer-mediated texts on the vocabulary learning and comprehension of intermediate-grade readers', *Journal of Reading Behavior*, 22: 395–411.

Reinking, D. and Watkins, J. (2000) 'A formative experiment investigating the use of multimedia book reviews to increase elementary students' independent reading', *Reading Research Quarterly*, 35: 384–419.

Repman, J., Cothern, N.B. and Cothern, J.S. (1992) 'Novice writers and word processing in the one-computer classroom', *Journal of Computing in Childhood Education*, 3: 203–14.

Roberts, G.C. and Mutter, G. (1991) 'A celebration of literacy: computer-assisted writing in the St James-Assiniboia School Division No. 2. How it started and how it works', *Education Canada*, 31: 4–7.

Roberts, G.I. and Samuels, M.T. (1993) 'Handwriting remediation: a comparison of computer-based and traditional approaches', *Journal of Educational Research*, 87: 118–25.

Rogier, L. L., Owens, J. L. and Patty, D. L. (1999) 'Writing to read: a valuable program for first grade?', *Reading Improvement*, 36: 24–34.

Rosenbluth, G.S. and Reed, W.M. (1992) 'The effects of writing-process-based instruction and word processing on remedial and accelerated eleventh graders', *Computers in Human Behavior*, 8: 71–95.

Ross, J.A., Hogaboam-Gray, A. and Hannay, L. (2001) 'Collateral benefits of an interactive literacy program for grade 1 and 2 students', *Journal of Research in Computing in Education*, 33: 219–34.

Rowley, K., Carlson, P. and Miller, T. (1998) 'A cognitive technology to teach composition skills: four studies with the R-WISE writing tutor', *Journal of Educational Computing Research*, 18: 259–96.

Russell, G. (1998) 'Elements and implications of a hypertext pedagogy', *Computers and Education*, 31: 185–93.

Seawel, L., Smaldino, S.E., Steele, J.L. and Lewis, J.Y. (1994) 'A descriptive study comparing computer-based word processing and handwriting on attitudes and performance of third and fourth grade students involved in a program based on a process approach to writing', *Journal of Computing in Childhood Education*, 5: 43–59.

Shaw, E.L., Nauman, A.K. and Burson, D. (1994) 'Comparisons of spontaneous and word processed compositions in elementary classrooms: a three-year study', *Journal of Computing in Childhood Education*, 5: 319–27.

Silver, N.W. and Repa, J.T. (1993) 'The effect of word processing on the quality of writing and self-esteem of secondary school English-as-second-language students: writing without censure', *Journal of Educational Computing Research*, 9: 265–83.

Sinatra, R., Beaudry, J., Pizzo, J. and Geisert, G. (1994) 'Using a computer-based semantic mapping, reading, and writing approach with at-risk fourth graders', *Journal of Computing in Childhood Education*, 5: 93–112.

Singleton, C. and Simmons, F. (2001) 'An evaluation of "Wordshark" in the classroom', *British Journal of Educational Technology*, 32: 317–30.

Smith, S. (2001) 'Using computers to improve literacy learning among low-achieving year 7 boys', *English in Australia*, 129–30: 163–70.

Snyder, I. (1994) 'Writing with word processors: the computer's influence on the classroom context', *Journal of Curriculum Studies*, 26: 143–62.

Snyder, I. (1995) 'Towards electronic writing classrooms: the challenge for teachers', *Journal of Information Technology for Teacher Education*, 4: 51–65.

Snyder, I. (1996) 'Integrating computers into the literacy curriculum: more difficult than we first imagined', *The Australian Journal of Language and Literacy*, 19: 330–44.

Spaulding, C.L. and Lake, D. (1992) 'Interactive effects of computer network and student characteristics on students' writing and collaborating', *High School Journal*, 76: 67–77.

Steelman, J.D. (1994) 'Revision strategies employed by middle level students using computers', *Journal of Educational Computing Research*, 11: 141–52.

Steg, D.R., Lazar, I. and Boyce, C. (1994) 'A cybernetic approach to early education', *Journal of Educational Computing Research*, 10: 1–27.

Stevens, K.B., Blackhurst, A.E. and Slaton, D.B. (1991) 'Teaching memorized spelling with a microcomputer: time delay and computer-assisted instruction', *Journal of Applied Behavior Analysis*, 24: 153–60.

Stoddard, B. and MacArthur, C.A. (1993) 'A peer editor strategy: guiding learning-disabled students in response and revision', *Research in the Teaching of English*, 27: 76–103.

Stromer, R. and Mackay, H.A. (1992) 'Spelling and emergent picture-printed word relations established with delayed identity matching to complex samples', *Journal of Applied Behavior Analysis*, 25: 893–904.

Stuhlmann, J.M. and Taylor, H.G. (1998) 'Analyzing the impact of telecommunications on learning outcomes in elementary classrooms', *Journal of Computing in Childhood Education*, 9: 79–92.

Sutherland, M.J. and Smith, C.D. (1997) 'The benefits and difficulties of using portable word processors with older dyslexics', *Dyslexia*, 3: 15–26.

Swanson, H.L. and Trahan, M.F. (1992) 'Learning disabled readers' comprehension of computer mediated text: the influence of working memory, metacognition and attribution', *Learning Disabilities Research and Practice*, 7: 74–86.

Tjus, T., Heimann, M. and Nelson, K.E. (1998) 'Gains in literacy through the use of a specially developed multimedia computer strategy', *Autism*, 2: 139–56.

Topping, K.J. (1997) 'Family electronic literacy: part 1 – home–school links through audiotaped books', *Reading*, 31: 7–11.

Topping, K.J. and Sanders, W.L. (2000) 'Teacher effectiveness and computer assessment of reading: relating value added and learning information system data', *School Effectiveness and School Improvement*, 11: 305–37.

Torgerson, C.J. and Elbourne, D. (2002) 'A systematic review and meta-analysis of the effectiveness of information and communication technology (ICT) on the teaching of spelling', *Journal of Research in Reading*, 25: 129–43.

Trushell, J., Burrell, C. and Maitland, A. (2001) 'Year 5 pupils reading an "interactive storybook" on CD-ROM: losing the plot?', *British Journal of Educational Technology*, 32: 389–401.

Turbill, J. (2001) 'A researcher goes to school: using technology in the kindergarten literacy curriculum', *Journal of Early Childhood Literacy*, 1: 255–79.

Underwood, J. (1996) 'Are integrated learning systems effective learning support tools?', *Computers and Education*, 26: 1–3.

Underwood, J.D.M. (2000) 'A comparison of two types of computer support for reading development', *Journal of Research in Reading*, 23: 136–48.

Utay, C. and Utay, J. (1997) 'Peer-assisted learning: the effects of cooperative learning and cross-age peer tutoring with word processing on writing skills of students with learning disabilities', *Journal of Computing in Childhood Education*, 8: 165–85.

Van Haalen, T. and Bright, G.W. (1993) 'Writing and revising by bilingual students in traditional and word processing environments', *Journal of Educational Computing Research*, 9: 313–28.

Varner-Quick, W.S. (1994) 'The effects of computer-assisted instruction on reading abilities: a comparison of fourth grade reading programs with and without computer technology', unpublished thesis, Wayne State University, USA.

Vaughn, S., Schumm, J.S. and Gordon, J. (1992) 'Early spelling acquisition: does writing really beat the computer?', *Learning Disability Quarterly*, 15: 223–8.

Vaughn, S., Schumm, J.S. and Gordon, J. (1993) 'Which motoric condition is most effective for teaching spelling to students with and without learning disabilities?', *Journal of Learning Disabilities*, 26: 191–8.

Vincent, J. (2001) 'The role of visually rich technology in facilitating children's writing', *Journal of Computer Assisted Learning*, 17: 242–50.

Vollands, S.R., Topping, K. and Evans, H. (1996) *Experimental Evaluation of Computer Assisted Self-assessment of Reading*, Dundee: Dundee University.

Vollands, S.R., Topping, K.J. and Evans, R.M. (1999) 'Computerized self-assessment of reading comprehension with the Accelerated Reader: action research', *Reading and Writing Quarterly: Overcoming Learning Difficulties*, 15: 197–211.

Walker, S.A. and Pilkington, R.M. (2000) *Computer-mediated Communication in the Development of Writing Skills at Key Stage 3*, Leeds: University of Leeds.

Watts, M. and Lloyd, C. (2001) 'Evaluating a classroom multimedia programme in the teaching of literacy', *Educational Research and Evaluation*, 7: 35–52.

Weller, L.D., Carpenter, S. and Holmes, C.T. (1998) 'Achievement gains of low-achieving students using computer-assisted vs regular instruction', *Psychological Reports*, 83: 834.

Wepner, S.B. (1992) '"Real-life" reading software and "at-risk" secondary students', *Reading Horizons*, 32: 279–88.

Wild, M. (1997) 'Using CD-ROM storybooks to encourage reading development', *Set Special 1997: Language and Literacy*, 6: 1–4.

Wild, M. and Ing, J. (1994) 'An investigation into the use of a concept keyboard as a computer-related device to improve the structure of young children's writing', *Journal of Computing in Childhood Education*, 5: 299–309.

Williams, H.S. and Williams, P.N. (2000) 'Integrating reading and computers: an approach to improve ESL students' reading skills', *Reading Improvement*, 37: 98–100.

Wise, B.W. and Olson, R.K. (1992) 'How poor readers and spellers use interactive speech in a computerized spelling program', *Reading and Writing*, 4: 145–63.

Wise, B.W. and Olson, R.K. (1995) 'Computer-based phonological awareness and reading instruction', *Annals of Dyslexia*, 45: 99–122.

Wise, B.W., Olson, R.K., Ring, J. and Johnson, M. (1998) 'Interactive computer support for improving phonological skills', in J. L. Metsala and L. C. Ehri (eds) *Word Recognition in Beginning Literacy*, Mahwah, NJ: Lawrence Erlbaum Associates Inc.

Wise, B.W., Ring, J. and Olson, R.K. (1999) 'Training phonological awareness with and without explicit attention to articulation', *Journal of Experimental Child Psychology*, 72: 271–304.

Wise, B.W., Ring, J. and Olson, R.K. (2000) 'Individual differences in gains from computer-assisted remedial reading', *Journal of Experimental Child Psychology*, 77: 197–235.

Wishart, E. (1994) 'Using a TTNS electronic mailbox in a junior class: a case study', in D. Wray (ed.) *Literacy and Computers: insights from research*, Royston: United Kingdom Reading Association.

Wolfe, E.W., Bolton, S., Feltovich, B. and Bangert, A.W. (1996) 'A study of word processing experience and its effects on student essay writing', *Journal of Educational Computing Research*, 14: 269–84.

Zhang, Y., Brooks, D.W., Frields, T. and Redelfs, M. (1995) 'Quality of writing by elementary students with learning disabilities', *Multimedia Today*, 3: 30–9.

Bibliography

Andrews, R. (2003a) 'ICT and literacies: a new kind of research is needed', *Literacy Learning: The Middle Years* (Journal of the Australian Literacy Educators' Association), 11.1, 9–12 (February 2003).

Andrews, R. (2003b) Keynote address, International Federation for the Teaching of English conference, Melbourne: University of Melbourne, July 2003.

Andrews, R., Burn, A., Leach, J., Locke, T., Low, G. and Torgerson, C. (2002) 'A systematic review of the impact of networked ICT on 5–16-year-olds' literacy in English' (EPPI-Centre Review), *Research Evidence in Education Library*, 1. London: EPPI-Centre, Social Science Research Unit, Institute of Education.

Andrews, R., Burn, A., Leach, J., Locke, T., Low, G., Torgerson, C. and Die, Z. (2003) 'A systematic review of the impact of networked ICT on 5–16-year-olds' literacy in English' (EPPI-Centre Review), *Research Evidence in Education Library*, 2. London: EPPI-Centre, Social Science Research Unit, Institute of Education.

BECTa (2001) *Building an ICT Research Network: Helping to Create Schools of the Future* (Report of a conference hosted by BECTa, 15 June 2001). Coventry: British Educational Communications and Technology Agency.

BECTa (2002) *Digital Divide: A Collection of Papers from the Toshiba/ Becta Digital Divide Seminar* (19 February 2002). Coventry: British Educational Communications and Technology Agency.

BECTa/DfES (2002) *ImpaCT2: The Impact of Information and Communication Technologies* (ICT in Schools Research and Evaluation series, no. 7). Coventry: British Educational Communications and Technology Agency and London: Department for Education and Skills.

BECTa (2003) *What the Research says about Portable ICT Devices in Teaching and Learning.* Coventry: British Educational Communications and Technology Agency.

BECTa (nd) *ICT Supporting Teaching: Developing Effective Practice.* Coventry: British Educational Communications and Technology Agency, plus DfES/NAACE/QCA/TTA.

Burn, A. and Leach, J. (2003) 'A systematic review of the impact of ICT on the learning of literacies associated with moving image texts in English, 5–16' (EPPI-Centre Review), *Research Evidence in Education Library*, 2. London: EPPI-Centre, Social Science Research Unit, Institute of Education.

Coles, M. (2002) *A Contribution to the Third Report on Vocational Training Research in Europe: Evaluating the Impact of Vocational Education and Training.* London: Qualifications and Curriculum Authority (revised version of 14 February 2003).

DfEE/QCA (1999) *The National Curriculum for England.* London: Department for Education and Employment/Qualifications and Curriculum Authority.

EPPI-Centre (2002) Guidelines for extracting data and quality assessing primary studies in educational research Version 0.9.4, London: Institute of Education, Social Science Research Unit.

Harrison, C., Cavendish, S., Comber, C. Fisher, T., Harrison, A., Haw, K., Lewin, C., McFarlane, A., Mavers, D., Scrimshaw, P., Somekh, B. and Watling, R. (1998) *The Multimedia Portables for Teachers' Evaluation.* Coventry: British Educational Communications and Technology Agency.

Lewin, C. *et al.* (2000) *The KS1 Literacy Evaluation Project Using Low Cost Computers.* Milton Keynes: The Open University, Centre for Language and Communication.

Locke, T. (2003) 'ICT and English' on Critical English Online (www.soe.waikato.ac.nz/english/EnglishNZ/ICT.html – accessed June 2003).

Locke, T. and Andrews, R. (2003) 'A systematic review of the impact of ICT on literature-based literacies in English, 5–16' (EPPI-Centre Review), *Research Evidence in Education Library*, 2. London: EPPI-Centre, Social Science Research Unit, Institute of Education.

Low, G. and Beverton, S. (2003) 'A systematic review of the impact of ICT on learners between 5–16, for whom English is a second or additional language' (EPPI-Centre Review), *Research Evidence in Education Library*, 2. London: EPPI-Centre, Social Science Research Unit, Institute of Education.

McFarlane, A. *et al.* (1995) 'Developing an understanding of the meaning of line graphs in primary science investigations using portable computers', *Journal of Computers in Mathematics and Science Teaching*, 14: 461–80

Ofsted (2001) *ICT in Schools: The Impact of Government Initiatives* (interim report, April 2001). London: Office for Standards in Education.

Ofsted (2002) *The National Literacy Strategy: The First Four Years 1998–2002.* London: Office for Standards in Education.

Parr, J.M. (2002) *A Review of the Literature on Computer-assisted Learning, Particularly Integrated Learning Systems, and Outcomes with Respect to Literacy and Numeracy.* Report to the New Zealand Ministry of Education (www.minedu.govt.nz – accessed June 2003).

Plewis, I. (2001) *Evaluating the Benefits of Lifelong Learning.* London: University of London, Institute of Education.

Torgerson, C. and Zhu, D. (2003) 'A systematic review and meta-analysis of the effectiveness of ICT on literacy learning in English, 5–16' (EPPI-Centre Review), *Research Evidence in Education Library*, 2. London: EPPI-Centre, Social Science Research Unit, Institute of Education.

Chapter 2

Evidence for the effectiveness of ICT on literacy learning

Carole Torgerson and Die Zhu

Introduction

The use of information and communication technology (ICT) in schools to support literacy learning is pervasive. Successive governments have, since the mid-1980s, invested large amounts of resources to develop ICT in schools, including more than £1 billion in the last five years in the UK. However, little robust evidence has been used to underpin this use of ICT.

Recent UK government policy on ICT is supported by five research reports from the British Educational Communications and Technology Agency (BECTa 1998; BECTa 1998–9; BECTa 2001a; BECTa 2001b; BECTa 2002). All five reports asserted that Government investment in ICT is justified in terms of its impact on pupil achievement.

In the most recent report (BECTa 2002) the aim was to investigate the associations between 'high' and 'low' use of ICT (networked technologies) and the educational attainment of pupils at key stages. There was a positive relationship for 'high' ICT and pupil attainment in 12 out of 13 associations (various subjects at different key stages) but in most cases this association was not statistically significant (7 out of 12 associations) and those associations that were statistically significant typically observed only very small effects.

A critical examination of the methods and data presented in the BECTa reports does not consistently support the conclusions drawn by the government policy documents. Indeed, some of the data can be interpreted as showing that ICT is ineffective or harmful. In addition, the evidence presented in the ImpaCT report (BECTa 2002) was based on observational data. It would not have been possible to establish a causal relationship between the level of ICT use and the educational attainment of the pupils because the observed effects could have been due to other known or unknown variables.

This absence of evidence for benefit in the UK was supported by a more recent evaluation of the introduction of computers into Israeli schools (Angrist and Lavy 2002). This study not only found an absence of benefit in Hebrew literacy but also noted a statistically significant decline in standards of mathematics associated with ICT use. The Israeli authors, unsurprisingly, concluded that the large financial investment would have been better spent on other educational inputs.

Whilst the BECTa and Israeli data were consistent in showing either no evidence of benefit or potential harm of ICT, they were not from randomized trials and were therefore susceptible to a range of biases that could make their results unreliable. To reliably assess the effects of ICT on literacy or any educational outcome requires an analysis of randomized controlled trials.

This contribution to the collection of articles in the book draws on a sub-review of a systematic review of the impact of ICT on 5–16-year-olds' literacy in English conducted by the EPPI English Review Group based at the University of York. The sub-review question was on the *effectiveness* of ICT on literacy learning in English, 5–16. This review used systematic review methods developed by the EPPI-Centre, and involved the initial identification of a research question; the searching of electronic databases for relevant primary research; the screening of the results of the searches using pre-established inclusion and exclusion criteria; a 'mapping' of the research in the field; the application of refined inclusion and exclusion criteria for the 'in-depth review'; quality appraisal of the included studies and synthesis of the findings. (The EPPI-Centre methodology and methods are discussed in detail in the chapter by Rees and Elbourne.)

The main aim of the sub-review on which this chapter is based was to investigate whether or not information and communication technology is effective in improving young people's literacy learning in English. We also wanted to assess the effectiveness of ICT on different literacy outcomes and, within those outcomes, to assess whether effectiveness varies according to different interventions. Therefore, the research question for this review was 'What is the evidence for the effectiveness of ICT on literacy learning in English, 5–16?' Before we consider the results of the review, we first discuss and justify the methodology of the studies included in our review.

The nature of evidence

The crucial question for any educational intervention should be: is it effective? or does it work? In research terms the only reliable way of assessing effectiveness is through the use of a randomized controlled trial (RCT). Because the focus of this review was on 'effectiveness', studies using rigorous study designs to assess effectiveness were required: this implies the identification of relevant randomized controlled trials (RCTs). The RCT is an experimental design that provides a way of reducing the risk of selection biases at entry to a study. Selection bias is where children are 'selected' into a group in such a way that this affects their educational outcome. Because children have been selected into a group (either by their teachers, parents or themselves) they are likely to have different characteristics from children who have been selected into another group. To avoid biases associated with this selection it is imperative to use the RCT method.

In an RCT, participants are randomly allocated to the interventions being evaluated. Typically, a participant will be allocated to the new intervention (so-called experimental group) or allocated to whatever is the usual practice (the control group). There are many variants to this design, for example allocating the participants to receive the new intervention either straightaway or later (a waiting list design), or to receive both the new and the old intervention but in different randomized sequences (reversal or cross-over design), or allocating groups (in the educational field, rather than individual students, this is usually intact classes or schools) in a cluster design. However, the essence of this design and all its variants is the *random* allocation. If participants are allocated on any other basis, one cannot be sure whether (except for chance differences) the experimental and control groups were similar before receiving (or not receiving) the intervention, and therefore it becomes impossible to disentangle the effects of the intervention from the characteristics of the people being allocated to the intervention. Techniques can be used to attempt to control for the potential confounding from known variables, but they cannot adjust for unknown variables. Thus, non-randomized designs cannot be certain to generate groups which do not differ (except by chance) in either known or unknown factors, and hence these designs always have the potential that selection biases may make comparisons between the two groups about the effect of the intervention uncertain. As well as controlling for confounding due to selection bias, randomization also controls for the statistical phenomenon of regression to the mean. Regression to the mean occurs when extreme test results occur partly by chance. Extreme results, such as low test-scores, will tend to 'regress to the mean' on re-testing irrespective of any intervention. Because randomization ensures that equal proportions of children with 'extreme' test results are present in each group, regression to the mean will affect all treatment groups equally and the change in test scores due to this phenomenon will be cancelled out. Therefore it is important that, for this review, studies were only included if they randomly allocated pupils to an ICT or no ICT intervention for the teaching of literacy.

The superiority of the RCT over other research designs has been recognised in the field of social policy innovations for a considerable time (Cook and Campbell 1979; Cook 2002). Although the RCT addresses the issue of selection bias it is also statistically a more efficient method than other quasi-experiments. An analysis of 74 meta-analyses of psychological, educational and behavioural interventions revealed that although in these fields the average effect sizes did not differ between 'true' and 'quasi' experiments, the standard deviation was much larger for the non-randomized experiments (Lipsey and Wilson 1993; Cook 2002). In other words the randomized experiments were more efficient than the controlled trials in their probing of causal hypotheses (Cook 2002). In addition, one-group pre-test and post-test designs for assessing the effectiveness of interventions can overestimate the size of the effects by up to 61 per cent compared with evaluations using designs that employ a control or comparison group (Lipsey and Wilson 1993).

Given the importance of the RCT, this review sought to identify all RCTs that evaluate interventions using ICT to increase literacy learning in order to assess whether or not ICT is effective in improving literacy learning.

Research background

Before we consider the primary research in the area of ICT and literacy, it is important to describe the existing secondary research in order to describe the conclusions from previous rigorous reviews.

As part of the overall review process five systematic reviews in the field of ICT and literacy were identified by Andrews *et al.* (2002) (Bangert-Drowns 1993; Blok *et al.* 2001; Fulk and Stormont-Spurgin 1995; MacArthur *et al.* 2001; Torgerson and Elbourne 2002). These reviews all used a systematic strategy to identify their included studies. All five reviews synthesised research in various aspects of literacy: spelling (Fulk and Stormont-Spurgin 1995; Torgerson and Elbourne 2002); writing (Bangert-Drowns 1993); verbal and vocabulary development (Blok *et al*. 2001), reading and writing (MacArthur *et al*. 2001). In some of the reviews the included studies focused on participants with specific learner characteristics, for example pupils experiencing learning disabilities (MacArthur *et al*. 2001; Fulk and Stormont-Spurgin 1995). Two of the reviews included papers of all study types (MacArthur *et al*. 2001; Fulk and Stormont-Spurgin 1995), whilst others were restricted to experimental research: randomized controlled trials or RCTs and CTs (Torgerson and Elbourne 2002; Blok *et al*. 2001; Bangert-Drowns 1993). Not all of the systematic reviews included detailed assessment of the quality of the included studies (Fulk and Stormont-Spurgin 1995).

Fulk and Stormont-Spurgin (1995) reviewed published research on spelling interventions for pupils with learning disabilities. They reviewed the effectiveness of four techniques for improving spelling, one of which was computer-assisted-instruction (nine studies). The authors of the review concluded that eight out of the nine studies in CAI reported positive effects for CAI. However, only two out of these nine included studies used an experimental design with random or non-random allocation to intervention (CAI) or control (traditional paper-and-pencil methods). The positive effects reported in the seven one-group studies could have been explained in other ways rather than by any causal relationship with ICT. These other explanations include: the statistical phenomenon of regression to the mean, where 'extreme' values either improve or decline, depending on which extreme of a distribution they lie; the Hawthorne effect, where merely the act of observation provokes a beneficial response; or temporal effects, whereby children tend to improve their spelling abilities irrespective of any intervention over the course of time.

In contrast, a more recent systematic review and meta-analysis of only randomized controlled trials evaluating the effectiveness of ICT interventions in the teaching of spelling (Torgerson and Elbourne 2002) suggested at best only a modest effect in favour of computer interventions on spelling. This benefit was not statistically significant.

Blok *et al*. (2001) investigated whether or not computers enabled young children to learn vocabulary more effectively than traditional teacher-led approaches. This 'effectiveness' review restricted inclusion by study type and therefore only studies with an experimental design were reviewed. In addition, the authors implemented fairly rigorous inclusion and exclusion criteria. Five studies were included, only one of which demonstrated a positive effect for the computer-condition. The review included a discussion of the quality of the five studies and concluded that there was little difference in effectiveness in vocabulary acquisition by computer or by teacher.

MacArthur *et al.* (2001) reviewed published research on the use of ICT to teach or support literacy in populations of students 'with mild disabilities'. They reviewed research in technology and three literacy areas: word identification, reading comprehension and writing. This review included only studies with either an experimental design or studies where quantified learning outcomes were reported. The authors concluded that 'cautious optimism' was justified about the technology potential to improve the literacy skills of students with learning disabilities. However, they also concluded that the methodological quality of the included studies was mixed and they outlined a number of methodological problems with some of the included studies; for example, ill-defined or weak control group treatments, insufficient information about the characteristics of the sample and small sample sizes.

Bangert-Drowns (1993) conducted a meta-analysis of 32 studies using an experimental method (with random or non-random assignment to treatment group) to evaluate the effectiveness of using the word processor to write assignments. Each included study compared two groups of students who received identical instruction in writing apart from the medium used for the writing process (word processor or by hand). Each study also measured treatment outcomes quantitatively. However, it is not possible to distinguish the randomized controlled trials from the controlled trials in the analysis and sizes of effect could not be calculated for all the trials. The included studies were published between 1983 and 1990, and only about half of them were conducted with populations of students between the ages of 5 and 16. Seventeen studies were conducted in college settings. The author concluded that the word-processing groups (especially the weaker writers) improved the quality of their writing more than the control groups.

The evidence to date, from previous systematic reviews, on the effectiveness of ICT on literacy learning in learners aged 5–16 is, therefore, equivocal. In summary, whilst there have been some systematic reviews relevant to the policy question of whether ICT is effective in improving literacy outcomes, the extant reviews were either insufficiently rigorous (in that they included non-randomized or poor quality trials) or they differed from this review in terms of scope: they either focused on one aspect of literacy only or they included learners of all ages.

Selecting studies for the review

For a paper to be included in the review, it had to be a study looking at the effect of ICT on the teaching of literacy to children in a school setting. Control treatments could take any form, such as routine classroom teaching, or other non-computer teaching. However, in order to investigate the effectiveness of ICT on literacy learning, included studies had to have an appropriate non-ICT control group that isolated the medium of instruction as the independent variable. Studies that did not explicitly have a control group that was not exposed to ICT were excluded. Included RCTs had to have a literacy intervention (students were exposed to an intervention that aimed to increase reading, writing or spelling abilities), and at least one quantified literacy outcome measure (reading, writing, spelling). If RCTs did not have both a literacy intervention (reading, writing, spelling) and at least one literacy outcome measure they were excluded.

For this review, studies were therefore only included if they randomly allocated pupils to an ICT or no ICT treatment for the teaching of literacy. Both individually randomized trials and cluster randomized trials were included, but cluster trials were only included if each arm contained more than four clusters, because trials with fewer than four clusters in each arm (eight in a two-arm trial) will be unlikely to produce statistically significant effects (Ukoumunne *et al.* 1998); and if the unit of analysis was at the cluster level (not the individual level) i.e. if there was no unit of analysis error. In order to establish effectiveness it was necessary to look at the effect sizes (with confidence intervals). If the authors did not present effect sizes, or if the reviewers were unable to calculate the effect sizes, an RCT was excluded. Essentially this means that the study had to report either means of post-tests or mean gain scores, numbers of participants in the intervention and control groups and the standard deviations of the mean scores, or the means and numbers of participants in each group and either a t-value or precise p-value in order that the reviewers could calculate the standard deviations. RCTs were included if they presented sufficient data.

We identified 45 RCTs. Three RCTs failed to meet our inclusion criteria. One of the 45 trials (Fuchs *et al.* 1991) was excluded because it randomized teachers rather than learners to an intervention. The intervention was not an ICT intervention in literacy for the pupils, but rather ICT methods for teachers to use in their assessments of the pupils' progress (some of which happened to be in literacy). A second RCT was excluded because it was not adequately randomized (Varner-Quick 1994). After randomizing 120 second-grade pupils to intervention or control, an unspecified number were excluded at fourth grade (all repeaters, transfers and subjects that did not participate in the programme from its inception) in order to create a 'random sample' of students to include in the data analysis. Therefore, the randomization procedure was violated. Because of this problem this study could no longer be considered an RCT. Two of the 45 papers described the same RCT (Matthew 1996 and Matthew 1997). Therefore these papers were considered together. This left a total of 42 trials.

To be included for a more detailed review, studies had to match the content-based and methodological criteria as outlined above. It was decided not to reanalyse poorly analysed cluster trials and not to approach RCT authors for further data.

Thirty of the initially identified 42 RCTs were excluded from the detailed review for the following reasons: no appropriate non-ICT control (19 RCTs); no literacy outcome measures (two RCTs); no data or insufficient data (six RCTs); cluster randomized trials with too few clusters or inappropriate analysis of cluster trial (three RCTs). This left 12 RCTs for the detailed review. A hierarchy for excluding studies was established, starting with exclusion one, continuing with exclusion two and so on. Therefore if a study was excluded on the basis of exclusion three (no or insufficient data) this means that there was an appropriate non-ICT control and there were literacy outcome measures in this trial. A number of trials were excluded on more than one criterion, but this has not been shown in the table.

Table 2.1 shows the reasons for exclusion for all the thirty excluded trials. Most were excluded because they did not have an appropriate non-ICT control.

The participants in the 12 included trials ranged in age from 5–13 (kindergarten to Grade 8). In 7 out of the 12 RCTs either all or half of the actual sample children were pupils who experienced 'learning disabilities' or 'specific learning disabilities'.

The 12 included RCTs were tabulated according to their literacy and ICT focus keywords. Table 2.2 presents the results, in alphabetical order.

A narrative synthesis of the included trials was undertaken. The conceptual framework which formed the basis of the synthesis

Table 2.1 Excluded RCTs and primary reasons for their exclusions

Exclusion 1	Exclusion 2	Exclusion 3	Exclusion 4
Barker 1994	Adam and Wild 1997	Braden et al. 1991	Allen and Thompson 1995
Barron et al. 1992	Dwyer and Sullivan 1993	Cato et al. 1994	Silver and Repa 1993
Bonk and Reynolds 1992		Grejda and Hannafin 1992	Spaulding and Lake 1992
Calvert et al. 1990		Harris and Bond 1992	
Cardinale and Fish 1994		Roberts and Samuels 1993	
Feldmann and Fish 1991		Topping 1997	
Foster et al. 1994			
Johnston 1996			
Laframboise 1991			
Leong 1992			
Leong 1995			
Leong 1996			
Lewin 2000			
Olson et al. 1997			
Palumbo and Prater 1992			
Rosenbluth and Reed 1992			
Utay and Utay 1997			
Wepner 1992			
Wise and Olson 1995			

Notes
Exclusion 1 = no appropriate non-ICT control
Exclusion 2 = no literacy outcome measure
Exclusion 3 = no data or insufficient data
Exclusion 4 = too few clusters in cluster randomized trial

focused first on different ICT interventions and second on different literacy outcomes. This resulted in two approaches to synthesising the evidence:

- interventions: an analysis of the effectiveness of different types of ICT interventions on a range of literacy outcomes
- outcomes: an analysis of the effectiveness of different types of ICT on specific literacy outcomes.

In the first synthesis the effectiveness of the different types of ICT interventions was established by a standard measure of effect for the range of literacy outcomes in the included trials (effect size). An effect size is a standardized measure that allows studies using different outcome measures to be compared using the same metric (i.e. the mean difference in test scores between groups divided by a pooled standard deviation). In order to present these effect sizes, the most appropriate literacy outcome measures at immediate post-test were selected. These outcomes were chosen by one of the authors of the review (C.T.), with advice from other reviewers involved in the data extraction and quality assessment of the included trials (D.Z. and two members of the EPPI-Centre). If a 'total' reading, writing or spelling test was used in addition to a variety of subtests, the 'total' test was selected. If a number of 'total' tests were used the outcome selected was the one felt to have the most important educational significance. The most appropriate outcome measures for reading were reading comprehension and accuracy. For writing, the most appropriate measures were holistic scoring (quality of writing) and word count (quantity of writing). For spelling, the outcome measure selected was spelling accuracy on a selection of words taught in the intervention. For phonological awareness, the outcome measure selected was total score on a phonological awareness test. Where there were two outcomes of equal importance both effect sizes were calculated for the syntheses.

Table 2.3 shows the range of five different kinds of ICT interventions that emerged from the 12 included RCTs in the review: computer-assisted-instruction (CAI), networked computer system (classroom intranet), word processing software packages, computer-mediated texts (electronic text) and speech synthesis systems. There were also three literacy outcomes: reading, including reading comprehension and phonological awareness (pre-reading understandings), writing and spelling. The table also shows how many RCTs there were in each ICT intervention/literacy outcome category.

Table 2.2 Trials included in the in-depth review with ICT focus (intervention) and literacy topic focus (literacy outcome)

Author	ICT intervention	Literacy outcome
Berninger et al. 1998	CAI	Spelling
Golden et al. 1990	Networked computer system	Reading (comprehension)
Heise et al. 1991	CAI	Reading
Jinkerson and Baggett 1993	CAI	Spelling
Jones 1994	Word processing	Writing
Lin et al. 1991	CAI	Reading
MacArthur et al. 1990	CAI	Spelling
Matthew 1996 (Matthew 1997)	Computer-mediated texts	Reading (comprehension)
Mitchell and Fox 2001	CAI	Reading (phonological awareness)
Reinking and Rickman 1990	Computer-mediated texts	Reading (comprehension)
Swanson and Trahan 1992	Computer-mediated texts	Reading (comprehension)
Zhang et al. 1995	Speech synthesis	Writing

Table 2.3 ICT interventions and literacy outcomes

ICT intervention	Literacy outcome (number of trials)
CAI	Spelling (3)
	Reading (2)
	Phonological Awareness (1)
	Reading (comprehension) (1)
Networked computer systems	Reading (comprehension) (1)
Word processing	Writing (2)
Computer-mediated texts	Reading (comprehension) (3)
Speech synthesis	Writing (1)

Synthesis of interventions: an analysis of the effectiveness of different types of ICT interventions on a range of literacy outcomes

There were six RCTs that evaluated CAI interventions (Berninger *et al.* 1998; Jinkerson and Baggett 1993; MacArthur *et al.* 1990; Heise *et al.* 1991; Lin *et al.* 1991; Mitchell and Fox 2001). The CAI interventions consisted of studies designed to increase spelling, reading abilities or phonological awareness (pre-reading understandings).

There was one networked computer system intervention (Golden *et al.* 1990), two word processing interventions, three computer-mediated texts interventions and one speech synthesis intervention.

Three of the RCTs contained two strata (Berninger *et al.* 1998; Lin *et al.* 1991; Swanson and Trahan 1992) because the pupils were divided into two groups with different learner characteristics (for example 'average' or 'learning disabled' readers) before being randomly allocated to the intervention or control groups. In all three cases the pupils with different learner characteristics were analysed separately by the authors, and therefore in the review they were treated separately.

One of the RCTs (Zhang *et al.* 1995) compared traditional word processing software with both a control group and with an innovatory word processing package with speech synthesis. The results of the two comparisons were reported separately: traditional word processing package v. control (Microsoft Word v. CT); Robo-Writer speech synthesis system v. control (RW v. CT); although only one of the comparisons was included in a meta-analysis because the same control group was used in both comparisons.

The effect sizes for literacy outcomes in each of the RCTs are presented in Table 2.4. In four of the RCTs (Golden *et al.* 1990; Jones 1994; Matthew 1996; Reinking and Rickman 1990), for the purposes of this synthesis the effect sizes on two literacy outcome measures were calculated because the outcomes were deemed to be equally appropriate for measuring the effectiveness of a particular ICT intervention. For example in Jones (1994) holistic scoring (writing quality) and word count (writing quantity) were both reported.

The syntheses reported are based on appropriate subsets of the 20 effect sizes for the five different ICT interventions.

As described elsewhere (Torgerson and Zhu 2003), included studies were quality appraised and rated according to three criteria:

Table 2.4 Effectiveness of ICT on literacy outcomes

Study	Literacy outcome	Weight of evidence	Effect size	95% confidence interval
CAI Intervention				
Berninger et al. 1998 (1)	Spelling	High	-0.054	-0.854 to 0.745
Berninger et al. 1998 (2)	Spelling	High	0.322	-0.484 to 1.128
Jinkerson and Baggett 1993	Spelling	Medium	-0.020	-0.897 to 0.856
McArthur et al. 1990	Spelling	High	0.387	-0.210 to 0.983
Heise et al. 1991	Reading	Medium	0.487	-0.044 to 1.019
Lin et al. 1991 (1)	Reading	Medium	-0.165	-0.732 to 0.401
Lin et al. 1991 (2)	Reading	Medium	-0.450	-1.051 to 0.136
Mitchell and Fox 2001	Phonological awareness	Medium	-0.604	-0.020 to -1.184
Networked computer systems				
Golden et al. 1990 (QAR2)	Reading 1	Medium	0.123	-0.594 to 0.841
(rule0based inference test)	Reading 2		0.610	-0.120 to 1.349
Word processing				
Jones 1994 (holistic scoring)	Writing 1	Medium	1.251	0.274 to 2.229
(word count)	Writing 2		0.470	-0.415 to 1.368
Zhang et al. 1995 (MS v. CT)	Writing	Medium	0.610	-0.248 to 1.469
Computer mediated texts				
Matthew 1996 (open ended questions)	Reading 1	High	-0.324	-0.783 to 0.134
(story re-telling)	Reading 2		0.545	0.081 to 1.010
Reinking and Rickman 1990	Vocabulary	Medium	0.925	0.391 to 1.460
	Reading		0.168	-0.338 to 0.675
Swanson and Trahan 1992 (1)	Reading	High	-0.267	-0.986 to 0.451
Swanson and Trahan 1992 (2)	Reading	High	0.639	-0.097 to 1.375
Speech synthesis				
Zhang et al. 1995 (RW v. CT)	Writing	Medium	2.740	1.516 to 3.964

methodological soundness; appropriateness of research design; and relevance of focus, context, sample and measures to the research question. They were also given an overall weighting based on the three aforementioned criteria (see Table 2.4). Four of the included trials had an overall weighting of high (Berninger *et al.* 1998; MacArthur *et al.* 1990; Matthew 1996; Swanson and Trahan 1992) and eight of the included trials had a weighting of medium (Golden *et al.* 1990; Heise *et al.* 1991; Jinkerson and Baggett 1993; Jones 1994; Lin *et al.* 1991; Mitchell and Fox 2001; Reinking and Rickman 1990; Zhang *et al.* 1995). All the trials were high quality in terms of appropriateness of study design as all the studies were RCTs. The most important quality assessment criterion is the soundness of the individual RCT (internal validity), and five studies were rated high and seven were rated medium for this criterion. A study could not be rated as overall high unless it achieved a high rating for internal validity.

In Table 2.4 we show the effectiveness results, with 95 per cent confidence intervals, of all the studies.

Overall results

Overall we included 20 comparisons among the 12 trials. Of these 20 effect sizes listed in Table 2.4, 13 were positive and seven were negative. Of the positive effect sizes, four were statistically significant, whilst one of the 7 negative trials was statistically significant. One RCT was equivocal, reporting two main outcomes going in opposite directions (Matthew 1996).

CAI

For CAI the overall data were suggestive of potential harm on literacy outcomes. Thus, for one of the eight strata in six trials there was a statistically significant harmful effect of CAI on literacy outcomes, whilst a further three noted a non-statistically significant harmful effect. Of the remaining three, which all showed a benefit of CAI, none was statistically significant.

Networked computer systems

The one study (Golden *et al.* 1990) that looked at networked computer systems noted a positive effect size in its two main outcomes. Neither of these effect sizes was statistically significant and in one the point estimate was only a small positive effect. However, the confidence intervals around the estimates were wide, potentially not ruling out a large benefit or moderate harmful effect.

Word processing

The effect of word processing on writing was evaluated in two trials (Jones 1994; Zhang *et al.* 1995). Jones (1994) presented two main outcomes. In one outcome (writing quality) there was a large positive benefit, which was statistically significant, whilst for the second outcome (writing quantity) there was a modest benefit, which was not statistically significant. In the other trial (Zhang *et al.* 1995) the positive effect for the word processing condition was not statistically significant.

Computer-mediated texts

In the three trials (two of which had two relevant outcomes and one had two strata), the evidence for the use of computer-mediated texts was somewhat equivocal. Whilst there was one outcome for one trial showing a strong, statistically significant benefit of computer-mediated text on vocabulary and another showing a modest benefit (which was statistically significant) on reading, two strata in another trial had effect sizes in opposite directions, although neither was significant.

Speech synthesis

Only one RCT evaluated the use of a speech synthesis system for composing on the computer (Zhang *et al.* 1995). The trial shows a large positive effect for the intervention that was statistically significant.

Synthesis of outcomes: an analysis of the effectiveness of different types of ICT on specific literacy outcomes

In the second synthesis the effectiveness of different types of ICT on three specific literacy outcomes (reading, writing, spelling) was established through a narrative synthesis and a series of meta-analyses where appropriate.

A meta-analysis essentially adds a number of studies together using a statistical method that gives the greatest weight to the studies with the smallest standard errors, which usually means the largest studies. Because there was more than one randomized trial measuring specific literacy outcomes, and the trials within these subgroups appeared to be relatively homogeneous, we undertook a series of pooled analyses (i.e. meta-analyses) that investigated effectiveness in different aspects of ICT and literacy.

CAI and spelling

We identified three relevant trials of CAI on spelling published since 1990 (Berninger *et al.* 1998; Jinkerson and Baggett 1993, MacArthur *et al.* 1990: Table 2.5). Two strata were reported in Berninger *et al.* 1998. The aim of this trial was to investigate whether the computer or the pencil was more effective in helping pupils to learn to spell words. Forty-eight children (24 in stratum (1) with spelling disabilities and 24 in stratum (2) with spelling and handwriting disabilities) were randomly allocated to computer or paper and pencil response mode. The methods for teaching and learning 48 easy, moderate and difficult words were identical in both conditions, except the children in the computer condition identified the letters on the computer keyboard, pressed the keys and then were able to see the letters on the monitor, and the children in the paper and pencil condition wrote the words as they learnt them. At post-test there were no significant differences for response mode.

The aim of the trial by MacArthur *et al.* (1990) was to compare computer-assisted instruction in spelling practice with traditional paper-and-pencil instruction in spelling practice. Forty-four fifth and sixth grade students with learning disabilities were randomly allocated to CAI (with immediate corrective feedback) or PPI (where the feedback was provided by self-checking). The instructional techniques for each condition utilized features typical of CAI and PPI. There was a non-significant positive effect for the computer condition.

The aim of the trial by Jinkerson and Baggett (1993) was to investigate whether or not the use of a spell checker would help students to identify and correct misspelled words in a story more effectively than students who identified and corrected by hand. Twenty pupils aged 9 to 11 were randomly allocated to a computer or a hand group. The same pre-written story was given to both groups to proofread for spelling errors. There were no significant differences between the groups at post-test.

The information from these three trials (four strata) is summarized in Table 2.5. Pooling these in a meta-analysis showed a small, but non-significant, benefit of CAI on spelling outcomes (Figure 2.1). The pooled effect size was 0.204 (CI −0.168 to 0.576). The heterogeneity 'Q' statistic was 1.1 (low). This shows that there was no statistical evidence for the studies being heterogeneous. Therefore we were justified in pooling them in a meta-analysis.

CAI and reading

Two RCTs (three strata) evaluated CAI and reading interventions (Lin *et al.* 1991; Heise *et al.* 1991).

The aim of the trial by Heise *et al.* was to investigate the role that CAI may play in the development of reading. Fifty-three third grade and sixth to eighth grade 'remedial' students were randomly allocated to computer-assisted instruction or teacher-directed instruction, using a matched pair design. The CAI group used a software package designed to teach new words, definitions and their usage. The conventional instruction group used teacher-directed instruction similar to the presentation on the software package. On a measure of total reading there was a positive effect for the intervention, but this was not statistically significant.

The aim of the trial by Lin *et al.* (1991) was to assess the effectiveness of CAI on the word recognition skills of 'mildly mentally handicapped' and 'non-handicapped' learners. Ninety-three 'mildly

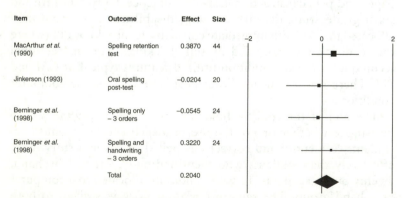

Item	Outcome	Effect	Size
MacArthur *et al.* (1990)	Spelling retention test	0.3870	44
Jinkerson (1993)	Oral spelling post-test	−0.0204	20
Berninger *et al.* (1998)	Spelling only – 3 orders	−0.0545	24
Berninger *et al.* (1998)	Spelling and handwriting – 3 orders	0.3220	24
	Total	0.2040	

Figure 2.1 Forest plot of effectiveness of CAI on spelling outcomes

Table 2.5 Effect of CAI on spelling outcomes

Subgroup	Item	Outcome	Group 1			Group 2			Hedges' g (corrected)	CI	
			N	M	SD	N	M	SD		lower	upper
CAI and spelling	MacArthur et al. 1990, 'Computer-assisted instruction with learning disabled students: achievement, engagement and other factors that influence achievement'.	Spelling retention test	22	8.450	5.460	22	6.360	5.150	0.387	-0.210	0.983
CAI and spelling	Jinkerson and Baggett 1993, 'Spell checkers: aids in identifying and correcting spelling errors'.	Oral spelling post-test	10	14.400	4.270	10	14.500	5.100	-0.020	-0.897	0.856
CAI and spelling	Berninger et al. (1) 1998. 'Teaching spelling to children with specific learning disabilities: the mind's ear and eye beat the computer or pencil'.	Spelling only – 3 orders	12	5.310	1.240	12	5.380	1.240	-0.055	-0.855	0.746

continued …

Table 2.5 continued

Subgroup	Item	Outcome	Group 1			Group 2			Hedges' g	CI	
			N	M	SD	N	M	SD	(corrected)	lower	upper
CAI and spelling	Berninger et al. (2) 1998, 'Teaching spelling to children with specific learning disabilities: the mind's ear and eye beat the computer or pencil'.	Spelling and handwriting – 3 order	12	5.130	1.890	12	4.420	2.340	0.322	–0.484	1.129
	Total								0.204	–0.168	0.576

Notes
Heterogeneity statistic Q = 1.1
Test statistic (combined effect) z = 1.07 p = 0.141
Meta-analysis method: Inverse Variance (fixed effects model)
N = number, M = mean, SD = standard deviation, CI = confidence intervals

mentally handicapped' and 'non-handicapped' students from various grades were randomly assigned to CAI or paper and pencil as the instructional medium for teaching word recognition skills. The outcome measurements were accuracy scores and response times. At post-test there were no significant differences between the groups for accuracy scores.

It was not possible to combine the two trials that evaluated the effectiveness of CAI interventions on reading because there was not sufficient homogeneity between the two groups of learners in the two RCTs. In one of the RCTs (Lin *et al.* 1991) the authors described the learners as 'bilingual' (Chinese American and Caucasian American). In the other RCT (Heise *et al.* 1991) the author described the learners' ethnicities but it was not clear whether the intervention was aimed at improving English as a first or second language. This decision was made a priori, i.e. before the reviewers looked at the results.

Word processing and writing

We identified two RCTs that investigated the effect of word processing on writing (Jones 1994; Zhang *et al.* 1995). The aim of the trial by Jones was to determine whether the use of a word processor would result in a larger quantity of writing and a higher quality of writing than when students composed with paper and pencil. Twenty second-grade students were randomly assigned to treatment or control condition. During the intervention period, the treatment group composed seven written assignments using a word processing program, whilst the control group used paper and pencil. At post-test both groups composed using paper and pencil. The overall quality of the treatment group's writing exceeded that of the control group, but there was no significant difference in mean word count scores (quantity of writing).

The aim of the trial by Zhang *et al.* (1995) was to assess the impact of specifically designed software tools on the quality of writing of children performing at least one year behind their grade level. Thirty-three students with 'learning disabilities' in grades 2–5 were randomly assigned to one of three groups (using a matched triad design). The MS group used a traditional word processing package; the RW group used an innovatory speech synthesis package; and the CT group used traditional paper and pencil. The pupils composed stories in their allocated treatment condition.

There was a pooled effect size of 0.890 (CI 0.245 to 1.535) (see Table 2.6 and Figure 2.2). This was quite a large positive effect for the word processing intervention that was statistically significant. The heterogeneity 'Q' statistic was 0.933 (very low). This shows that, statistically, the studies were similar and therefore we were justified in performing a meta-analysis.

Computer-mediated texts and comprehension

Three RCTs (one with two strata) evaluating the effectiveness of computer-mediated texts interventions on reading comprehension outcomes were included in the in-depth review (Matthew 1996; Swanson and Trahan 1992; Reinking and Rickman 1990). The aim of the trial by Matthew (1996) was to compare the reading comprehension of third grade children who read interactive storybooks with children who read traditional print storybooks. Seventy-four pupils were randomly allocated to intervention or control (using a matched pair design). Students in the experimental group read CD-ROM storybooks on the computer. Students in the control group read the same books in a traditional print format. Two outcome measures were used to measure reading comprehension: ten open-ended questions and story re-telling. There were no statistically significant differences in reading comprehension as assessed by open-ended questions. There was a positive and statistically significant effect for the intervention as assessed by story re-telling.

The aim of the trial by Reinking and Rickman (1990) was to investigate whether or not sixth grade readers' vocabulary learning and comprehension would be improved through the use of computer-mediated texts. Sixty students were randomly assigned to one of four conditions: control – dictionary or glossary condition – (passages were presented on typed pages and accompanied by either dictionary or typed glossary page); computer-mediated intervention – select

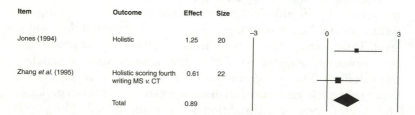

Figure 2.2 Forest plot of effectiveness of word processing on writing

Table 2.6 Effect of word processing on writing outcomes

| Subgroup | Item | Outcome | Group 1 | | | Group 2 | | | Hedges' g | CI | |
			N	M	SD	N	M	SD	(corrected)	lower	upper
Word processing and writing	Jones 1994, 'The effect of a word processor on the written composition of pupils'.	Holistic scoring	10	7.100	1.940	10	4.770	1.610	1.252	0.274	2.229
Word processing and writing	Zhang et al. 1995, 'Quality of writing by elementary students with learning disabilities'.	Holistic scoring fourth writing MS v. CT	11	4.020	1.040	11	3.460	0.690	0.610	−0.249	1.470
		Total							0.890	0.245	1.535

Notes
Heterogeneity statistic Q = 0.933
Test statistic (combined effect) z = 2.7 p = 0.00344
Meta-analysis method: Inverse Variance (fixed effects model)
N = number, M = mean, SD = standard deviation, CI = confidence intervals

definitions or all definitions condition – (pupils could request the definitions of words on screen or they had to view the meanings of target words before proceeding to the next section of text). For the purposes of this review the two print control groups and the two computer intervention groups were combined in order to calculate the effect size. There was a small positive effect for the intervention, but this was not statistically significant.

The aim of the trial undertaken by Swanson and Trahan (1992) was to determine the degree to which computer-mediated texts influenced 'learning disabled' children's reading comprehension. One hundred and twenty fourth, fifth and sixth grade pupils were randomly assigned to one of four conditions: control (all pre- and post-test measures but no reading comprehension intervention, other than normal classroom instruction); paper offline (traditional and cloze comprehension passages in printed form); computer presentation – no re-reading (traditional and cloze story passages in computer-mediated form); computer re-reading (readers were directed to re-read all or portions of the passages before answering comprehension items or cloze items). For this effectiveness review, the paper offline condition was compared with the computer no re-read condition. In stratum (1) ('learning disabled' readers) there was a small positive effect for the control condition that was not statistically significant. In stratum (2) ('average' readers) there was quite a large positive effect for the treatment condition, but this was not statistically significant.

Two separate meta-analyses were undertaken for the trials investigating computer-mediated texts and reading comprehension (Tables 2.7 and 2.8 and Figures 2.3 and 2.4). This is because Matthew (1996) used two outcomes for reading comprehension (open-ended questions and story re-telling) that the reviewers judged to be equally appropriate for measuring reading comprehension.

There was a non-statistically significant positive effect for the control. The effect size was –0.047 (CI –0.330 to 0.236). Again, with a low 'Q' statistic there was no evidence of heterogeneity. Therefore we were justified in performing a meta-analysis.

There was a small positive effect for the computer-mediated texts group which was of borderline statistical significance (effect size 0.282 CI –0.003 to 0.566). Again the 'Q' statistic was low. Therefore there was no evidence of heterogeneity and we were justified in performing the meta-analysis.

Table 2.7 Effect of computer-mediated texts on reading outcomes

Subgroup	Item	Outcome	Group 1			Group 2			Hedges' g	CI	
			N	M	SD	N	M	SD	(corrected)	lower	upper
Computer-mediated texts and reading (1)	Matthew 1996, 'The impact of CD-ROM storyboks on children's reading comprehension and reading attitude'.	Open-ended questions	37	46.080	5.010	37	47.680	4.740	−0.325	−0.784	0.134
Computer-mediated texts and reading (1)	Swanson and Trahan (1) 1992, 'Learning disabled readers' comprehension of computer-mediated text: the influence of working memory, metacognition and attribution'.	Nelson comprehension (learning disabled)	15	12.300	5.020	15	13.550	4.850	−0.246	−0.965	0.472
Computer-mediated texts and reading (1)	Swanson and Trahan (2) 1992, 'Learning disabled readers' comprehension of computer-mediated text: the influence of working memory, metacognition and attribution'.	Nelson comprehension (average readers)	15	18.070	4.820	15	15.770	6.090	0.407	−0.317	1.132

continued ....

Table 2.7 continued

Subgroup	Item	Outcome	Group 1			Group 2			Hedges' g	CI	
			N	M	SD	N	M	SD	(corrected)	lower	upper
Computer-mediated texts and reading (1)	Reinking and Rickman, 1990, 'The effects of computer-mediated texts on the vocabulary learning and comprehension of intermediate-grade readers'.	Comprehension computer v. no computer	30	3.650	2.800	30	3.160	2.946	0.168	−0.339	0.675
		Total							−0.047	−0.330	0.236

Notes

Heterogeneity statistic Q = 3.91

Test statistic (combined effect) z = 0.326 p = 0.628

Meta-analysis method: Inverse Variance (fixed effects model)

N = number, M = mean, SD = standard deviation, CI = confidence intervals

Table 2.8 Effect of computer-mediated texts on literacy outcomes

Subgroup	Item	Outcome	Group 1			Group 2			Hedges' g	CI	
			N	M	SD	N	M	SD	(corrected)	lower	upper
Computer-mediated texts and reading (2)	Matthew 1996, 'The impact of CD-ROM storybooks on children's reading comprehension and reading attitude'.	Story re-telling	37	24.990	2.960	37	23.170	3.610	0.546	0.081	1.010
Computer-mediated texts and reading (2)	Swanson and Trahan (1) 1992, 'Learning disabled readers' comprehenson of computer-mediated text: the influence of working memory, metacognition and attribution'.	Nelson comprehension (learning disabled)	15	12.300	5.020	15	13.550	4.850	−0.246	−0.965	0.472
Computer-mediated texts and reading (2)	Swanson and Trahan (2) 1992, 'Learning disabled readers' comprehension of computer-mediated text: the influence of working memory, metacognition and attribution'.	Nelson comprehension (average readers)	15	18.070	4.820	15	15.770	6.090	0.407	−0.317	1.132

continued ...

Table 2.8 continued

Subgroup	Item	Outcome	Group 1			Group 2			Hedges' g	CI	
			N	M	SD	N	M	SD	(corrected)	lower	upper
Computer-mediated texts and reading (2)	Reinking and Rickman 1990, 'The effects of computer-mediated texts on vocabulary learning and comprehension of intermediate-grade readers'.	Comprehension computer v. no computer	30	3.650	2.800	30	3.160	2.946	0.168	−0.339	0.675
		Total							0.282	−0.003	0.566

Notes
Heterogeneity statistic Q = 3.62
Test statistic (combined effect) z = 1.94 p = 0.0261
Meta-analysis method: Inverse Variance (fixed effects model)
N = number, M = mean, SD = standard deviation, CI = confidence intervals

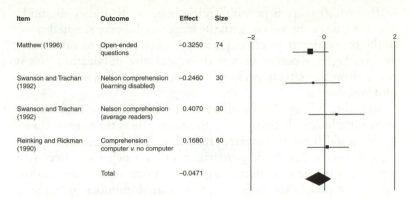

Figure 2.3 Forest plot of effectiveness of computer-mediated texts on reading comprehension (1)

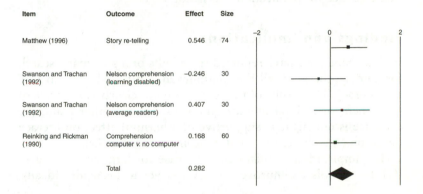

Figure 2.4 Forest plot of effectiveness of computer-mediated texts on reading comprehension (2)

Publication bias

One source of bias for systematic reviews is through publication bias. If studies showing a positive (beneficial) effect are more likely to be published than negative or inconclusive studies, this will give a biased estimate of effect. One method of determining the existence of publication bias is to draw a funnel plot. This plots the effect size of a study (on the x-axis) against its sample size (on the y-axis). Very small studies will have a high probability of showing an inconclusive effect even if the intervention is effective, just as they will have a raised probability of showing a positive effect if the intervention is ineffective. If there is no publication bias, small studies should be scattered along the x-axis, with the larger trials being situated closer to the true estimate of effect (as they are less subject to variability). To investigate whether or not there was any publication bias in research in the effectiveness of ICT on literacy learning a funnel plot was drawn.

In Figure 2.5 we plot the effect size of the identified trials against their sample size. If there is no publication bias then the included trials should form an 'inverted' funnel with the largest trials at the top. In Figure 2.5 the largest trial reports a negative effect size; however, the studies with the largest effect sizes tend to be positive. There is a possibility, therefore, that a small number of 'missing' trials may have negative effect sizes. The absence of these trials will tend to make any estimates of effect biased towards the positive. The evidence for publication bias is not large.

Findings and implications

In this chapter we have reported the results of a systematic search for, and synthesis of, all the randomized controlled trials in ICT and literacy. The results of the review are not clearly supportive of the benefit of ICT on literacy outcomes. On the other hand, the evidence is not strongly supportive of a harmful effect on literacy development. Therefore, the data seem to be equivocal.

The implication of this is that the case for large investment in ICT by schools to improve literacy has yet to be made. Ideally,

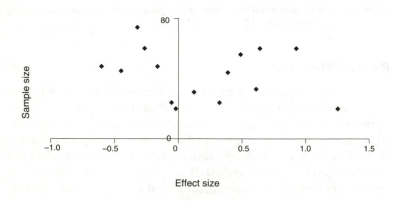

Figure 2.5 Funnel plot of included trials

therefore, large robust trials that could confirm any benefit of ICT on literacy need to be undertaken, otherwise the continued high investment in ICT could be wasted.

We identified 12 relatively small RCTs for a detailed review. Some were so small that they could only really be considered to be pilot studies. These tiny trials are the sum of the most rigorous evidence available to date upon which to justify or refute the policy of spending millions of pounds on ICT equipment, software and teacher training.

In the first synthesis for five different ICT interventions overall we included 20 comparisons from the 12 RCTs; 13 were positive and 7 were negative. Of the positive ones three were statistically significant, whilst of the seven negative trials one was statistically significant. These data would suggest that there is little evidence to support the widespread use of ICT in literacy learning in English. This also supports the findings from previous systematic reviews that have used data from rigorous study designs. It also supports the most recent observational data from the ImpaCT study (BECTa 2002). These findings support the view that ICT use for literacy learning should be restricted to pupils participating in rigorous randomized trials of such technology.

In the second synthesis we undertook three principal meta-analyses: one for the effect of CAI on spelling, one for the effect of word processing on writing, and one for the effect of computer-mediated texts on reading. In two there was no evidence of benefit or harm (i.e. in spelling and reading the small effect sizes were not statistically significant). In writing there was weak evidence for a positive effect, but it was weak because only 42 children altogether were included in this meta-analysis.

Policy makers should refrain from any further investment into ICT and literacy until at least one large and rigorously designed randomized trial has shown it to be effective in increasing literacy outcomes. Teachers should be aware that there is no evidence that non-ICT methods of instruction and non-ICT resources are inferior to the use of ICT to promote literacy learning. A series of large, rigorously designed RCTs to evaluate ICT and literacy learning across all age ranges is urgently required.

Randomized controlled trials

Studies selected for in-depth review are marked with asterisks.

Adam, N. and Wild, M. (1997) 'Applying CD-ROM interactive storybooks to learning to read', *Journal of Computer Assisted Learning*, 13: 119–32.

Allen, G. and Thompson, A. (1995) 'Analysis of the effect of networking on computer-assisted collaborative writing in a fifth grade classroom', *Journal of Educational Computing Research*, 12: 65–75.

Barker, T.A. (1994) *An Evaluation of Computer-assisted Instruction in Phonological Awareness with Below Average Readers*, Florida, US: Florida State University.

Barron, R.W., Golden, J.O., Seldon, D.M., Tait, C.F., Marmurek, H.H.C. and Haines, L.P. (1992) 'Teaching prereading skills with a talking computer: letter-sound knowledge and print feedback facilitate nonreaders' phonological awareness training', *Reading and Writing: An Interdisciplinary Journal*, 4: 179–204.

*Berninger, V., Abbott, R., Rogan, L., Reed, E., Abbott, S., Brooks, A., Vaughan, K. and Graham, S. (1998) 'Teaching spelling to children with specific learning disabilities: the mind's ear and eye beat the computer or pencil', *Learning Disability Quarterly*, 28: 106–22.

Bonk, C.J. and Reynolds, T.H. (1992) 'Early adolescent composing within a generative-evaluative computerized prompting framework', *Computers in Human Behavior*, 8: 39–62.

Braden, J.P., Shaw, S.R. and Grecko, L. (1991) 'An evaluation of a computer-assisted instructional program for elementary hearing-impaired students', *Volta Review*, 93: 247–52.

Calvert, S.L., Watson, J.A., Brinkley V. and Penny, J. (1990) 'Computer presentational features for poor readers' recall of information', *Journal of Educational Computing Research*, 6: 287–98.

Cardinale, P. and Fish, J.M. (1994) 'Treating children's writing apprehension with word processing', *Journal of Personality and Clinical Studies*, 10: 1–15.

Cato, V., English, F. and Trushell, J. (1994) 'Reading screens: mapping the labyrinth', in D. Wray (ed.) *Literacy and Computers: Insights from Research*, Royston: United Kingdom Reading Association.

Dwyer, H.J. and Sullivan, H.J. (1993) 'Student preferences for teacher and computer composition marking', *Journal of Educational Research*, 83: 137–41.

Feldmann, S.C. and Fish, M.C. (1991) 'Use of computer-mediated reading supports to enhance reading comprehension of high school students', *Journal of Educational Computing Research*, 7: 25–36.

Foster, K.C., Erickson, G.C., Foster, D.F., Brinkman, D. and Torgersen, J.K. (1994) 'Computer administered instruction in phonological awareness:

evaluation of the DaisyQuest Program', *Journal of Research and Development in Education*, 27: 126–37.

Fuchs, L.S., Fuchs, D., Hamlett, C.L. and Allinder, R.M. (1991) 'Effects of expert system advice within curriculum-based measurement in teacher planning and student achievement in spelling', *School Psychology Review*, 20: 49–66.

*Golden, N., Gersten, R. and Woodward, J. (1990) 'Effectiveness of guided practice during remedial reading instruction: an application of computer-managed instruction', *Elementary School Journal*, 90: 291–304.

Grejda, G.F. and Hannafin, M.J. (1992) 'Effects of word processing on sixth graders' holistic writing and revisions', *Journal of Educational Research*, 85: 144–9.

Harris, E.A. and Bond, C.L. (1992) 'A holistic approach to guided writing: using the WICAT Program supplemented with peer critique', *Journal of Computing in Childhood Education*, 3: 193–201.

*Heise, B.L., Papalewis, R. and Tanner, D.E. (1991) 'Building base vocabulary with computer-assisted instruction', *Teacher Education Quarterly*, 18: 55–63.

*Jinkerson, L. and Baggett, P. (1993) 'Spell checkers: aids in identifying and correcting spelling errors', *Journal of Computing in Childhood Education*, 4: 291–306.

Johnston, C.B. (1996) 'Interactive storybook software: effects on verbal development in kindergarten children', *Early Child Development and Care*, 132: 33–44.

*Jones, I. (1994) 'The effect of a word processor on the written composition of pupils', *Computers in the Schools*, 11: 43–54.

Laframboise, K.L. (1991) 'The facilitative effects of word processing on sentence-combining tasks with at-risk fourth graders', *Journal of Research and Development in Education*, 24: 1–8.

Leong, C.K. (1992) 'Enhancing reading comprehension with text-to-speech (DECtalk) computer system', *Reading and Writing*, 4: 205–17.

Leong, C.K. (1995) 'Effects of on-line reading and simultaneous DECtalk in helping below-average and poor readers comprehend and summarize text', *Learning Disability Quarterly*, 18: 101–16.

Leong, C.K. (1996) 'Using microcomputer technology to promote students' "higher-order" reading', in B.E.M. Gorayska and L. Jacob (eds) *Cognitive technology: in search of a humane interface. Advances in psychology, Vol. 113*, New York: Elsevier Science.

Lewin, C. (2000) 'Exploring the effects of talking book software in UK primary classrooms', *Journal of Research in Reading*, 23: 149–57.

*Lin, A., Podell, D.M. and Rein, N. (1991) 'The effects of CAI on word recognition in mildly mentally handicapped and nonhandicapped learners', *Journal of Special Education Technology*, 11: 16–25.

*MacArthur, C.A., Haynes, J.A., Malouf, D.B., Harris, K.R. and Mowings, M. (1990) 'Computer assisted instruction with learning disabled students: achievement, engagement, and other factors that influence achievement', *Journal of Educational Computing Research*, 6: 311–28.

*Matthew, K.I. (1996) 'The impact of CD-ROM storybooks on children's reading comprehension and reading attitude', *Journal of Educational Multimedia and Hypermedia*, 5: 379–94.

Matthew, K.I. (1997) 'A comparison of the influence of interactive CD-ROM storybooks and traditional print storybooks on reading comprehension', *Journal of Research in Computing in Education*, 29: 263–75.

*Mitchell, M.J. and Fox, B.J. (2001) 'The effects of computer software for developing phonological awareness in low-progress readers', *Reading Research and Instruction*, 40: 315–32.

Olson, R.K., Wise, B., Ring, J. and Johnson, M. (1997) 'Computer-based remedial training in phoneme awareness and phonological decoding: effects on the post-training development of word recognition', *Scientific Studies of Reading*, 1: 235–53.

Palumbo, D.B. and Prater, D.L. (1992) 'A comparison of computer-based prewriting strategies for basic ninth-grade writers', *Computers in Human Behavior*, 8: 63–70.

*Reinking, D. and Rickman, S.S. (1990) 'The effects of computer-mediated texts on the vocabulary learning and comprehension of intermediate-grade readers', *Journal of Reading Behavior*, 22: 395–411.

Roberts, G.I. and Samuels, M.T. (1993) 'Handwriting remediation: a comparison of computer-based and traditional approaches', *Journal of Educational Research*, 87: 118–25.

Rosenbluth, G.S. and Reed, W.M. (1992) 'The effects of writing-process-based instruction and word processing on remedial and accelerated eleventh graders', *Computers in Human Behavior*, 8: 71–95.

Silver, N.W. and Repa, J.T. (1993) 'The effect of word processing on the quality of writing and self-esteem of secondary school English-as-second-language students: writing without censure', *Journal of Educational Computing Research*, 9: 265–83.

Spaulding, C.L. and Lake, D. (1992) 'Interactive effects of computer network and student characteristics on students' writing and collaborating', *High School Journal*, 76: 67–77.

*Swanson, H.L. and Trahan, M.F. (1992) 'Learning disabled readers' comprehension of computer-mediated text: the influence of working memory, metacognition and attribution', *Learning Disabilities Research and Practice*, 7: 74–86.

Topping, K.J. (1997) 'Family electronic literacy: part 1 – home–school links through audiotaped books', *Reading*, 31: 7–11.

Utay, C. and Utay, J. (1997) 'Peer-assisted learning: the effects of cooperative learning and cross-age peer tutoring with word processing on writing skills of students with learning disabilities', *Journal of Computing in Childhood Education*, 8: 165–85.

Varner-Quick, W.S. (1994) 'The effects of computer-assisted instruction on reading abilities: a comparison of fourth grade reading programs with and without computer technology', unpublished thesis, Wayne State University, USA.

Wepner, S.B. (1992) ' "Real-life" reading software and "at-risk" secondary students', *Reading Horizons*, 32: 279–88.

Wise, B.W. and Olson, R.K. (1995) 'Computer-based phonological awareness and reading instruction', *Annals of Dyslexia*, 45: 99–122.

*Zhang, Y., Brooks, D.W., Frields, T. and Redelfs, M. (1995) 'Quality of writing by elementary students with learning disabilities', *Multimedia Today*, 3: 30–9.

References

Andrews, R., Burn, A., Leach, J., Locke, T., Low, G. and Torgerson, C. (2002) 'A systematic review of the impact of networked ICT on 5–16-year-olds' literacy in English' (EPPI-Centre Review), *Research Evidence in Education Library*, 1, London: EPPI-Centre, Social Science Research Unit, Institute of Education.

Angrist, J. and Lavy, V. (2002) 'New evidence on classroom computers and pupil learning', *The Economic Journal*, 12 (October): 735–65.

Bangert-Drowns, R.L. (1993) 'The word processor as an instructional tool: a meta-analysis of word processing in writing instruction', *Review of Educational Research*, 63: 69–93.

Blok, H., Van Daalen-Kapteijns, M.M., Otter, M.E. and Overmaat, M. (2001) 'Using computers to learn words in the elementary grades: an evaluation framework and a review of effect studies', *Computer Assisted Language Learning*, 14: 99–128.

British Educational Communications and Technology Agency (BECTa) (1998–9), *A Preliminary Report for the DfEE on the Relationship Between ICT and Primary School Standards*, Coventry: BECTa.

British Educational Communications and Technology Agency (BECTa) (1998) *The UK Evaluations Final Report*, Coventry: BECTa.

British Educational Communications and Technology Agency (BECTa) (2001a) *Primary Schools of the Future – Achieving Today*, Coventry: BECTa.

British Educational Communications and Technology Agency (BECTa) (2001b) *The Secondary School of the Future*, Coventry: BECTa.

British Educational Communications and Technology Agency (BECTa) (2002) *The Impact of Information and Communication Technologies on Pupil Learning and Attainment*, Coventry: BECTa.

Cook, T.D. and Campbell, T.D. (1979) *Quasi-experimentation: Design and Analysis Issues for Field Settings*, Boston: Houghton Mifflin.

Cook, T.D. (2002) 'Reappraising the arguments against randomized experiments in education: an analysis of the culture of evaluation in

American schools of education', paper for presentation at the SRI International Design Conference on Design Issues in Evaluating Educational Technologies (www.sri.com/policy/designkt/found.html).

Fulk, B.M. and Stormont-Spurgin, M. (1995) 'Spelling interventions for students with disabilities: a review', *The Journal of Special Education*, 28: 488–513.

Lipsey, M. and Wilson, D. (1993) 'The efficacy of psychological, educational and behavioral treatment: confirmation from meta-analysis', *American Psychologist*, 48: 1181–209.

MacArthur, C.A., Ferretti, R.P., Okolo, C.M. and Cavalier, A.R. (2001) 'Technology applications for students with literacy problems: a critical review', *The Elementary School Journal*, 101: 273–301.

Torgerson, C.J. and Elbourne, D. (2002) 'A systematic review and meta-analysis of the effectiveness of information and communication technology (ICT) on the teaching of spelling', *Journal of Research in Reading*, 25: 129–43.

Torgerson, C.J. and Zhu, D. (2003) 'A systematic review and meta-analysis of the effectiveness of ICT on literacy learning in English, 5–16' (EPPI-Centre Review), *Research Evidence in Education Library*, 2. London: EPPI-Centre, Social Science Research Unit, Institute of Education.

Ukoumunne, O.C., Gulliford, M.C., Chinn, S., Sterne, J.A.C. and Burney, P.G.J. (1998) 'Evaluation of healthcare interventions at area and organization level', in N. Black, J. Brazier, R. Fitzpatrick and B. Reeves (eds) *Health Services Research Methods*, London: BMJ Publications.

Chapter 3

The impact of networked ICT on literacy learning

Richard Andrews, Andrew Burn, Jenny Leach, Terry Locke, Graham Low and Carole Torgerson

The study of the impact of networked ICT on literacy learning was undertaken in three stages. First, a mapping study was undertaken in late 2001, revealing a wide range of aspects of ICT that required in-depth study. The decision to focus on *networked* ICT was taken by the English Review Group and an in-depth study followed. A first version of this study was published six months later as Andrews *et al.* (2002) During the second year of in-depth reviews deriving from the mapping study (which itself was updated to take into account new publications in the field), the networked ICT review was updated. This chapter consists of a summary and commentary on that updated review. The review itself is published in the Research Evidence in Education Library (http://eppi.ioe.ac.uk/reel) as Andrews *et al.* (2003)

The main research question for this particular review was:

* What is the impact of *networked* ICT on literacy learning in English, 5–16?

By 'networked ICT' we mean information and communication technologies that operate by linking computers or mobile phones to each other, thereby creating a network of communication possibilities. The most common applications are texting, email and the Internet, though we include in the definition local area networks and intranets.

The definitions of 'literacy' and 'impact' were important to establish at the outset, and are defined in Chapter 1.

We confined our searches to the teaching and learning of English in the curriculum from 5–16. While the principal focus was on the use of ICT in English in schools, there is also important research on the individual use of ICT in, for example, the creation of websites (e.g. Abbott 2001) and other home or out-of-school use, as we did not wish to exclude related research that might shed light on the issues we were trying to address.

In order to delimit the scope of the review further, and because of the rapidly changing nature of ICT, we focused on research published since 1990: the beginning of the decade in which the Internet became widely used and in which schools began to use it in significant numbers.

Furthermore, the review is delimited by its focus on literacy learning *in English*. That is to say, we have included studies that focus on English as a mother tongue and as a second or additional language, but not on English as a foreign language. In other words, the studies come from contexts in which English is used as a first, second or additional language in home, school and other environments.

Justification for range of study types

Because our research question seeks to address *impact* rather than just *effect*, it casts its net wider than randomised controlled trials – which are generally accepted as the best way to gauge effect within a scientific cause-effect paradigm. Other study types were included in order to shed light on the multi-faceted nature of 'impact', i.e. influence which brings about change in strategic and contextual ways as well as in practical, observable effects. These study types included, within the outcome evaluation category, the following: non-randomised trials, pre- and post-test designs, and post-test designs. It might be said that these study types represent a descending hierarchy of methods in terms of reliability. Additionally, within a broad process evaluation category, we included process evaluations and needs assessments. As we undertook the update of the review between 2002 and 2003, the categorization of study types was revised by the EPPI-Centre. Studies that were previously classified as 'process evaluations' were re-classified as 'explorations of relationships', and as it turned out, some of the best studies in this particular field were of that nature. Qualitative data or quantitative data might appear in either major category and almost within every study type. Overall, we sought a spectrum of evidence to answer our research question.

Synthesis

We were unable to statistically synthesise the data in a meta-analysis because there was an absence of the kind of quantitative data that could fit into a meta-analysis. Therefore the synthesis took the form of a qualitative overview: a qualitative description of the main findings of the 'sound' trial and its methodological strengths and weaknesses; and a description of the methodological shortcomings of the five trials that, in the first review, were judged to be 'not sound' according to the EPPI Reviewer criteria.

The synthesis takes a narrative form. It has been drafted, discussed, revised and redrafted by the review team and its advisory group, which consists of teachers, school board advisers, parent governors and policy-makers.

Results

The results of the mapping and in-depth review parts of the study are initially presented in tabular form. Tables 3.1 and 3.2 present information on the number of studies identified for the mapping study and the specific in-depth review. Tables 3.3 and 3.4 present, in summary form, the titles of the articles reviewed in the in-depth study and a description of each of the articles. These are then discussed in more detail in the following section.

Discussion of results

This section focuses on the results of the in-depth review. Readers interested in a discussion of the methodological issues that have arisen are referred to the full technical report on http://eppi.ioe.ac.uk/reel. Because the nature of the results and the methodological issues differ according to the types of study design used, we have discussed the research study-type by study-type: first, randomised controlled trials and controlled trials, then pre- and post-test designs, then process evaluations/explorations of relationships and needs assessment studies.

Randomised controlled trials and controlled trials

Randomised controlled trials, and, to a lesser extent, non-randomised controlled trials, are the most appropriate methods that can be used

Table 3.1 The process of retrieval of the 24 included papers in the in-depth review

Total number of 'hits'	2,319
Met mapping study inclusion criteria on the basis of the title or abstract	428
Not received or unavailable	34
Full reports available	394
Full reports that did not meet mapping study inclusion criteria	182
Met mapping study inclusion criteria and keyworded	212
Keyworded as networked ICT and included in in-depth review	24

Table 3.2 The number of studies that reached the in-depth review by study type

Study type	
Exploration of relationships	8
Evaluation – naturally occurring	2
Evaluation – researcher-manipulated	14
Researcher-manipulated	
RCT	3
Trial	7
Other	4

to assess whether networked computers are actually *effective* in improving literacy learning (though note that our focus is on *impact*) In this section we consider all the experimental studies identified in our systematic review.

Ten randomised controlled trials or controlled trials met our inclusion criteria for the in-depth review. Three were randomised controlled trials: Allen and Thompson (1995); Golden *et al.* (1990); Spaulding and Lake (1992). Seven studies were controlled trials: Casey (2001); Clouse (1992); Erickson *et al.* (1992); McKeon and Burkey (1998); Moore and Karabenick (1992); Stuhlmann and Taylor (1998); Watts and Lloyd (2001). However, only two of the studies, Golden *et al.* (1990) and Watts and Lloyd (2001), were judged 'sound' on the basis of the EPPI Reviewer criteria. Therefore,

Table 3.3 Summary of articles included in in-depth review by study type

Exploration of relationships	Abbott, 2001
	Baker, 2001
	Bigum *et al.* 1997
	Ewing, 2000
	McKeon and Burkey, 1998
	McKeon *et al.* 2001
	McNamee, 1995
	Morgan, 1997
	Morgan, 2001
	Stuhlmann and Taylor 1998
Evaluation – naturally occurring	Collins, 1993
	Wishart, 1994
Evaluation – researcher-manipulated:	
RCT	Allen and Thompson, 1995
	Golden *et al.*, 1990
	Spaulding and Lake, 1992
Trial	Casey, 2001
	Clouse, 1992
	Erickson *et al.* 1992
	McKeon and Burkey, 1998
	Moore and Karabenick, 1992
	Stuhlmann and Taylor, 1998
	Watts and Lloyd, 2001
Other	Garner *et al.* 2000
	Love, 1998
	Nettelbeck, 2000
	Peyton, 1991

only these trials were available to establish the impact of networked ICT on literacy learning.

The study by Golden *et al.* (1990) can help to show whether or not the use of a low-cost networked computer system for guided practice can have an impact on the reading comprehension and inferential learning of low-achieving students compared with the use of a worksheet for the same purpose. The study can also help to show levels of student engagement on task, and the impact of this use of networked computers on student satisfaction.

Golden *et al.* (1990) investigated the effectiveness of the use of guided practice in teaching reading comprehension to middle-school students in a remedial reading class. Teachers used a low-cost computer networking system to immediately assess and tabulate student performance to determine which segments of the curriculum required additional remediation.

There is a significant main effect for the instructional method (intervention) for the rule-based inferences test. On both testing occasions the guided practice group performed significantly better than the comparison group:

> the results indicate that the guided practice had a significant positive effect on students' acquisition of the more complex material in the rule-based inferences curriculum but had no discernible effect on their performance on the more familiar material in the QAR (Question-Answer Reading strategy) test. The effect on the rule-based inferences was maintained over a 2-week period.
>
> (Golden *et al.* 1990: 298)

Pre- and post-test studies

Peyton (1991), Clouse (1992), Erickson *et al.* (1992), Garner *et al.* (2000), Casey (2001) and Watts and Lloyd (2001) are all outcome evaluations, using a pre- and post-test or a post-test design. The shortcomings that we have identified in these studies are not so much to do with the nature of pre- and post-test research designs, as with the way in which most of these studies have been carried out.

Peyton (1991) is one of the most useful as far as the present study is concerned. It explores the use of a local area network within a classroom for written real-time communication with students who have hearing problems and other learning difficulties. The hypotheses generated by the research from the Electronic Networks for Interaction (ENFI) Project – a wider project referred to in the 1991 paper – are that all writing does not have to consist of extended, autonomous text; that writing does not have to grow from signed or oral communication; and that a small amount of writing can serve as a starting point for communication in speech and other media. A range of outcomes is reported, some attitudinal ('students were more motivated and willing to write') and others more skills-based ('They have begun to initiate topics, maintain and elaborate on topics, request and provide clarification, ask and respond appropriately to questions, and write increasingly sophisticated and complex English'). But these outcomes are illustrations or supporting evidence for hypotheses or propositions generated from previous research in the ENFI project. They cannot be taken as attempts to prove or disprove the hypotheses. We have no evidence to doubt the author's conclusions, most of which are suggestive of the capacity of ENFI to motivate deaf students to write. The study shows that immediate guided practice can also facilitate engagement with tasks and satisfaction with learning tasks.

The aim of the research reported in Clouse (1992) was to establish whether US Grade 1–4 students using a Teaching and Learning with Computers system and following the Jostens reading, writing and math curriculum for K-4 made gains in main skills and selected sub-skill areas. Although the greatest absolute gains are reported as being made by Grade 1 students (a 23.4 per cent gain for reading), methodological weaknesses in the study make it impossible to draw conclusions about the impact of ICT on literacy learning. A large-scale study compared to national norms could have indicated what sort of learners gain what sort of benefit from ICT support in language skills.

Erickson *et al.* (1992) examined the independent home behaviours of fourth graders on a network in terms of online choices of videotext. They found that students did use online programs over the summer vacation and that the usage peaked at an average rate which exceeded that observed in the latter part of the previous term. Some programs were preferred (on average) over others. The study provides limited evidence that elementary school students in socially-disadvantaged circumstances might be motivated to engage in literacy-related work online from home during the summer vacation.

The broad aim of the Garner *et al.* (2000) study is to try to determine whether writing on networked computers in an out-of-school environment can motivate young people to write more freely than within school. The authors use not-very-clearly defined measures of student behaviour to conclude that students taking part in an online newsletter in the out-of-school environment appear to have written as if they were in school; and they see the failure rate (50 per cent) on completion of writing assignments as indication of such a response from the students. However, the data presented do not substantiate the conclusion presented in the abstract (that it was mainly the adult audience that was unmotivating for the children) though the lack of motivation could have been one of the reasons.

Casey (2001) is the report of a non-randomised controlled trial that aims to see if computers make a difference in the learning that occurs in the classroom, especially with regard to reading and writing development. Although a range of methods was used to gauge the impact of various kinds of software on 5–6-year-olds in a school in southern California, data are not presented in the report, even though it is claimed that 'all students in the experimental classrooms using Writing to Read averaged at least 2 writing levels higher based on a holistic evaluation than those in the control classrooms'. There are probably data published elsewhere that would provide evidence for the conclusions, but overall, on the basis of the published report we found, little data and no analysis were presented. Nettelbeck (2000) is another study where, perhaps, the nature of the text-type used for the reporting of the study (brief article in this case as opposed to brief report for Casey) limits the significance of the research. Although the aim of the study is explicit – to find out whether the use of computers in one Australian secondary school led to the types of literacy activities required for examinations and syllabuses in that particular context – and the findings are plausible, the conclusions are presented without any discussion of the design, methodology, validation or analysis of the data.

The paper by Watts and Lloyd (2001), on the other hand, provided a more explicit account of a research study, the aim of which was to evaluate a complete and compact ICT service, 'Espresso for Schools'. Espresso was compared with other forms of ICT provision: there were four experimental and four 'comparative' schools in which 10-year-old pupils were studied. The children were presented with a series of journalistic tasks and classroom activities that they resolved through the use of a compact and coordinated information system. Via pre-test and post-test, gains in achievement from the pre-teaching to the post-teaching task were measured. The outcomes demonstrated that children can become self-directed and very active, exploratory learners in a very short period of time. A clear majority of pupils did manage to increase the quality of their work within the middle range of scores. To what extent these gains were sustainable, and whether or not they could transfer to other parts of the curriculum or to other more generic skills and attitudes were not explored.

Overall, there is not much that can be concluded from the pre-test and post-test studies.

Love's (1998) study, however, looks at how English teachers are using computers in their classrooms and how they are being helped to integrate computer technology into their teaching. It is one of the few research studies that has investigated the need for the management techniques necessary in the light of new developments in technology and literacy/ies. The unevenness 'in terms of [pupils'] conceptual and technical expertise' is matched by that of teachers, who need to become more aware of technology's limitations as well as its possibilities. Such unevenness suggests the need for national strategies in professional development at both pre- and in-service stages of teaching, and the nurturing of a critical approach to computer use in literacy development for both teachers and pupils alike.

Process evaluations and explorations of relationships

There is a total of eight process evaluations and explorations of relationships in the in-depth review. Process evaluations tend to focus on *how* to research a particular topic rather than on definable outcomes of research. Explorations of relationships often take the form of case studies or other largely qualitative designs which aim to explore factors or variables at play in a particular situation, and to begin to define relationships between those factors or variables.

The studies by Ewing (2000) and Morgan (1997) were defined in the first version of the review as process evaluations, but their focus is not entirely methodological. In both papers, there are projections from available data – a process of hypothesis-forming about practice as well as questions raised about how best to move forward research in the field.

Ewing's paper, 'Enhancement of online and offline student learning' looks at a range of views about using ICT in support of learning and postulates a model for ICT in support of learning. Its focus is not only on literacy learning. The paper takes a constructivist approach to the enhancement of learning, and because constructivism (in the wake of Vygotsky, e.g. 1986) assumes communication is at the heart of a social, collaborative learning process, literacy learning is central to the process. While collaborative learning, it is suggested, requires enhanced literacy skills in speaking and listening, there are implications for reading and writing on screen (both online and offline). A useful distinction is made in the paper between network literacy skills and computer literacy skills (see OECD 2001). Network literacy skills include 'accessing and creating resources and communication with others' (p.212) The paper proceeds by evaluating data from three projects in the light of a composite model for ICT in support of learning. The other most significant elements of the model for the purposes of the present study are that:

- computer-based learning must include electronic mail and conferencing facilities
- the computer learning environment should provide opportunities for student activities other than word processing
- student use of hard copies of electronic learning material may be the preferred approach offline.

For a full account of the model, readers are recommended to consult the original paper. Methodological issues arising from the paper are the fact that the emerging model is based on qualitative research outcomes and that the data are used to illuminate the model.

The paper by Morgan (1997) is based on a keynote address to a Teacher Refresher Course Conference in New Zealand in January 1997. The research is part of a larger project, reported in Bigum *et al.* (1997) – also part of the present in-depth review – and takes the form of evaluative 'snapshots' of practice at the interface of technology and literacy education. The examples on which the report is focused come from the BushNet project in northern Queensland, a series of linked websites between rural schools. These examples are used to suggest implications for our understanding of the relationship between literacy, networked technologies and education; to suggest that we need critical frames with which to make sense of new literacies; and that 'empowerment' and 'ownership' are essential for young people who are engaged with these new literacies.

While Morgan's focus might be said to be primarily on the processes of implementing initiatives like BushNet, the larger study (Bigum *et al.* 1997) from which her paper is derived tends toward a descriptive study. It does not set out to test a hypothesis, nor attempt to intervene in ongoing practice or measure effect. The project is driven more by a notion of a symbiotic relationship between new technologies and literacy development, rather than by a scientific or causal paradigm. As such, it does not seek to deliver 'results'; rather, to shed light on current practice, to suggest implications for future practice, and to inform further policy-making in the field.

The aim of the study is to investigate relationships between literacy and technology, as well as to explore the impact of technology on the nature, definition and views of literacy. Through a study of a wide range of types of educational institution, of children's ages and geographical and socio-economic settings, the project generates a general theory of literacy learning as promoted by ICT: this includes a notion of dynamic text, extended meta-knowledge of literacy, new genres, and new audiences and presentational opportunities online. It provides and tests a model of patterns and principles to explain why, how and in what contexts new technologies work or are impeded from working; and also provides empirical evidence in support of its emerging theory. In its kaleidoscopic form, it operates via snapshots of current practice plus commentaries which shape the principles and patterns of emerging theory. It therefore operates via a 'grounded theory' approach.

The aim of the McNamee study was to discover what the effects were of telecommunications opportunities on children's writing development in an after-school computer club (see also Garner *et al.* 2000) Findings are based on small-scale case study evidence, and suggest a growth in confidence and communicative ability of the child in question over the year of the study. There is also a suggested growth in the confidence of the mentor, an African-American community worker operating under the supervision of a university-devised scheme; and – while not strictly within the parameters of the present study – a transformation in the ability of the community workers to manage the communicative tools and forms of language for the benefit of their children (e.g. an assertion of the need to incorporate African-American forms of English into the email exchanges). However, our cautious use of 'suggested' as a qualifier to the reported findings (not 'results') indicates that the claims are not all fully supported by evidence.

McKeon and Burkey's (1998) paper describes 'the nature of an email collaborative between pre-service teachers and fourth and fifth graders in which literature was used as a vehicle for language and reading enhancement'. The authors claim that 'the motivation for the project was evident' and that parents were impressed with 'the students' increased interest in reading and purposeful computer usage' (p.90) Furthermore, 'the elementary students had the opportunity to enhance their critical reading and social skills using the computer, while pre-service teachers developed their teaching and communication skills' (p.91). However, the evidence for all these claims is thin, as it is for enhanced reading and social skills.

The purpose of Stuhlmann and Taylor's (1998) research is to look at the impact of telecommunications on learning outcomes in elementary classrooms. It provides limited evidence on the literacy benefits of networked exchanges between students in different schools; and of 'success factors', assuming the reported success to be the case. The authors claim that a) students became involved in complex learning and that b) the self-esteem of many children was increased; furthermore, c) motivation increased, as did use of email for third graders. The enthusiasm of the teachers was noted as a critical success factor, and other factors were seen as significant: the provision of training, the close monitoring of the project and a limited timeframe to keep the project fresh and dynamic. As these factors are described, the impact of ICT on literacy learning is implied, possibly through the anonymity provided by email exchanges as a communicative element in the project as a whole.

It is in the explorations of relationships that some of the best studies in this field have emerged, particularly in the first years of the twenty-first century. Abbott (2001) sets out to create a typology of web uses (rather than users) based on the different literacy practices and 'philosophies' of a small sample of users. He examines three young male website owners whom he characterizes as the technological aesthete, the community builder and the professional activist, thus defining them according to the function of their website creation and use. The technological aesthete primarily aims to represent himself in a particular way rather than to elicit contacts; the community builder aims to communicate an interest to other similarly interested individuals; and the activist uses his site to change some aspect of the real world. The study shows that it is important for educationalists to recognize how the web can contribute to young people's developing sense of identity, how aspects of learning can take place informally outside or inside the classroom, and how the process of engagement with networked ICT can differ for different people. Unlike many of the studies in the other study types, this one takes full account of the social contexts of literacy and literacy development, and is intended to have a longitudinal dimension.

Baker's (2001) study looked at four dimensions of literacy in a technology-rich fourth grade classroom. The first dimension was the public side, in which students read and commented on each other's work as projects proceeded; the second was a semiotic side, in which children used different sign systems that were independent. These were more available because of multimedia technologies, forcing educators to widen their conceptions of literacy. The third dimension looked at the 'transitory' side in which compositions cannot be viewed as 'static, done or complete' (p.179); and the fourth considered the publishing dimension of children's work, along with their notions of audience. The naturalistic design of the case study made sense in a complex literacy environment; it would have been hard to explore the transitoriness of literacy without such an approach. Although the report of the study could have been more explicit about why the particular class or teacher was chosen for research and how the enquiry team was selected (or, indeed, how they designed the study and reported it), such problems can be lived with because the author acknowledges the fact that the technology-rich class was not representative. Again, despite the fact there were not enough data presented nor examples of children's work for us to weigh up evidence against conclusions, the study was well-designed and the conclusions appeared to be valid.

A similar methodological and procedural conundrum is found in Morgan (2001). This study, which aims to explore how particular forms of cultural difference are being produced through different practices of ICT-enhanced literacy pedagogy, takes three teachers and their classrooms and investigates their practices. Based, like Abbott's work, on theories of situated practice and on functional and social analyses of literacy, it reveals paradoxes and uncertainties about the impact of ICT on literacy learning. Through analyses of three chosen groups 'on the edge' of educational research, the study uses ethnographic methods to reveal the ideologies underlying different practice. One of the conclusions is that it is not so much the nature of networked ICT that is important in developing literacy, but the nature of the networked communities created and the mediation of the teacher who controls the discourse of the particular classroom. The essential findings are that literacy is not a context-free skill; that success in literacy means being able to appropriate texts and articulate meanings for one's own context; and that it is important to provide explicit support for learners as they negotiate sociological variables in their use of networked ICT. Conclusions deriving from these findings are that ICT can be used for trans-formative work in which a text in one hybrid format is transformed into another as a learning exercise; that it can be used for 'meta-cognitive understanding of how texts and contexts ... are open to negotiation' (p.44); and that all these practices around ICT involve enculturation. A further fascinating aspect of Morgan's study (which also applies to her 1997 article, discussed above) is that her post-modernist narrative style of delivery asks some interesting questions about the nature of research and of its reporting in the ICT field. It is not possible to discuss these within the confines of the present chapter and book, but they are the focus of a forthcoming article on research paradigms in the investigation of ICT and literacy by Andrews.

The comparison with McKeon et al. (2001) is at the heart of this methodological issue. This article is also an exploration of relationships and based on case study methodology, but within a more explicit 'scientific' paradigm. Its aim is to examine an email collaboration between a 10-year-old, Donna, and a pre-service teacher in order to understand the nature of the email partnership. Methods such as think-aloud protocol, exit interview, observation, self-completion report and diary, and analysis of the email correspondence itself were used to build up a rounded picture of the interactions. Triangulation by method and inter-rate reliability were used to validate the data and make them more reliable, at least within the limitations of the case study approach where generalizability is not at a premium. The results of this study showed that Donna became more motivated towards her literacy development, based on interest, social engagement and self-esteem; and that the exercise provided an optimal challenging opportunity to use literacy to make decisions and gain greater ownership of her reading and writing. But although we can feel confident in the outcomes of this particular study, because of the high degree of rigour in the explication of the methodology, we cannot be sure that the motivation of the learner was sustained. Issues of the sustainability of motivation also arise in Wishart (1994) where a junior class 'learned about their own environment purposefully and sought to present this information interestingly and accurately in order to send it to their [email] correspondents' (p.26) but when the 'human element' was removed, motivation decreased.

Other study types

There is one other study in the in-depth review: that of Collins (1993). This is essentially a needs assessment study of English teachers in secondary schools in Belfast, through whose views we access information about the use of computers by 11–16-year-old pupils for the purposes of extending the range of their writing practices. There is a suggestion that word processing was still the predominant use of the computer in secondary English classrooms in the city – in 1993 at least – with 75 per cent of respondents reporting such a perception. Under half of the teachers in the sample believed that email and computer conferencing could be used to develop writing skills, although two-thirds at that time had access to computers. On the basis of these perceptions, the author proposes a need for in-service training in email and computer conferencing, if ICT is to fulfil its potential in secondary English classes. Because the methodological approach is relatively weak, however, these results have to be taken as provisional; there is insufficient evidence to justify the claims, so it is hard to determine the relationship between data and conclusions.

Conclusion

When we undertook the first review of the topic in 2001/2, we felt the answer to the research question for the in-depth review – 'What is the impact of networked ICT on literacy learning in English, 5–16?' – was inconclusive and patchy because there was insufficient research of high quality. The updated review, undertaken in 2002/3, revealed a number of articles published at the beginning of the new decade which have suggested that the quality of research in this field is increasing. These articles – we are thinking of Abbott (2001), Baker (2001), McKeon *et al.* (2001) and Morgan (2001) in particular – are all reports of case studies and all of medium and/or high quality according to the EPPI Reviewer criteria.

Many of the studies in the in-depth review as a whole focus on the primary/elementary school sector, with at least six studies concentrating on fourth/fifth graders (i.e. 9–10-year-olds) Four of the studies look at out-of-school activities, and only three (and all indirectly) turn their attention to the impact of ICT on literacy at secondary or high school level. The principal areas of interest for the studies are reading and writing, but those twin aspects of literacy are often narrowly conceived, so that we are looking at the impact of new technologies on old practices rather than at the symbiosis between new technologies and new forms of literacy. Four of the studies look at word processing; four at new conceptions of literacy; one is on speaking and listening; and two are on special educational needs.

In general, as suggested above, conceptions of literacy are narrow. Many of the studies show *how an impact can* be made, rather than whether it *is* made; or whether the nature of literate practice itself changes under the influence of ICT. They tend to show how ICT can help in terms of 'exchange of information' rather than in the quality of writing or comprehension or some other aspect of literacy; as such, they highlight a practice that ICT has made more accessible to children and young people.

Overall, ten of the studies provide no firm basis for accepting their findings and therefore can have little bearing on the answering of the main research question for the in-depth review. Of the remaining fourteen, three or four provide theoretical and practical insights into widening conceptions of literacy; six suggest increased motivation and/or confidence in pupils as a result of ICT use with regard to literacy development; and three see empowerment and ownership as an important factor to bear in mind in an increasingly diverse digital world.

Methodologically, there is a wide variety of study types in the in-depth review, characteristic of education research in general but not reflective of the types of study found in the overall review on the impact of ICT on literacy learning – the majority of which, unsurprisingly, are outcome evaluations. The range of study types in the in-depth review on the impact of *networked* ICT on literacy learning makes synthesis difficult. Meta-analysis was not possible, because only one of the studies with quantitative outcomes was judged to be sound; and also because data collection methods among the outcome evaluations were different. The synthesis is therefore narrative in nature.

Eleven of the twenty-four studies examined in the in-depth review were judged poor or weak in design and/or execution and/or reporting; a further three were deemed problematic. Of the remaining ten, all were generally well designed for their purpose. More specifically, ten experimental or quasi-experimental studies were identified in this review, nine of which were judged 'not sound'. The remaining study was weak methodologically, so its results should be treated with caution. Nevertheless, it did indicate that using a networked system which allowed teachers to respond immediately to the comprehension levels of their class was beneficial. There is no good evidence from the outcome evaluations that the widespread use of network technologies will lead to an improvement in children's literacy; however, this does not mean that there is no impact.

In the pre- and post-test studies, process evaluations and explorations of relationships and other studies, the findings are suggestive rather than conclusive.

Recommendations for future research

At the end of our two-year review of the interface between ICT and literacy/literacies, we offer overleaf a table that sets out areas for future research in networked literacies. Our belief is that each of the areas has only just begun to be thoroughly examined. Although we have pointed out shortcomings, as we see them, in many of the studies we have examined, we also wish to acknowledge that each of the studies in the in-depth review has indicated (sometimes indirectly) new areas for research and has made a positive contribution to a complex field of study. We feel that the field of research into networked ICT and literacy/literacies is in a 'pre-paradigmatic' stage where explorations of relationships are the most convincing approach to date. It may be the case that we will arrive at a more achieved state of research into the field shortly, but we feel that such a state will have to recognize that hybrid, multimedia practice requires hybrid, multimedia forms of representation, analysis and research; if such a challenge cannot be met, we will be forced to conclude that research itself, in the forms we have conceived it so far, is inadequate for the task of understanding networked ICT practice in relation to new conceptions and practices of literacy.

Table 3.4 shows where work has been undertaken and where there are gaps. It provides a map of where future research on the impact of networked ICT on literacy learning might take place.

Coda

Even though we have limited the period of review to studies since 1990, many of the earlier studies will be outdated, describing ICT arrangements that are no longer typical. We have updated the review in 2003 to take account of recent research; and, importantly, of research we missed in the previous year's review. We welcome correspondence that will help us improve the quality and range of our study, both with regard to the present review of the impact of ICT on literacy learning which focuses on *networked* ICT, and for the rest of the review in the wider field of ICT and literacy.

Most of the studies we have unearthed seem to assume a similar conceptual framework to that of the present study, namely one which sees literacy learning practices at home and at school being affected by changing information and communication technologies. We are aware that our contribution to the wider question of the symbiotic relationship between ICT and literacy development is a partial one; we hope, nevertheless, as a ground-clearing exercise, it is a useful one.

Table 3.4 A map for future research on the impact of networked ICT on literacy learning

Aspects of ICT → Aspects of literacy ↓	Computer-mediated networked systems	Wider conceptions of information and communication technology	Email, conferencing and the Internet	Software systems	Videotext, moving image
Word processing	Allen and Thompson (1995)	Love (1998) McNamee (1995) Bigum et al. (1997) Morgan (1997) Morgan (2001)	Collins (1993		
New literacies				Watts and Lloyd (2001)	
Writing skills	Garner et al. (2000) Spaulding and Lake (1992)		Collins (1993) Wishart (1994) Nettelbeck (2000) Casey (2001)	Clouse (1992) Moore and Karabenick (1992)	
Reading skills		Love (1998)	McKeon and Burkey (1998) Stuhlmann and Taylor (1998) McKeon et al. (2001) Casey (2001)	Clouse (1992) Golden et al. (1990)	
Videotext					Erickson et al. (1992)
Speaking and listening		Ewing (2000)			
Hybridity	Baker (2001	Morgan (2001)	Abbott (2001)	Baker (2001)	
Special needs	Peyton (1991		McKeon et al. (2001)		

Selected studies for in-depth review

Abbott, C. (2001) 'Some young male website owners: the technological aesthete, the community builder and the professional activist', *Education, Communication and Information*, 1: 197–212.

Allen, G. and Thompson, A. (1995) 'Analysis of the effect of networking on computer-assisted collaborative writing in a fifth grade classroom', *Journal of Educational Computing Research*, 12: 65–75.

Baker, E.A. (2001) 'The nature of literacy in a technology-rich, fourth-grade classroom', *Reading Research and Instruction*, 40: 159–84.

Bigum, C., Durrant, C., Green, B., Honan, E., Lankshear, C., Morgan, W., Murray, J., Snyder, I. and Wild, M. (1997) *Digital Rhetorics: Literacies and Technologies in Education – Current Practices and Future Directions* (Executive Summary and Volumes 1, 2 and 3), Canberra: Department of Employment, Education, Training and Youth Affairs.

Casey, J.M. (2001) *A Path to Literacy: Empowering Students in Your Classroom*, California: California State University.

Clouse, R.W. (1992) 'Teaching and learning with computers: a classroom analysis', *Journal of Educational Technology Systems*, 20: 281–302.

Collins, J. (1993) 'Beyond the word processor: computer-mediated communication with pupils and teachers', *Computer Education*, 73: 13–17.

Erickson, B., Allen, A. and Mountain, L. (1992) 'Telecommunications promotes summer reading and writing: a pilot project report', *Journal of Computing in Childhood Education*, 3: 295–302.

Ewing, J. (2000) 'Enhancement of online and offline student learning', *Education Media International*, 37: 205–17.

Garner, R., Tan, S. and Zhao, Y. (2000) 'Why write?', *Computers in Human Behavior*, 16: 339–47.

Golden, N., Gersten, R. and Woodward, J. (1990) 'Effectiveness of guided practice during remedial reading instruction: an application of computer-managed instruction', *Elementary School Journal*, 90: 291–304.

Love, K. (1998) 'Old cyborgs, young cyborgs (and those in between)', *English in Australia*, 121: 63–75.

McKeon, C.A. and Burkey, L.C. (1998) 'A literature based e-mail collaborative', in E.G. Sturtevant and J. Dugan (eds) *Literacy and Community: The Twentieth Yearbook*, Carrollton, GA: College Reading Association.

McKeon, C.A., Sage, M.C.G. and Gardiner, H.W. (2001) 'E-mail as a motivating literacy event for one struggling reader: Donna's case', *Reading Research and Instruction*, 40: 185–202.

McNamee, G. D. (1995) 'A Vygotskian perspective on literacy development', *School Psychology International*, 16: 185–98.

Moore, M.A. and Karabenick, S.A. (1992) 'The effects of computer communications on the reading and writing performance of fifth-grade students', *Computers in Human Behavior*, 8: 27–38.

Morgan, W. (1997) 'From the margins to the centre: schools online', *English in Aotearoa*, 32, 3–11.

Morgan, W. (2001) 'Computers for literacy: making the difference?', *Asia Pacific Journal of Teacher Education*, 29: 31–47.

Nettelbeck, D. (2000) 'Using information technology to enrich the learning experiences of secondary English students', *Literacy Learning: The Middle Years*, 8: 40–9.

Peyton, J.K. (1991) 'Electronic communication for developing the literacy skills of elementary school students: the case of ENFI', *Teaching English to Deaf and Second Language Students*, 9: 4–9.

Spaulding, C.L. and Lake, D. (1992) 'Interactive effects of computer network and student characteristics on students' writing and collaborating', *High School Journal*, 76: 67–77.

Stuhlmann, J.M. and Taylor, H.G. (1998) 'Analyzing the impact of telecommunications on learning outcomes in elementary classrooms', *Journal of Computing in Childhood Education*, 9: 79–92.

Watts, M. and Lloyd, C. (2001) 'Evaluating a classroom multimedia programme in the teaching of literacy', *Educational Research and Evaluation*, 7: 35–52.

Wishart, E. (1994) 'Using a TTNS electronic mailbox in a junior class: a case study', in D. Wray (ed.) *Literacy and Computers: Insights from Research*, Royston: United Kingdom Reading Association.

Bibliography

Abbott, C. (2001) 'Some young male website owners'. Paper given at BFI Colloquium, British Educational Communications and Technology Agency (BECTa), Coventry, January 2000. *Education, Communication, Information*, 1(2).

Andrews, R. (2001) *Teaching and Learning English: A Guide to Recent Research and its Applications*, London: Continuum.

Andrews, R., Burn, A., Leach, J., Locke, T., Low, G. and Torgerson, C. (2002) 'A systematic review of the impact of networked ICT on 5–16-year-olds' literacy in English' (EPPI-Centre Review), *Research Evidence in Education Library*, 1, London: EPPI-Centre, Social Science Research Unit, Institute of Education.

Andrews, R., Burn, A., Leach, J., Locke, T., Low, G. and Torgerson, C. (2003) 'A systematic review of the impact of networked ICT on 5–16-year-olds' literacy in English' (EPPI-Centre Review), *Research Evidence in Education Library*, 2, London: EPPI-Centre, Social Science Research Unit, Institute of Education.

Burn, A. (1999a) 'Grabbing the werewolf: digital freezeframes, the cinematic still and technologies of the social', *Convergence*, 3(4).

Burn, A. (1999b) 'Digiteens: media literacies and digital technologies in the secondary classroom', *English in Education*, 33(3) (also website with Kate Reed: http://www/nyu.edu/education/teachlearn/ifte/burn1.htm).

Burn, A. and Parker, S. (2001) 'Making your mark: digital inscription, animation, and a new visual semiotic', *Education, Communication, Information*, 1(2), 155–79.

EPPI-Centre (2001a) *Core Keywording Strategy: Data Collection for a Register of Educational Research, version 0.9.4*, London: University of London, Institute of Education, EPPI-Centre, Social Science Research Unit.

EPPI-Centre (2001b) *Review Guidelines for Extracting Data and Quality Assessing Primary Studies in Educational Research, Version 0.9.4*, London: University of London, Institute of Education, EPPI-Centre, Social Science Research Unit.

Gamble, N. and Easingwood, N. (eds) (2000) *ICT and Literacy: Information and Communications Technology, Media, Reading and Writing*, London: Continuum.

Goodwyn, A. (ed.) (2000) *English in the Digital Age*, London: Continuum.

Haas, C. (1996) *Writing Technology: Studies on the Materiality of Literacy*, Hillsdale, NJ: Lawrence Erlbaum Associates.

Lanham, R. (1993) *The Electronic Word*, Chicago: Chicago University Press.

Lankshear, C. and Snyder, I. (2000) *Teachers and Techno-literacy*, St Leonards, NSW: Allen & Unwin.

Leask, M. and Meadows, J. (eds) (2000) *Teaching and Learning with ICT in the Primary School*, London: RoutledgeFalmer.

Leu, D.J. (2000) 'Literacy and technology: deictic consequences for literacy education in an information age', in Kamil, M.L., Mosenthal, P.B., Pearson, P.D. and Barr, R. (eds) *Handbook of Reading Research*, Hillsdale, NJ: Lawrence Erlbaum Associates.

Loveless, A. and Dore, B. (eds) (2002) *ICT in the Primary School*, Buckingham: Open University Press.

Loveless, A. and Ellis, V. (eds) (2001) *ICT, Pedagogy and the Curriculum*, London: RoutledgeFalmer.

McFarlane, A., Harrison, C., Somekh, B., Scrimshaw, P., Harrison, A. and Lewin, C. (2000) *Establishing the Relationship between Networked Technology and Attainment*, ImpaCT2 project, preliminary study 1, April 2000, Coventry: British Educational and Communication Technology Agency.

Monteith, M. (ed.) (2002) *Teaching Primary Literacy with ICT*, Buckingham: Open University Press.

Moseley, D. and Higgins, S. (1999) *Ways Forward with ICT: Effective Pedagogy Using Information and Communications Technology for Literacy and Numeracy in Primary Schools*, Newcastle: University of Newcastle.

Organisation for Economic and Collaborative Development (2001) *Review of Assessment Activities*, OECD/INES/Network A newsletter, issue 14, November 2001, Paris: OECD.

Snyder, I. (1999) *Hypertext*, Melbourne: University of Melbourne Press.

Tyner, K. (1998) *Literacy in the Digital Age*, Mahwah, NJ: Lawrence Erlbaum Associates.
Vygotsky, L. (1986) *Thought and Language* (newly revised and edited by Alex Kozulin), Cambridge MA: MIT Press.

Chapter 4

ICT, literacy learning and ESL learners

Graham Low and Sue Beverton

Introduction

There is now a very large number of computer-based teaching materials and articles and books advising teachers how to make productive use of ICT with students who are attempting to acquire a second or foreign language. As Chapelle (1990: 199) puts it, 'Computer-assisted language learning is now used routinely in language instruction'. At a general policy level, the UK government has justified its investment in ICT in schools in terms of its positive impact, citing four research reports from the British Educational Communications and Technology Agency (BECTa 1998; BECTa 1998–9; BECTa 2001a; BECTa 2001b). While there are numerous anecdotal eulogies of the role of computer-assisted learning in language and literacy situations, it remains unclear whether there is well-researched evidence of a positive impact. Chapelle's stark comment from her 1990 paper on research studies in Computer-assisted Language Learning (CALL) published before 1990 – in English as a Foreign Language (EFL) as well as English as a Second Language (ESL) – establishes that there is a serious need for a detailed review of research conducted post-1990:

> Progress in this area ... does not appear to be forthcoming from current research on ... CALL.
> Little if any current CALL research can offer unambiguous evidence concerning effects of CALL activities because current research methods fail to elucidate exactly what students do while they work with language learning software.
> Much current CALL research (e.g. Kleinmann 1987) shares the pitfalls of investigations of second language classroom teaching methods of the 1950s and 1960s.... As Long (1980),

Allwright (1988), and Chaudron (1988), among others, point out, this research was inconclusive because too many factors influencing students' performance were not accounted for. One of these factors was what students and teachers actually did and said in the classrooms under investigation. Classroom research requires more than general (method) labels for instruction; it requires precise descriptions of the interaction that occurs in classrooms.

(Chapelle 1990: 199–200)

Similar caution is expressed by Hyland (1993) on the more specific topic of word processors. Hyland briefly compared positive, negative and unclear research findings up to 1991 and concluded that, 'Research is unable to confirm that the quality of computer written texts is superior to conventionally produced work', though 'studies of motivational and attitudinal changes ... tend to be more positive' (p.22). Hyland was writing with respect to EFL rather than ESL students, but his conclusion about the importance of teaching/learning support and its methodology (allied to collaborative learning and integration with the regular curriculum) resembles that of Chapelle and should be taken to imply a major line of approach in any review of ESL-related ICT research in the 1990s and after: 'There is little doubt that support is a critical variable in this process. Quite simply, the most convincing improvements in student writing are not due to computers, but teachers' (p.28).

Chapelle was particularly concerned with the need to describe interaction accurately, but her finding introduces a possible worry that other areas of research methodology might be equally problematic. A systematic review of studies in the last decade of the twentieth century and at the start of the twenty-first was thus felt to be needed.

The present review restricts Chapelle's focus in two ways: first, it treats just research on written literacy and, second, it considers only learners who are acquiring English as a second (rather than a foreign) language. The reasons for this are as follows.

EFL involves a relatively well-defined cluster of contexts and has been the subject of large amounts of research worldwide for half a century at least. ESL situations are somewhat different (see below) and in general less well researched. This is not to say that research or survey reports do not exist – witness for example in a UK context the recent Ofsted reports, *Managing Support for the Attainment of Pupils from Minority Ethnic Groups* (2001) and *More Advanced*

Learners of English as an Additional Language in Secondary Schools and Colleges (2002) – it was simply felt that the EFL literature requires a separate review. The reason for selecting writing was slightly different. While it was self-evident that oral skills often develop before writing skills and that many tasks both in and out of school require language skills to be mixed or integrated, it nevertheless remains the case that writing is the key to academic success at virtually all levels of education in probably the majority of countries, for mother tongue and ESL learners alike.

Definitional and conceptual issues

English as a second/additional language

The expression 'English as an additional language' (EAL) tends to be used as a cover term when it is unclear whether a situation/ community should be treated as English as a Foreign Language (EFL) or English as a Second Language (ESL) (Görlach 2002). The term is also used by Ofsted (2001, 2002) as an alternative to ESOL (English for Speakers of Other Languages) to describe the language situation of many children from 'minority ethnic groups'; the label is assumed to be transparent and not in need of any precise definition. EAL may thus be somewhat general or indeterminate, but is useful for the present study as a search term, as long as a secondary check is made to eliminate EFL or mother tongue/first language situations.

The term 'English as a second language' (ESL) is far commoner in the international literature on language learning than EAL, and as such needs to be treated as the main keyword in this review. The term is, however, used variably in the research and teaching literature. It is often used, for example, within Sociolinguistics to refer to English in ex-colonies, where there was a small native English speaking group of administrators, and where English was accordingly a, or the, official administrative language, but where there was little use of English in the general community (Görlach 2002). This is *not*, however, the sense in which ESL will be used in this report. It is used here in the sense in which it is commonly employed in UK educational circles, namely to refer to students in the education system of a largely English-speaking host culture, who, in theory, are immersed in that culture and environment. This latter view has pedagogical implications, as one might expect issues of cultural identification and assimilation (or rejection) to be taught rather differently in EFL and ESL situations.

The above characterization of ESL also has implications with respect to the identification of studies for the review. While it is relatively easy to isolate ESL students in schools in the UK, USA, Australia, Canada and New Zealand, it becomes correspondingly harder to categorize students in English-speaking schools in say, Hong Kong, India, Holland, or Uganda, where English is an official language, but the bulk of the population cannot be said to be immersed outside school in a rich English-speaking culture. Even in the 'English-speaking' countries, it is not always uncontroversial how to categorize particular groups. Refugees, for example, represent a border category between a second and a foreign language; if they were isolated from the host culture, then they would be treated as EFL, but if they were allowed to live relatively freely in the host culture they would be effectively ESL. The children of second- or third-generation immigrants are likely to have adapted more to the host country and its language, but it does not necessarily follow that their English is of high proficiency and that they should not be categorizable (for some purposes at any rate) as ESL. Black, Caribbean or African-American students in the USA represent a different categorization problem. The linguistic literature is divided about whether 'Black English' (BEV), or its more recent appellation 'African American Vernacular English' (AAVE), should be treated as a dialect of standard English (arguing for categorizing its speakers as native speakers of English) or as a Creole approaching standard English (arguing for categorization as ESL). It was decided that speakers of AAVE would be categorized for this report as native speakers, thus differentiating them from, say, Hispanic students in the USA, who would, if their command of standard English was reasonably low, be categorized as ESL. Indigenous groups, such as the Maoris in New Zealand, whose settlement in the area predates that of the dominant English-speaking group, represent yet another categorization problem. If their linguistic situation is such that their command of English is relatively poor and they are not free agents in the economy (e.g. the job market), then they are categorized as ESL. The effect here, as with Hispanic students in the USA, is that some Maori students must be treated as native speakers, while others might be reasonably categorizable as ESL.

In short, an ESL situation is hard to define, but may be characterized prototypically as one where English is (a) not the primary language of the learner or the home, but is (b) the current medium of instruction, (c) the language of the wider community and (d) an official language at national level. It needs to be stressed that US researchers sometimes use ESL to refer to what UK researchers call EFL; this means that for this review, the reviewers need to re-screen studies to remove ones which are actually EFL-oriented.

Bilingualism

Categorization as ESL implies a philosophical position on the notion of bilingualism. This, like ESL, is variably treated in the literature. If ESL groups are partly characterized by a less than 'perfect' command of English, and an imbalance between their languages, then the only appropriate view of bilingualism is a so-called 'inclusive' view whereby bilingualism is relative, not absolute, or balanced. Establishing a minimum cut-off point remains controversial, however, and somewhat subjective (Baker 2001). For the present review any degree of proficiency over zero will be treated as evidence of bilingualism.

Types of bilingualism

Research suggests that students who choose to learn a second language can show greater gains than those who are forced to learn it (Baker 2001) and that those who see the L2 as adding to their repertoire make more progress than those who see it 'subtractively', as involving a loss of their L1 and/or home culture (Lambert 1974; Ellis 1985; Baker 2001). Again, students who live in a situation where it is expected that everyone will acquire the nation's languages (individual bilingualism) may well progress differently from students in situations where there are different language groups, but these remain relatively monolingual (i.e. there is social, but not individual bilingualism) (see Fasold 1984; Romaine 1995; Gardner 2002). It is highly likely that the use of ICT in formal (or even informal) educational situations will be affected by the ways in which the students concerned perceive the nature of their bilingualism. The topic has considerable current interest, as a number of academics are beginning to find paradoxes in the assumed link between additive bilingualism and learning efficiency, and to question its inevitability (see particularly Gao 1994, 2001, 2002). Although the keywording system (described below) did not take features of bilingual situations into account, the reviewers felt that it would be important to note all such detail mentioned in the included studies.

Impact

We have preferred to review studies for evidence of 'impact' rather than 'effect', because it tends to be generally understood in a broader way in the context of research studies (see Andrews *et al.* 2002; Coles 2002). We have avoided the term 'outcomes' in the title simply because the word is often used in both a narrow and a broad sense. For present purposes, 'impact' may be defined in a global way as 'the totality of change, or altered capacity for change, in people or processes related to those involved in the research'. Thus outcomes, whether 'immediate/long-term' or 'direct/indirect', contribute to such change or capacity for change. Moreover, while 'effects' tend to be local, specific and measurable (whence indices such as effect size), the 'impact' of a literacy programme might be felt in various ways by parents, employers and school administrators as well as by the learners. Moreover, it might also be delayed, involve paths through life that might not have been selected otherwise, or serve to create connections between seemingly unrelated entities. Although few of these broader issues were in fact addressed by most of the studies included in the review, the object was to establish a framework broad enough to discuss them, if the opportunity arose.

Literacy

The term 'literacy' has been interpreted in several different ways in the applied linguistics literature, but in general, one may take a narrow or a broad view. The narrow view is that to be literate means that you can read and write (often popularly interpreted as reading relatively difficult texts and/or writing without breaking the 'rules of grammar'). Though Lemke (1998) and others have argued that there is no principled reason for isolating reading and writing as literacy, Gillen (2002) points out that it can still be useful for particular purposes. The broader view, held by for example Barton and his colleagues (2000), is that reading and writing are not discrete stand-alone skills, but are standardly used in complex ways to help achieve social tasks. Thus a preferable framework is to distinguish between 'literacy events' (which require reading/writing in some reasonably central way) and 'literacy practices' (which are the ways in which an individual copes with an event). A slight extension of this view leads researchers like Street (1993) to talk of 'multiple literacies' or 'multi-literacies'. This variation in treatment does not cause great difficulties for the present review and a neutral, if slightly subjective, position could be taken. If a study explored the influence of ICT on tasks that centrally involved reading and writing, then it would be included – whether a more psychological or a more sociological position was taken by the authors was not important, nor was the integration of reading/writing with other skills.

A related, and currently controversial question concerns the idea of the language learner developing and/or being taught to develop a personal 'voice'. As with 'literacy' itself, 'voice' can be treated narrowly, as 'aspects of the L2 that are sufficiently me-like to accept', or more broadly as the expression of 'a speaking subject's perspective, conceptual horizon, intention and world view' (Bakhtin, cited by Wertsch 1991: 51). While Kramsch (2002) argues that voice is important at all levels of language learning, Stapleton (2002) takes a more sceptical view and argues that the 'voice' proposal has been taken to extremes and is far less important pedagogically than its proponents are claiming. One might argue, however, that voice is more important for ESL learners (in the sense that we are defining ESL) than for EFL learners, as ESL learners have a greater need to function effectively in English in the local environment. The notion of voice would also seem in theory to be relevant in several ways to ICT. First, working alone at a computer would appear to encourage personal reflection and self-expression. Second, the appearance of a real-life task or real-life reader would appear to introduce the need to orient one's own literacy practices with respect to the other person's, either converging or diverging. Lastly, the use of groupwork in CALL would seem to reduce the likelihood of an individual voice predominating or developing. Clearly, a focus on voice as a research topic is not criterial for inclusion in the present review, but, as with additive and subtractive bilingualism, it was hoped that some relevant data would be presented.

Policy and practice background

The present review examines research studies produced from 1990. The feeling then was one of excitement that computers were starting to show their value and had great potential. As Huss *et al.* noted in the 1990 ERIC digest 'Using computers with adult ESL literacy learners':

> The prospects for using computer-assisted instructional programs and other technological media with adult ESL literacy learners are excellent, provided that programs are designed or adapted especially for these learners and that instructors are willing to try new and innovative approaches.
>
> (Huss *et al.* 1990)

The comment is equally applicable to learners between 5 and 16 years.

From around the middle of the 1990s, there has been a vast and worldwide explosion of educational use of interactive technologies, centred on the Internet, and even a basic Web search will now bring up hundreds of teacher- and materials-oriented websites for use with EFL and ESL students. For all practical purposes, the assumption now made is that CALL materials are here to stay and that their value is self-evidently positive. However, few of the sites seen by the present reviewers are concerned with evaluating usefulness in a systematic way. There is thus an ever-increasing need for research studies which explore impact and effectiveness with rigour and non-commercial objectivity.

Along with the explosion of websites and Internet use is the increase in powerful, fast multimedia computers, often networked within a school or college. As Levy (1997) put it,

> the convergence of once separate media such as video and the computer, or telecommunications technologies and the computer, moves us towards a multi-user, multi-site environment for interaction and learning, stretching far beyond the confines of the traditional computer laboratory.
>
> (Levy 1997: 44)

While these facilities have been enthusiastically received by EFL teachers, and huge international link-up networks, such as Ruth Vilmi's 'International Writing Exchange' (Vilmi 2000), have been created, it is less clear how far ESL students (in the sense defined here) have benefited from increased hardware and access to it.

Methodological considerations

In the light of the above discussion, there were two research questions:

- What is the evidence with respect to the impact of ICT on literacy learning in English of learners between 5 and 16, for whom English is a second language (ESL) or an additional language (EAL)?
- What conclusions may be drawn with reasonable confidence from the evidence?

To be included in the in-depth review, a paper had to be about literacy teaching/learning by children between 5–16 years old, in a school or school-related setting. After-school activities organized by, say, a local community centre would be acceptable if the other criteria were met, but a private project organized by a learner at home would not.

To meet the criterion of ESL, the language of instruction had to be primarily English and the teaching/learning to take place in an English-speaking environment – though it was accepted that the learners' homes or the immediate community might be L2–speaking. As this information was not available from the keywording, all ESL/EAL studies were re-screened to ensure they met the required definitions (above). Where different types of student were included in the same study, the paper needed to identify and report separately on the ESL students. This had been intended as a quite unproblematic requirement, but the vagueness or lack of discussion of ESL issues in several papers meant that even where studies were included, the quality of the evidence was at times severely reduced.

It was decided to restrict the review to studies based on a clear body of empirical data which had been collected in a systematic way and retained for examination and analysis. Studies were excluded if they (a) had no clear body of data, (b) employed very subjective and/or inconsistent field coding, or (c) drew conclusions without establishing comparability of data, definable analyses or adequate justifications.

Given that the present review concerned the ability to draw conclusions about impact, it was decided that case studies involving a single learner would only be included if they involved an evaluated intervention.

In short, the inclusion and exclusion criteria were as follows:

Inclusion criteria

- must involve children between 5 and 16 years old
- must involve/report on a research study of a written literacy-based intervention (reading, writing or spelling)
- must collect and analyse a defined body of empirical data
- must report on progress (process, product or both) of ESL learners
- the language of instruction must be English (or primarily English)
- the language of the wider community (or a large part of it) must be English
- English must be the (or an) official language.

Exclusion criteria

- not a research study
- no literacy-related intervention
- learners of wrong or indeterminate age
- no body of empirical data or systematic analysis
- learners not ESL.

Results

Inclusions and exclusions

A total of ten studies were isolated on the basis of the original keywording. Of these, two studies failed to meet the criteria. One of these, the three-volume *Digital Rhetorics*, by Bigum *et al.* (1997), contained a very extensive review of previous research and thinking about literacy and literacy teaching, but was excluded on three grounds. Primarily there was no definable body of systematically-gathered data that could be (or had been) subjected to detailed analysis, but secondarily there was use of considerable, seemingly subjective, field coding and ESL students were not reported separately in a clear way. A second report, McNamee (1995), was restricted to African-American students, so was excluded on the grounds of not meeting the criteria for being ESL.

In four of the eight included studies, namely Lin *et al.* (1991), Decosta (1992), Sinatra *et al.* (1994) and Parr (1997), it was not clear whether the students were genuinely ESL.

Lin *et al.* (1991) have a Chinese American group, but all the students are above the twenty-first percentile on the English Language Assessment Battery, which is used by the New York City Board of Education to determine eligibility for 'bilingual services'. The researchers include 'cultural background' as a factor in their analysis, but do not discuss the topic, beyond suggesting the universal value of their treatment (p.24).

Decosta (1992) describes the local community as predominantly 'Italian and Eastern European in heritage' with 35 per cent Afro-Americans (p.17). The make-up of the sample observed is not, however, reported, so the proportion of Afro-Americans, who are not here classified as ESL, is not known. Also, the children are described as being second or even third generation immigrants, but no English language proficiency data or home language background is provided, so it is hard to know whether even the Italian or East European children can validly be seen as ESL. The paper was given the benefit of the doubt.

The third study, Sinatra *et al.* (1994), resembles Decosta, in that it gives a linguistic breakdown of the local area, but does not directly state the profile of the group(s) studied. Again like Decosta, the local area contains a mixture of possibly ESL and (for this review) clearly non-ESL inhabitants: 46 per cent Hispanic, 26 per cent speakers of languages other than Spanish, 6 per cent Afro-Caribbean and 22 per cent undefined – but presumably native English-speaking and white. The reader is led to infer a research group profile of 72 per cent ESL, but the scores of these children are not reported separately. The study was given the benefit of the doubt and classified as ESL, but its overall weight of evidence for the review questions could not be high.

In Parr (1997) there are two ESOL groups from whom data is gathered, but whose results are not reported. There is also a Maori ethnic group in the classes whose results are reported, but these have similar reading scores to their 'European' peers. Lastly, a Form 3 Learning Support Group and a Waipareria group are noted, but the ethnic/linguistic composition is not reported for either. The Parr paper was given the benefit of the doubt, but the overall weight of evidence with respect to the review questions was necessarily low.

A different situation was posed by the Williams and Williams (2000) study. The title used EFL rather than ESL and no background information was reported about the students studied. However, as the term ESL was used consistently in the body of the article and the initial discussion related to mainstreaming within the regular education system, the study was given the benefit of the doubt and categorized as ESL-related.

The Williams and Williams paper illustrated a further classification problem. This was the fact that although there was an intervention and the students typed words into a computer, it was not clear whether the computer had played any real part in the gains made. Again, the paper was given the benefit of the doubt, though its value in answering the review questions was hence inevitably low.

The Decosta (1992) study involved a second problem with respect to the in/exclusion criteria, in addition to the ESL one discussed above. This was the fact that the paper claimed to be a spin-off from an ongoing study involving six intact classes. The paper involved a commentary on selected texts drawn from the study, but no research design or research questions were reported, no research methodology was described and no systematic analysis (even of the texts cited) was described or evident. The paper was thus marginal about whether it could be said to be a literacy-based research project, where data was systematically collected and analysed. With some misgivings, the paper was given the benefit of the doubt, largely on account of the fact that it included more discussion of situational and pedagogical details than the other studies.

The final result is that just three of the eight studies are clearly classifiable as ESL: Nwogu and Nwogu (1992), Silver and Repa (1993) and Van Haalen and Bright (1993), though even in the latter, the bilingual and monolingual speakers were relatively balanced as regards English language proficiency.

The overall inclusion situation is summarized in Table 4.1.

Table 4.1 All studies keyworded as ESL/EAL indicating numbers included and excluded

Total number of keyworded ESL/EAL	10
Excluded for failure to meet criteria	2
Not ESL	1
No analysed data	1
Total number of studies in in-depth review	8

Comparing the included studies

The eight studies in the in-depth review vary with respect to the aspect(s) of literacy involved, the country where the study was carried out and the type of research involved. These details are summarized in Table 4.2.

The eight studies also vary in terms of the age group and the nationalities involved. Essentially, four studies involve secondary-level students (here defined as 11–16) and four primary level students (5–10). One study (Van Haalen and Bright 1993) involves US Grade 5; this has been classed as primary. As regards nationality, there is a wide variety; the only common factor is that three studies (Van Haalen and Bright 1993, Silver and Repa 1993, Sinatra *et al.* 1994) have a high proportion of (American) Hispanic students. The situation is summarized in Table 4.3.

It had been hoped to compare the studies on the basis of features of bilingualism, but none of the included studies devoted much discussion to the topic. Indeed, most studies had no discussion at all on questions of bilingualism, so it was not possible to analyse this topic further. Chapelle's (1990) insistence on the importance of linking classroom behaviour to classroom language was not reflected in the eight, so again, no further analysis of this important topic was possible. Gillen (2002) has recently argued for a stronger position, that by itself even classroom language data allow for few explanations; what is needed is supplementary information from the participants about what they were trying to do and how they were using the ICT. The included studies shed no light on this.

Hyland (1993), in a paper examining the factors likely to promote learning via CALL with EFL/ESL classes, noted the likely importance of integrating the CALL sessions and content with the regular curriculum. This is inherently a very plausible hypothesis, and one which we had hoped to check in the present review. Unfortunately, none of the papers details clearly whether integration took place and if so, how. Silver and Repa certainly imply that the 'Introduction to Literature 1' course was a normal part of the curriculum and Decosta implies that the writing work was integrated into part of the children's school day (indeed both also comment on the collaborative learning that Hyland was also concerned about). Parr implies fairly clearly that the reading work was not integrated – indeed, several of the teachers complained about the fact – and the work in Lin *et al.*, Van Haalen and Bright, and Nwogu and Nwogu

Table 4.2 Focus and type of research of included studies

Study	Country	Literacy	Evaluation type
Decosta (1992)	USA	Writing: narrative	Unclear
Lin et al. (1991)	USA	Reading: word recognition	RCT
Nwogu and Nwogu (1992)	UK	Reading + writing? (unclear)	Naturally occurring
Parr (1997)	NZ	Reading generally	Naturally occurring
Silver and Repa (1993)	USA	Writing: (genre unclear)	Researcher manipulated
Sinatra et al. (1994)	USA	Reading + writing: narrative	Researcher manipulated
Van Haalen and Bright (1993)	USA	Writing: narrative	Researcher manipulated
Williams and Williams (2000)	USA	Reading + writing: transcription	Naturally occurring

Table 4.3 Student age and nationality in included studies

Study	Country	Age	Ethnicity of ESL students
Decosta (1992)	USA	5–10 Kindergarten + Grade	Italian, Eastern European American
Lin et al. (1991)	USA	7–8 Grade 2	Chinese American
Nwogu and Nwogu (1992)	UK	11–16? Secondary	Mainly 'of Asian origin'
Parr (1997)	NZ	13–16 F3–F6	Maori, Poly/Melanesian
Silver and Repa (1993)	USA	15 Grade not reported	46%? Hispanic American
Sinatra et al. (1994)	USA	9–10 Grade 4	Mainly Hispanic American
Van Haalen and Bright (1993)	USA	10–11 Grade 5	Mexican American
Williams and Williams (2000)	USA	11–16? Ages not reported	Mainly East African

seems not to have been integrated. The relationship between the intervention and the regular curriculum in Williams and Williams is not made clear. Given the apparent absence (or low level) of integration in four of the eight studies and the lack of detail or clarity in three more, the question of integration is not pursued in any real depth.

The relative weight of evidence

The relevance and value of the eight studies for the present review are summarized in Table 4.4.

Synthesis of the evidence

The majority of the eight studies focus more on lower level literacy skills, though several studies do report that they had hoped students would carry out more higher level editing. There is a lack of Internet-based studies, but this can be accounted for by the fact that the majority date from the early 1990s.

Table 4.4 General and review-specific weight of evidence (summary)

Study	A	B	C	D
Decosta (1992)	Medium	Medium	Low	Low
Lin et al. (1991)	Medium	High	Medium	Medium
Nwogu and Nwogu (1992)	Medium	Medium	Medium	Low*
Parr (1997)	Low	Medium	Low	Low
Silver and Repa (1993)	Medium	Medium	High	Medium
Sinatra et al. (1994)	Low	Medium	Low	Low
Van Haalen and Bright (1993)	Medium	Medium	Medium	Medium
Williams and Williams (2000)	Low	Medium	Low	Low

Note
* Categorized as 'low' due to the absence of empirical data and the lack of information about how the method was implemented. The focus is however fairly relevant, and the research design could have been implemented more systematically and reported more comprehensively.

Key
General
A   Can findings be trusted in answering study question(s)? (EPPI Q.M11)

Review-specific
B   Appropriateness of research design and analysis   (EPPI Q.A2)
C   Relevance of focus of study   (EPPI Q.A3)
D   Overall weight of evidence   (EPPI Q.A4)

The eight studies comprise a range of investigatory approaches. Some studies (Parr; Sinatra *et al.*) are designed to test out/explore the impact of a commercial CALL package. Parr in particular is concerned to observe the impact of a US package in a non-US environment. Nwogu and Nwogu are more concerned to observe what happens in a classroom and to document problems. There is just one RCT (Lin et al.), though two other studies employ some form of control group and a pre-test/post-test design (Silver and Repa; Sinatra *et al.*). One study (Van Haalen and Bright) has a control condition, rather than a control group, and all students receive both the control and experimental treatments. The Williams and Williams study is a before and after evaluation (the term being used to refer to a more informal situation than pre-test/post-test) of a single group that was formed to resolve a learning need and who all underwent the same teaching. Finally, one study, Decosta, is more a qualitative interpretation of selected text data from an evaluation study.

The relationship between investigator and teacher appears to be relatively homogeneous. In seven cases the researcher seems not to have been the teacher, but in one case (Williams and Williams) one of the authors was.

Only one study explicitly builds students with mild learning difficulties into the research design (Lin *et al.*), though other studies may have a number of similar students in the sample (Nwogu and Nwogu, for example, mention their existence in the class, but do not report any numbers, or analyse them separately).

Comments on the individual studies

In this section we comment briefly on each of the eight studies individually, dividing them into primary (under 11 yr) and secondary level (11 yr and over).

Primary

Decosta (1992) differs from all the other studies in that it is not a report of a systematic observation or intervention. Rather, it is an interpretation/evaluation of text fragments produced by US kindergarten and Grade 1 children who lived in an area of unemployment and social problems, and who were exposed to word processing. The ICT teaching was heavily integrated into the school day and the class environment, and involved a high level of teacher support, collaborative work, redrafting and editing, plus a 'user-friendly' environment. The paper is held to be derived from a larger, ongoing study, but details of this are not reported. Decosta claims that all the children involved were very positive about writing using the computers. She also shows that some 5–6-year-old children, when encouraged by the teacher and freed from overconcern about the mechanics of writing, will describe their psychological and home problems in their texts. This intensely personal writing is held to be good from a writing point of view as well as allowing teachers or other appropriate persons to help the students concerned. The results of the study are intuitively very plausible and match Hyland's criteria for progress using CALL, but it is hard to be at all definite, as there are a number of methodological problems: (a) it is unclear how many ESL students are involved in the larger group, (b) only nine children are actually cited in the paper, (c) there is no research design and no systematic sampling or analysis, (d) the timeframe is unclear, and (e) it is unclear how far any effects are due to the computer or a result of good teaching.

Lin *et al.* (1991) represents the only study to overtly include students with mild learning difficulties as part of the research design. The researchers were interested to discover whether CAI improved word recognition skills. The sample of 93 children came from ten US elementary schools and involved 'Caucasian' and 'Chinese American' children. The mean chronological age of those without difficulties was 7.8 yr and of students with mild learning difficulties 8.7 yr (their reading age was on the Grade 2 level). Allocation to treatment groups was random. Retention in the study depended on achieving 45–85 per cent accuracy and a response time of over 100 seconds in the pre-test. The intervention consisted of ten lessons. Pre- and post-testing involved the same multiple choice test, where students were presented with a word and asked to select the correct version from a set of four choices. The results were complex. With respect to response time, both groups of students improved significantly ($p<.001$), but those without difficulties ($p<.001$) and the CAI students ($p<.001$) performed significantly faster, with the latter also being less variable ($p<.01$). The students with mild learning difficulties showed less variance, however ($p<.05$). Further analysis indicated that the greatest response time gains were made by the students with the slowest initial times. With respect to accuracy, the sample had again improved significantly ($p<.001$). This time, however, the pen and paper group was more accurate than the CAI group (p<.01) and the group without difficulties more accurate and less variable than the group with difficulties (both p<.05). Cultural background had no effect. The authors conclude that CAI and pen and paper methods have differing effects on learning, with the pen and paper group being more accurate and the CAI group being faster. These results do help answer the review question in this one restricted domain, but their generalizability and validity need to be tempered by the following difficulties: (a) it is not clear how far the learners are genuinely ESL, (b) few details of the pen and paper tests are given, (c) no sample test items are given, (d) there is a clear assumption that multiple choice tests without a discourse context genuinely measure reading ability and that m/c format represents a valid way to teach reading, (e) there is no reporting of how far the teaching and testing reflect, or are integrated into, current classroom practice, (f) it is unclear whether the sample is at all representative, and (g) there appear to be ceiling effects in the outcome scores. It is also just possible that there was a halo effect; the CAI group had to be trained how to use a keyboard, so it may be that computers were *per se* felt to represent something new and exciting.

Sinatra *et al.* (1994) used a commercial program, seemingly developed by two of the authors, 'Thinking Networks for Reading and Writing Program' to test whether teaching 'at risk Chapter 1' fourth Grade ESL students in New York to compose structured story-board outlines served to improve the quality of their narratives. The procedure was called 'semantic mapping' (though it appears to be heavily discourse rather than semantics oriented) and meant that this was the one study of the eight to be devoted to higher level skills (though Van Haalen and Bright did include them in the analysis). Writing was assessed by using texts taken before and after the intervention and holistically scored using both an overall scale and a composite scale. Attitudes towards computers and towards writing were also gathered. There were originally 260 students from intact classes in six elementary schools, divided into an experimental group of 160 and a control group of 100, who were to be examined over a year's teaching. Unfortunately, 80 students moved from the control to the experimental situation in January, thereby severely unbalancing the groups and reducing the control group to 20. The results showed the experimental group's writing improving significantly (p<.05) and the small control group's scores decreasing. Differential rates of gain indicated that some teachers were more successful than others, with the teachers of the two 'half-year' groups being the most enthusiastic and successful. Ethnicity or L2 was not included in the analysis. Gender was; it proved non-significant as regards writing quality but when attitude was measured, girls scored significantly higher than boys on (a) the importance of writing (p<.01), (b) recognizing a link between writing skill and achievement (p<.001) and (c) having a positive view of oneself as a writer. While the role of enthusiasm on the part of the teacher is highly likely to be an important factor in success with CALL, it is hard to use the results of the study to answer the review question. The reasons are: (a) the description of the linguistic make-up of the observed sample is hedged, (b) no separate analysis for the ESL students, or for separate L2s, is carried out, (c) the statistical analysis is seriously impaired, as the authors admit, by the 80 students shifting conditions, (d) attitudes are only measured after the end of the study, not before, (e) the experimental group differs from the control on two major counts, not one – the control used neither a computer nor semantic mapping – (f) no baseline data on initial English levels is reported and (g) the authors admit (p.108) that the control group lacked 'a cohesive plan for in-depth development of a particular discourse form ... the narrative'.

Van Haalen and Bright (1993) investigated whether word processing aided a sample of 42 fifth grade monolingual and bilingual Mexican American students in their writing. The sample was from a southern US city and appeared to be reasonably representative of the local community. The monolingual group were essentially English language only, though their receptive skills were not reported. Each group received four writing tasks, the first two word processed, the second two pen and paper. The task involved a pictorial stimulus and students underwent a three-day writing cycle to produce a written narrative. The texts were scored holistically and five types of revision were counted; these ranged from low-level spelling and punctuation to higher level sentence rearrangement and resequencing. The main findings were that (a) significantly more revisions were made in the pen and paper condition than the word processing condition (p<.05), except for word-level revisions, (b) females made more revisions overall than males (p<.01), (c) monolinguals made more surface revision than bilinguals but bilinguals made significantly more phrase-level revisions (p<.05) and (d) keyboarding was a significant regressor in predicting revisions. With respect to the holistic scores, performance was better in the pen and paper condition than the CALL condition (p<.001), but neither bilingualism nor gender affected the results significantly. However, when keyboarding scores were factored in, bilingual students did score significantly higher (p<.05). At a general level, the authors noted that most revisions were at word-level and few students made higher level sentence revisions, especially when using the computer. The researchers concluded that both higher level revision and keyboarding skills need to be taught to all students, irrespective of language; lack of keyboarding skills can hold students back from realising their writing potential. The findings do help answer the review question, but a number of methodological or reporting difficulties, in addition to the ESL classification problem mentioned above, limit the definiteness with which one may apply the conclusions. First, there are few details about the writing tasks or the teaching procedures; the seeming lack of any collaborative work or integration with regular schoolwork may have limited the quality of the texts or the number and type of revisions (this despite the flagging of integration as potentially important on p.314). Second, the research design would have been improved if there had been random assignment to treatments and both groups had not received the experimental and control conditions and in the same order. Third, the absence of English proficiency data makes it hard to draw conclusions about linguistic thresholds for tasks. Indeed there is very little baseline data reported.

Secondary

Nwogu and Nwogu (1992) observed a class of ESL children in a Birmingham (UK) secondary school for four months, then interviewed the teacher and gave a 26-item questionnaire to a random selection of ten children. The school had been selected as the only one found matching seven criteria. These included: having timetabled CALL sessions for ESL students, reasonable access times, CALL materials and a CALL trained teacher. The sample is not clearly described, but was largely of South Asian origin and comprised a mixture of students, from recent arrivals in the UK to children with (moderate) hearing difficulties. No age profile is reported, but most of the children had a reading age of less than 8 yr. The researchers noted that there were very few computers available to the ESL children (namely one BBC computer), that access time was severely limited and that the CALL programs available were designed for native speakers (their drill-like structure making them unsuited to modern ideas of communicative or task-based language teaching).

The results of the questionnaire, however, showed that the children were very enthusiastic about the CALL sessions and attributed considerable learning gains to them. The finding that few computers were available to ESL students in Birmingham schools in the early 1990s is very plausible, as is the claim that little real progress can be expected without CALL programs that are compatible with good language teaching practice. However, as there are no real data, the study cannot be held to really show anything about ICT and ESL learners. On top of this, the study is let down by (a) the absence of any analysis of the observations, (b) conflating the results from other schools, or conclusions from general knowledge, with those of the class observed, (c) not reporting what CALL was in fact observed and (d) reporting the questionnaire results and procedure in an anecdotal and unquantified way.

Parr (1997) is a study of how intact classes of New Zealand secondary children, both ESL and non-ESL, reacted to the use of the American 'SuccessMaker' program, designed to improve reading and maths skills. A range of students with ages, academic levels and exposure times was observed over an academic year and their learning gains rechecked several months later. Parr concludes that there were initial reading gains by Form 3, Form 3 Learning Support and Form 4 students, but that, when standard reading tests were used, the gains did not last. Parr suggests that the multiple choice questions initially confused the New Zealand students (who were unused to the concept), but that they mastered the idea rapidly and made considerable gains. However, the multiple choice format did little to enhance learning in the longer term. Comparisons between Maori and European students were non-significant, though there was a gender effect; girls scored significantly higher than boys ($p < .05$). Sixty-three students, both frequent and non-frequent users of 'SuccessMaker', were interviewed. Seventy per cent felt they had made good progress on 'SuccessMaker'. Roughly a third had been bored ($n = 21$) and a third had been motivated ($n = 26$). Ten students liked the absence of writing and ten liked being in control. Unquantified effects on the teachers were that several felt their role had been eased by the program, but some disengaged. There are serious difficulties in using these results to answer the research question in this review. The main problems are that (a) the progress of the ESL students is not reported, (b) it is unclear whether the Maori students in F3 and F4 should be seen as ESL, as their English proficiency was similar to that of the European students, (c) the make-up of the F3 Learning Support Group (who made the most gains) is unreported, (d) comparing reading scores with those of the previous year's students can only be a very partial and non-ideal control, (e) baseline data on reading skills was available, but does not appear to have been used, (f) the questionnaire and interview data are mostly reported in anecdotal form, or not reported at all (e.g. the self-report questionnaire) and (g) no statistical test for the standardized reading test scores is reported. Lastly, it has to be said that both reviewers found it extremely hard to disentangle the precise details of the sample, the research design and some of the results.

Silver and Repa (1993) examined whether word processing would improve the writing skills and self esteem of 66 beginning ESL students (aged 15–16 yr) in an urban New York secondary school. The authors took four intact classes studying 'Introduction to Literature 1' and conducted a pre-test/post-test study lasting 13 weeks. The experimental group met for 18 sessions of 70 minutes and learned, during the classes, to compose on the computer using 'Wordperfect Junior'. Self-esteem was measured using the Cooper-smith Self-Esteem Inventory and a teacher-report Behavioural Academic Self-Esteem scale. Writing proficiency was measured using text samples rated holistically in accordance with the CUNY Writing Skills Assessment Test Evaluation Scale. The findings were that the experimental group's writing quality increased significantly (p < .05), but that self-esteem ratings did not, though 'all but two students developed a positive attitude toward writing' (p.277). The authors concluded that (a) 13 weeks was possibly not long enough to increase self-esteem, (b) that collaborative assignments were 'aided by using word processing' (p.275), (c) collaborations 'were made easier when each member of the group was given a legible printout' (p.275), (d) use of the computer generated more writing (than not using it) and (e) teachers in computer-aided sessions tended to become facilitators. The study is let down slightly by not using the pre-test data when measuring post-test gain (i.e. Analysis of Covariance is not employed) and by the fact that the experimental group appears to have done more writing than the control group. The lack of comparison with a non-ESL group, or between the L2 groups involved also limits the value of the findings, as does the lack of investigation of the textual and strategic differences between the writing samples. The four unquantified results are of particular interest, as they match Hyland's proposed criteria for learning gains using CALL, but the very fact of the comments being vague in scope and unquantified means that one cannot really generalize from them. One should perhaps also note that the school was an alternative school, with a very high commitment to and provision of student support.

Williams and Williams (2000) were concerned to test out a new way of teaching 21 ESL students in a North Western US secondary school who could not follow the teacher or the course successfully. The aim was to improve students' reading by use of a combination of reading (and reading aloud), oral repetition and copying/ transcribing the text (words then phrases then sentences) into the computer. The authors measured progress after one semester and claimed a marked improvement. The study is let down by a number of factors. Apart from the classification problems noted above, the main difficulties are that the research question and the nature of the students' problems are not adequately discussed, the pre-test data are unclear, the relative contribution of the different aspects of the treatment (such as repetition, writing, using the computer) is neither addressed nor discussed, and the nature of 'correctness' is not addressed. The result is that, while the idea of measuring learning gain from an integrated-skill treatment is good in outline, the lack of theoretical discussion, of an appropriate research design, of attempts to address validity or reliability, and of appropriate statistical analysis make it impossible to draw any real conclusions about the role of ICT in helping the students improve their literacy skills.

The impact of ICT on literacy

In the final analysis, several studies have produced suggestive ideas, but just three studies rate as having 'medium' weight of evidence to answer the review question of the impact of ICT on literacy among ESL students (Lin *et al.*; Silver and Repa; Van Haalen and Bright). Of these, there is some doubt about the validity of the ESL status of Lin *et al.* and Van Haalen and Bright. Our conclusions below are based primarily on the medium weight studies. Where details of the low weight studies are not problematic, these have at times been drawn on; on other occasions, a detail from a low weight study has been mentioned, but either the weighting has been explicitly noted, or information from the medium weight studies has been used in support or contrast.

Impact on the educational system

Despite a lack of generalizable empirical evidence, Nwogu and Nwogu's conclusion seems reasonable, namely that no proper CALL teaching or learning can take place with ESL students, unless there are adequate numbers of available computers, CALL programs are adaptable and fit current approaches to language teaching, there are CALL-trained ESL teaching staff, students each receive adequate access time and CALL sessions are timetabled/integrated into the regular school programme. This agrees with Silver and Repa's task-based approach, whereby CALL students worked collaboratively and had a goal (publishing on the web). Decosta's findings do not carry a medium or high weight of evidence for this review, but they do support the need to integrate CALL classes and work into the regular curriculum and a user-friendly, collaborative environment. Hyland's proposal to this effect is thus supported by the studies in this review. Impact on the 'system' may be taken to indicate impact on the classroom.

Chapelle (see Introduction) considered what actually goes on in the classroom to be a key determinant of success with CALL. Though a successful classroom is described by Decosta, her description is rather lyrical and at a general level. The remaining studies touch periodically on classroom activity, but there is no detailed account and no attempt at recording or measuring it. There is, moreover, no indication of ways in which classrooms or class activities were modified as a result of the observations or interventions.

Impact on the student

The effect of word processing proved variable; Van Haalen and Bright's primary students wrote better narratives using pen and paper, while Silver and Repa's secondary students wrote better on the computer. In spite of the methodological problems with the study, Sinatra et al. identified the enthusiasm of the class teacher as a major determinant of success with CALL, but neither Van Haalen and Bright nor Silver and Repa examined this.

Lin et al. commented that, at least for low level tasks like word recognition, there may be a trade-off between speed (using a computer) and accuracy (using pen and paper). The notion of differ-ent media enhancing different skills is intuitively very plausible, but unfortunately none of the other studies address it. Van Haalen and Bright's distinction between number and type of revisions and overall quality is not quite the same.

Though Sinatra et al. did ask for discourse level activities and approached them in a structured way, other studies, such as Van

Haalen and Bright, found that few students used word processors to carry out sentence level revisions. Even though the Sinatra *et al.* study does not directly answer the question for ESL students, our conclusion is that some discourse level revision is likely to be possible with ESL primary and secondary students, but only with strong support from the teacher, the CALL materials and the teaching environment. Van Haalen and Bright recommend that such techniques are worth teaching; we support this but feel that more research is needed to indicate the limitations and the possibilities.

Two studies found that students with lower starting proficiency made the greatest gains. Parr found that the F3 Learning Support Group made the greatest reading score gains (using a multiple choice approach) and Lin *et al.* found that the greatest response time gains for word recognition were made by the students with the slowest initial times. Both studies involved fairly mechanical learning tasks and this may be the key. It is unclear whether Parr's Learning Support Group contained any ESL students, but the Nwogu and Nwogu study may provide some indirect support, in that the observed group contained students with learning difficulties and the teaching involved fairly mechanical approaches to pre-reading activities, but all the ten students who responded to the questionnaire attributed personal learning gains to the CALL sessions.

There is some evidence from Decosta that ICT experience, when supported by good teaching and collaborative work, can foster the development in some young primary children of a personal 'voice' when writing. Decosta does not use the term voice, but is in effect employing it in the broad sense of a means to express a personal and deeply felt perspective. The problem is, as indicated above, that the report suffers from a number of methodological difficulties and the evidence cannot be treated as other than low weight for this review. The claim is sufficiently important, however, to imply a strong need for further research.

Impact with respect to gender

Three studies found a gender effect in favour of girls (Parr; Sinatra *et al.*; Van Haalen and Bright). Parr's sample for this effect contains primarily F3 and F4 children who appear not to be ESL, so the gender effect cannot really be endorsed in the context of this review. Van Haalen and Bright found that while the quality of narratives was similar for girls and boys, girls made significantly more revisions than boys. Sinatra *et al.* also found a gender difference among attitudes, with girls developing a better attitude towards writing, and in particular being more aware of the importance of writing, the link between writing and achievement and showing a more positive view of themselves as writers. All of these findings could easily be accounted for if the girls were slightly more mature than the boys, but as the evidence stands, no common underlying factor can be clearly identified from the studies reviewed.

Impact with respect to ethnicity

Only Van Haalen and Bright report a significant difference for ESL students, with respect to the type of revisions made, but this result may well be due more to the fact of relatively balanced bilingualism on the part of those who performed better. This would indeed support the notion that bilingualism can confer advantages with respect to cognitive skills, but this conclusion requires a linguistic threshold to have been reached. Lin *et al.* did not find a language or ethnicity effect, but they did comment on the notion of a threshold, noting that certain tasks might work against ESL students whose English is below a certain threshold. With no more evidence, all that can be concluded here is that thresholds are likely to be important in several aspects of CALL, but more detailed research is needed. In sum, the studies in the review suggest that, where the task is appropriate to students' needs, and their language and intellectual level, CALL materials are as useful for teaching ESL students, whether with mild learning difficulties or without, as they are for teaching English mother tongue students.

Impact with respect to student attitude/opinion

Though the opinions of students of all ages, primary and secondary, tended to be more or less positive about the use of computers, this trend was not universal. Twenty-one of the 63 students in Parr's study who reported their opinions considered 'SuccessMaker' boring – though again it is unclear if any of these were genuinely ESL. The reviewers had expected to find a marked gender effect, with girls being more negative than boys, but the effect only occurred in Sinatra *et al.* and that was the inverse. The data in the eight studies are not adequate to decide which students liked what sort of CALL programs and what sort of tasks/work.

Impact with respect to staff attitude or behaviour

To Hyland, teachers not computers are the key to successful learning via CALL. The point is strongly endorsed by writers from Farrington (1989: 70) to Sussex (1991: 21) and Levy (1997: 231). Unfortunately the studies in the review did not focus on teachers in any great detail. Rather, impact on and of the teacher tended to be reported anecdotally in all cases – even where precise data collection measures had apparently been adopted. Both Silver and Repa, and Decosta noted that the CALL teacher became a facilitator, rather than imparter of wisdom, bringing CALL teaching into line with modern views of regular class-based language teaching. Sinatra *et al.* also noted that the greatest learning gain was made by the two classes with highly enthusiastic teachers; there is little data about teacher enthusiasm in the other studies, though Parr reported that some teachers (unquantified) were less enthusiastic than others and simply disengaged in the CALL classes. This situation presumably supports Nwogu and Nwogu's assertion that trained CALL teachers are an important requirement for success in using ICT with ESL, or, one suspects, any other students.

Strengths and limitations of this review

Strengths

The general approach taken in this analysis is an applied linguistic one (rather than say a psychological one). The primary strength of the review thus lies in a close analysis of the sample, the task and the investigatory method; it is, we trust, informed by research and concepts in language education.

The review also has a possible strength that was not anticipated, with respect to the question of collaborative work between students. Most of the included studies happened to date from the early 1990s, when there were fewer computers in schools for students to use. This lack of hardware is likely to make extensive individual use of machines difficult, so shared or collaborative work may well be suggested by the teacher simply as a means of overcoming the problem, or else arise spontaneously among students who would otherwise have to compete for scarce resources.

Limitations

The primary limitation of the review is that it is small. There are only eight included studies and of these, none were deemed to provide a 'high' weight of evidence to answer the question at hand; indeed, only three were deemed 'medium'. The reasons for not categorizing the weight as 'high' differed, but the result inevitably remains that it is hard to draw any firm conclusions or draw much in the way of implications for policy.

Unlike Andrews *et al.* (2002) this report looked specifically for relevant details of the learning environment and sample: for characteristics of bilingualism in the individual or society, for example, or for details of classroom practice. The virtual absence of any such detail from seven of the studies included means that the review is far more limited in scope than had originally been intended.

The fact that most of the included studies (6/8) dated from the early 1990s also imposes limitations on the value of the review for policy-making in the twenty-first century. The first limitation stems from the simple fact that technology has moved on. Even 'basic' entry-level computers are far faster and displays are no longer text-based. Computer programs are larger, more visual, more inclusive, more interactive in many cases, more integrated to email and the web and more likely to form part of an integrated suite. Thus, a 1990 study which reported solely on word processing, for example, was making a more inclusive and universal statement then than it would now. Perhaps the most important change, however, lies in the explosion of email and web-based communication by children in their own homes. This may well link with the explosion of mobile phone use by the same generation, with the consequent widespread use of texting. There are two significant implications of this for the present review. The first is that students are far more confident about and competent at using the hardware than a decade ago. The second implication is that the degree of constant exposure to emails and webpages is likely to have reduced (or entirely removed) the feeling that ICT is something new and exciting. A third implication, which none of the included studies addresses, is that children's use of ICT for such things as fast games, alters the nature of pre-course training from how to cope with a computer to how to slow down and concentrate.

Although it is not really a limitation, there is a small problem which needs to be mentioned which is inherent in the basic concept of evidence-based reviewing. This is, somewhat paradoxically, the very fact that all studies should be treated in an equivalent fashion when it comes to evaluating them. The reason why this can be a problem (rather than a big advantage) is that not all articles or research reports are written with an identical purpose, or an identical audience, in mind. They are also constrained by editorial conventions and a strong demand by journals in disciplines such as psychology to be of minimal length and to omit much methodological description or discussion. As a result, the systematic reviewer may berate a brief 'readable' summary written, for example, for teachers, as method-ologically unsound research, and of low value for the review. While such a study cannot in truth be categorized as other than of low value for the review, it may nevertheless be felt that there is inevitably a tacit implication of incompetence by the researcher or author and that the paper has been wrongly treated as something which it never set out to be. In the case of the present review, it could be argued that there is an element of this problem with the Nwogu and Nwogu paper and possibly with the Williams and Williams article. All one can say is that any such implications deriving from the source are unintended.

Our final point concerns future reviews. The present review used ESL and EAL as keywords, but given the adoption of ESOL (English for Speakers of Other Languages) by the UK Basic Skills Agency and one or two other organizations, future reviews should really employ ESOL as well as ESL and EAL.

Implications

Given that five of the eight studies included in the in-depth review were allocated a 'low' level of overall weight of evidence, and that all the remaining three studies were allocated a 'Medium' rating in this respect, the overall implication is that there is an insubstantial body of evidence pointing in any direction regarding the research question. The following points are presented, therefore, with a high degree of caution.

Implications for policy

- Introduction and development of ICT-based ESL programmes should be on the basis of careful preliminary consideration of the intended role of the computer and software. To what use would the ICT be put? There was a lack of clarity in some studies over whether the computer/software was in fact adding anything unique into the learning process that could not be achieved by other means;

- Where the ICT equipment has a specific and unique role, and where that is clear and observed by practitioners, then it can have a beneficial impact on improving literacy, especially writing skills;
- ICT can help create more motivated ESL learners. More positive attitudes are reported as resulting more often from groups using computers in ESL learning than non-ICT groups of ESL learners;
- Development of ESL using ICT requires systematic evaluation so that policy-makers obtain essential information regarding what is effective;
- It is not clear what ICT has to offer ESL as a group of learners as distinct from other learner groups (such as SEN, EFL, at-risk learners). Until such evidence is forthcoming, policy-makers should review evidence from wider-ranging studies on the impact of ICT.

Implications for practice

- There appears to be evidence in a number of studies that suggests the use of ICT in the ESL classroom can alter the role of the teacher. The shift tends to be away from being a 'traditional' teacher and towards the role of being a facilitator;
- The level of sophistication which ESL software can bring to literacy tasks is often kept to a low level in the classroom. Teachers and learners seem to use ICT more readily for basic work, such as word-level operations and proof-reading. Greater use of ICT's potential in text manipulation and other higher order literacy skills is needed;
- Appropriate training for staff using ICT as a teaching medium with ESL learners is necessary.

Implications for research

A number of robust studies are needed to address the research question. These should systematically record, monitor and investigate:

- learners' ethnicity and existing level of proficiency in English

- the learning processes which particular items of ESL software engender
- the relationship between those processes and the learning processes of the mainstream classroom and the culture at large
- learning gains and attitude changes
- these and other outcomes of the ESL ICT-based learning programmes compared with those of other forms of ESL learning programmes.

Studies included in map and synthesis

Bigum, C., Durrant, C., Green, B., Honan, E., Lankshear, C., Morgan, W., Murray, J., Snyder, I. and Wild, M. (1997) *Digital Rhetorics: Literacies and Technologies in Education – Current Practices and Future Directions* (Executive Summary and Volumes 1, 2 and 3), Canberra: Department of Employment, Education, Training and Youth Affairs.

Decosta, S.B. (1992) 'Sociological findings in young children's word-processed writings', *Computers in Human Behaviour*, 8: 17–25.

Lin, A., Podell, D. and Rein, N. (1991) 'The effects of CAI on word recognition on mildly mentally handicapped and non-handicapped learners', *Journal of Special Education Technology*, 11: 16–25.

McNamee, G.D. (1995) 'A Vygotskian perspective on literacy development', *School Psychology International*, 16: 185–98.

Nwogu, K. and Nwogu, E. (1992) 'Computers and ESL in the West Midlands', *Language Learning Journal*, 6: 74–6.

Parr, J.M. (1997) 'Computer assisted learning with an integrated learning system: another front for raising literacy and numeracy amongst secondary students?', *New Zealand Journal of Educational Studies*, 32: 37–51.

Silver, N.W. and Repa, J.T. (1993) 'The effect of word processing on the quality of writing and self esteem of secondary school English-as-second-language students: writing without censure', *Journal of Educational Computing Research*, 9: 265–83.

Sinatra, R., Beaudry, J., Pizzo, J. and Geisert, G. (1994) 'Using a computer-based semantic mapping, reading and writing approach with at-risk fourth graders', *Journal of Computing in Childhood Education*, 5: 93–112.

Van Haalen, T. and Bright, G.W. (1993) 'Writing and revising by bilingual students in traditional and word processing environments', *Journal of Educational Computing Research*, 9: 313–28.

Williams, H.S. and Williams, P.N. (2000) 'Integrating reading and computers: an approach to improve EFL students' reading skills', *Reading Improvement*, 37: 98–100.

References

Allright, D. (1988) *Observation in the Language Classroom*, New York: Longman.

Andrews, R., Burn, A., Leach, J., Locke, T., Low, G.D. and Torgerson, C. (2002) 'A systematic review of the impact of networked ICT on 5–16 year olds' literacy in English' (EPPI-Centre Review), *Research Evidence in Education Library*, 1, London: EPPI-Centre, Social Science Research Unit, Institute of Education.

Baker, C. (2001) *Foundations of Bilingual Education and Bilingualism*, Clevedon: Multilingual Matters.

Barton, D., Hamilton, M. and Ivanic, R. (2000) *Situated Literacies: Reading and Writing in Context*, London: Routledge.

British Educational Communications and Technology Agency (BECTa) (1998–9) *A Preliminary Report for the DfEE on the Relationship Between ICT and Primary School Standards*, Coventry: BECTa.

British Educational Communications and Technology Agency (BECTa) (1998) *The UK Evaluations Final Report*, Coventry: BECTa.

British Educational Communications and Technology Agency (BECTa) (2001a) *Primary Schools of the Future – Achieving Today*, Coventry: BECTa.

British Educational Communications and Technology Agency (BECTa) (2001b) *The Secondary School of the Future*, Coventry: BECTa.

Chapelle, C. (1990) 'The discourse of computer-assisted language learning: toward a context for descriptive research', *TESOL Quarterly*, 24: 199–224.

Chaudron, C. (1988) *Second Language Classrooms: Research on Teaching and Learning*, Cambridge: Cambridge University Press.

Coles, M. (2002) *The Impact of Reforming Vocational Education and Training Organisation and Financing in Europe: Evaluating the Impact of Vocational Education and Training*, London: Qualifications and Curriculum Authority.

Ellis, R. (1985) *Understanding Second Language Acquisition*, Oxford: Oxford University Press.

Farrington, B. (1989) 'AI: "grandeur" or "servitude"', in K.C. Cameron (ed.) *Computer-Assisted Language Learning: Programme Structure and Principles*, Oxford: Intellect Books.

Fasold, R. (1984) *The Sociolinguistics of Society*, Oxford: Blackwell.

Gao, Y. (1994) 'Productive bilingualism: an empirical study', *Foreign Language Teaching and Research*, 97: 59–64.

Gao, Y. (2001) *Foreign Language Learning: '1+1>2'*, Beijing: Peking University Press.

Gao, Y. (2002) 'Productive bilingualism: 1+1>2', in D.W.C. So and G.M. Jones (eds) *Education and Society in Plurilingual Contexts*, Brussels: VUB Brussels University Press.

Gardner, R.C. (2002) 'Social psychological perspective on second language acquisition', in R. Kaplan (ed.) *The Oxford Handbook of Applied Linguistics*, Oxford: Oxford University Press.

Gillen, J. (2002) 'Methodological issues involved in studying children's interactions with ICT', in K. Spelman Miller and P. Thompson (eds) *Unity and Diversity in Language Use*, London: BAAL and Continuum.

Görlach, M. (2002) *Still More Englishes*, Amsterdam/Philadelphia: Benjamins.

Huss, S. and others (1990) 'Using computers with adult ESL literacy learners', ERIC Digest ED343462, Washington, DC: National Clearinghouse on Literacy Education. Online. Available HTTP: //www.ericfacility.net/ericdigests/ed343462.html>(accessed 6 Feb 2003).

Hyland, K. (1993) 'ESL computer writers: what can we do to help?', *System*, 21: 21–30.

Kleinmann, H. (1987) 'The effect of computer-assisted instruction on ESL reading achievement', *The Modern Language Journal*, 71: 267–76.

Kramsch, C. (2002) 'Beyond the second vs foreign language dichotomy: the subjective dimensions of language learning', in K. Spelman Miller and P. Thompson (eds) *Unity and Diversity in Language Use*, London: BAAL and Continuum.

Lambert, W.E. (1974) 'Culture and language as factors in learning and education', paper presented at the eighth Annual TESOL Conference.

Lemke, J.L. (1998) 'Multimedia literacy demands of the scientific curriculum', *Linguistics and Education*, 10: 247–71.

Levy, M. (1997) *Computer-Assisted Language Learning*, Oxford: Clarendon.

Long, M. (1980) 'Inside the "black box": methodological issues in classroom research on language learning', *Language Learning*, 30: 1–42.

Ofsted (2001) *Managing Support for the Attainment of Pupils from Minority Ethnic Groups*, London: Ofsted (Office for Standards in Education) Publications Centre.

Ofsted (2002) *More Advanced Learners of English as an Additional Language in Secondary Schools and Colleges*, London: Ofsted (Office for Standards in Education) Publications Centre.

Romaine, S. (1995) *Bilingualism* (second edn), Oxford: Blackwell.

Stapleton, P. (2002) 'Critiquing voice as a viable pedagogical tool in L2 writing: returning the spotlight to ideas', *Journal of Second Language Writing*, 11: 177–90.

Street, B. (ed.) (1993) *Cross-Cultural Approaches to Literacy*, Cambridge: Cambridge University Press.

Sussex, R.D. (1991) 'Author languages, authoring systems and their relation to the changing focus of computer-aided language learning', *System*, 19: 15–27.

Vilmi, R. (2000) 'Collaborative writing projects on the internet: more than half a decade of experimentation', in P. Howarth and R. Herington (eds) *ESP Learning Technologies*, Leeds: Leeds University Press.

Wertsch, J.V. (1991) *Voices of the Mind: A Sociocultural Approach to Mediated Action*, Cambridge, MA: Harvard University Press.

Chapter 5

ICT and literature: A Faustian compact?

Terry Locke and Richard Andrews

> Mephist.: Here, take this book, peruse it well:
> The iterating of these lines brings gold....
> Faustus: Thanks, Mephistophilis, for this sweet book:
> This will I keep as chary as my life.
> Christopher Marlowe, *Dr Faustus*

Books play an ambivalent role in *Dr Faustus*. On the one hand, they can be seen as repositories of accumulated wisdom. On the other hand, they have the potential to charm and ensnare readers in search of power and various forms of self-gratification. Within a short space of time, the learned Faustus of Marlowe's play turns his back on one use of reading and opts for another – one that will deliver almost godlike power into his grasping hands.

Within the drama, set at a time when the printing press was revolutionising the production of texts, the place of books is assured. And so is the assumed nexus between textual practice and power. Four hundred years later, the latter assumption remains a truism. But the assured place of books, both as a medium and as in a narrower sense enshrining the collective intellectual endeavour of a people, is under threat. In respect of the former, one increasingly finds references to 'a post typographic world' (Reinking *et al.* 1998) and the death of the book. In respect of the latter, challenges to various constructions of *the* canon of hallowed texts and even to the idea of a canon itself have become commonplace in the latter decades of the last century (e.g. Eagleton 1983, Guillory 1995, West 1994).

Like other contributions to this collection, this one draws on a sub-review of a systematic review of the impact of ICT on 5–16-year-olds' literacy in English conducted by the EPPI Review Group for English based at the University of York. The sub-review question was on the impact of ICT on literature-related literacies in English, 5–16. This review used systematic research review methodology developed by the EPPI-Centre, moving from a stage of identifying the research question in a protocol or plan; through searching and screening according to inclusion and exclusion criteria; mapping of the field; further application of the criteria to determine the core papers for in-depth review; the review itself; and subsequent synthesis of the findings. (This methodology will be referred to in this article but not detailed since it is discussed elsewhere in this book in Chapter 7.)

Literature, then, for all its troubled and troubling status, is the theme of this chapter. We begin with a discussion of the concepts embedded in and related to the sub-review questions. We then move to a consideration of the sorts of research agendas underpinning the studies included in (and also excluded from) the in-depth review of core papers. We look at some of the findings and suggestions contained in these studies and conclude with a section on implications. Here we will discuss not only policy and pedagogical implications, but also implications for a future research agenda (including the need for further theorisation).

Towards a conceptual map

Any study of the impact of ICT on literature-related literacies is complicated by the fact that it is effectively addressing three moving targets: ICT itself, literature and literacy. Indeed, it might be suggested that the noun 'impact', itself, is a moving target (see below). It has become a kind of orthodox commonplace to describe literacy as a social practice and therefore subject to change (Leu 2000). Literacy has become a plural – literacies – and more often than not prefaced by terms such as 'technological', 'digital', 'computer', 'multiple', 'new' and sometimes 'old', i.e. the one(s) academic researchers grew up with (see, for example, Cope and Kalantzis 2000, Lemke 1998).

For such reasons, the term *literacy*, as used in the overarching protocol for this project (Andrews *et al.* 2002), was broadened first to include social as well as cognitive aspects of literacy, and second to accommodate texts where written language has been complemented by a graphic or pictorial dimension. The protocol also defined *ICT* as including stand-alone computers, networked technologies with a multimodal interface, mobile phones with the capacity for a range of types of communication, and other technologies which allow multimodal and interactive communication.

The fluidity of the current social milieu has been summed up by Leu (op. cit.) in his use of the word 'deictic' to refer to the rapidity with which definitions of literacy are regularly redefined 'not by time or space, but by new technologies and the continuously changing envisionments [sic] they initiate for communication' (Leu 2000: 745). It is not only ICTs as systems which are changing; it is the envisionments of their use. While changes in technology have a role to play in the transformation of literacy, so new literate practices can serve to transform technology use. For this reason, *impact* needs to be thought of symbiotically, with technologies and literate practices mutually transforming each other. (As they always *have* done, we might add. Literacy has always been a technologised practice.)

An instance of this symbiosis can be found in a report on the American BookRead Project (Jody and Saccardi 1998). What is significant about this project, though the report authors do not comment on it directly, is that the intervention (networked ICT), while apparently being utilized to serve traditional educational ends, actually works transformatively. That is, the intervention actually transforms the literature-based literacy practice. If one thinks of reading as the interpretative, meaning-making conversation (even with oneself) one conducts around a text, then the introduction of networked ICTs alters that conversation (in ways that Jody and Saccardi report on at length). In the case of the BookRead Project, if the authors of the texts studied had not been included in the conversation, the readers would have had to resort to establishing, say, authorial intention, through interpretation and speculation – a different kind of meaning-making practice, we would suggest.

Finally, there are a number of reasons why 'literature' must be viewed as a shifting target, despite its continued overt presence in national English curriculum statements. On the one hand, as has been mentioned previously, its status as a category has been affected by the attack on the literary canon. Questions such as 'What should be categorized as literature?' are not settled ones. And the question is complicated by the current high status of 'children's literature' and 'literature for young adults'. On the other hand, changes in critical theory have meant the proliferation of approaches to literary study. Putting it bluntly, there is no simple answer to the question, 'What constitutes literature-related literacy?' Indeed, some theorists would challenge the validity of such a construction.

Such problematisation, however, has done little to challenge the secure place of literature in the national curricula of most English-speaking countries. In England, literature has a set of objectives to itself in the Reading section of each of Key Stages 1–4. In addition, Key Stages 3–4 add a section of aims related to 'English literary heritage' (DfEE and QCA 1999). One of the six basic outcomes of the New Zealand national English curriculum is that students 'respond personally to and think critically about a range of texts, including literary texts' (Ministry of Education 1994: 9). In the Australian situation, the words 'literature' and 'literary' are notably absent from 'Reading and Viewing' outcomes for any level of *English – a curriculum profile for Australian schools*. However, in the discussion of types of evidence for level-related attainment, one finds frequent references to literary genres and the terminology of literary study, e.g. 'allegory', 'point of view', 'character' (Curriculum Corporation 1994). In the United States, the IRA/NCTE 'Standards for the English Language Arts' include: 'Students read a wide range of literature from many periods in many genres to build an understanding of the many dimensions (e.g., philosophical, ethical, aesthetic) of human experience' (IRA and NCTE 1996: 3). Indeed, such statements taken collectively would appear to belie the problematisation of literature as a concept.

A further complicating factor is the place of writing in the context of 'literary study', however the latter is defined. Scholes (1985) points out the privileging of reading over writing in traditional 'literary study' courses and comments on the unthinkability of students being viewed as producing 'literature' themselves. It appears 'natural' for curriculum documents to relate literature to reading (or responding) rather than to writing (or producing). The hegemonies implicit in such an analysis probably persist, but one can suggest that a challenge to this situation might come from classroom programmes that recognize the interactive potential and productive capabilities of digital technologies.

Taking these factors into consideration, we have defined literature-related literacy as a range of competences enabling students to read, interpret and critique literary texts (however defined) and to engage in the production of such texts. Such a definition accommodates, for example, theoretical positions which distinguish between operational, cultural and critical literacies (Green and Bigum 1996) or which utilize the notion of 'technological literacy' (Lankshear and Knobel 1997).

Literature and ICT: some recent studies

In undertaking the sub-review, we were not aware of any systematic or non-systematic literature reviews that dealt with the impact of ICT on literature-related literacies. With a national survey of Australian schools indicating relatively little use of computers in teaching literary texts (Durrant and Hargreaves 1995), we did not expect the field to be rich in research on the impact of ICT on literature-related literacies. This expectation was fulfilled. What a rich field might look like in the future will be discussed later in this chapter.

This lack of research stands in pointed contrast to the increased use of ICT in schools aimed at 'supporting' literacy learning. Successive governments, across a range of English-speaking countries, have, since the mid-1990s, invested large amounts of resources to develop ICT in schools. What appears to have been lacking in all this noise and endeavour has been the articulation of a rationale for ICT integration into the English/literacy programme. Indeed, to take the New Zealand case, a recent issue of *English in Aotearoa* (2001), despite a reported increase in ICT access and use in New Zealand schools, quoted research indicating relatively low levels of integration of ICTs in the classroom practices of English teachers, especially at secondary level (Ham 2001, Halliday 2001).

Part of the background to our sub-review was an emerging picture suggestive of a disjunction between policy and practice, with governments advocating increased ICT 'take up' and a classroom reality where ICT integration has been piecemeal and sometimes lacking in terms of a rationale. The three-volume report on the state of ICT integration in Australian schools, *Digital Rhetorics* (Bigum *et al.* 1997), suggests such a picture for that country.

The research question for the review, then, was: 'What is the impact of ICT on literature-related literacies in English 5–16?' This research question was developed because of the prominent (if not central) role accorded literary study in secondary school English classrooms and the wide use of children's literature ('literary' texts for younger readers) in primary literacy programmes. The question acknowledged that 'literature-related literacy' was a contestable term. It also deliberately viewed 'impact' as an outcome that was emergent rather than predetermined and anticipated. We saw literature-related literacy/ies as not static but as something susceptible to transformation under the pressure of ICT, both in the classroom and in changing textual forms and practices in the world at large.

The following research goals are illustrative of the focus (not always reflected in the studies identified) we brought to the review process:

- an evaluation of the impact of a particular ICT-based intervention or practice on one or more aspects of literature-related literacy as conceptualised by the researchers
- the last, but coupled with a comparison with the impact of, say, print-based texts
- an evaluation of the impact of a particular ICT-based intervention or practice on a literature-related pedagogy as conceptualised by the researchers
- the last, but coupled with a comparison with the impact of, say, a print-based pedagogical practice
- an evaluation of ways in which literature-related literacies are being affected or re-conceptualised under pressure from the 'new' technologies and the text types (genres and hybrids) they have spawned.

Selecting studies

For a detailed account of the process of identifying and describing the twelve studies that were included in the systematic map see Locke and Andrews (2003). We were constrained to exclude studies which fell outside the range of children aged 5–16. A study by Bain *et al.* (2000) on the use of a hypertext discussion tool for teaching English literature, for example, was excluded because its student sample averaged 17.5 in age.

For a study to be included in the in-depth review, it had to deal with an intervention utilizing ICT in some way in teaching/learning contexts where the object of study was literature and which analysed in some way the impact of one or more ICTs on the development of literature-related competences (or which began with the identification of specific literature-related competences and studied ways in which ICT could foster the development of these). Study types included descriptive studies (where these included evaluation), explorations of relationships and both 'naturally occurring' and 'researcher-manipulated' evaluations.

Subsequently, five of the studies included in the systematic map were excluded from the in-depth review. Of these, four (Bigum *et al.* 1997, McKeon and Burkey 1998, McKeon 2001, Moore and

Karabenick 1992) were excluded because their focus was on general literacy (reading and writing or attitudes to these) rather than literature-related literacy. The fifth (McClay 2002) was excluded because it was a descriptive study of one student's experimentation with 'new' literary writing forms but lacked an evaluative element.

Table 5.1 provides summary information on those studies selected for the in-depth review in respect of educational setting, ICT focus and aspect of literature-related literacy focused on. Three studies were from the USA and four from Australia. Studies were evenly divided between older and young children, perhaps reflecting a strong sense that children's literature is a 'legitimate' focus for literary study. Most of the studies investigated mixed sex classes or groups. Where participants were one sex only, there was generally a lack of rationale for the choice, i.e. gender was incidental. Educational settings were evenly divided between primary and secondary schools, perhaps indicating a widespread sense that 'literary' study is an appropriate focus for all levels of schooling.

Most of the studies approached literature-related literacy from a social/cultural rather than a psychological/cognitivist perspective. However, as we discuss later, these two perspectives, while they might usefully be kept distinct for the sake of theorising the object of inquiry, are not necessarily mutually exclusive. Finally, most studies

Table 5.1 Studies included in in-depth review with educational setting, ICT focus and literacy focus

Author, date	Educational setting	ICT focus	Literacy focus
Chu (1995)	Primary	Electronic books	Reading
Love (1998)	Secondary	Word processing, multimodal presentational software, WWW	Reading, composition, research, critical literacy
Morgan (1995)	Secondary	CD Rom	Reading, critical literacy
Meskill and Swan (1996)	Primary/Secondary	Multimedia software	Reading
Meskill and Swan (1998)	Primary	Multimedia software	Reading, writing
Nettelbeck (2000)	Secondary	Online discussion	Reading
Wild (1995)	Primary	Electronic books	Reading

were researcher-manipulated evaluations. However, the distinction between researcher-manipulated and naturally occurring interventions is not always clearcut.

As we have described elsewhere (Locke and Andrews 2003), included studies were subjected to a system of evaluation where they were rated according to three criteria of methodological soundness, appropriateness of research design and relevance of focus vis-à-vis the review question. They were also given an overall weighting – which was not always reflective of the ratings received in relation to one or more of these three criteria. Three studies were given an overall weighting of 'medium' (Chu 1995, Love 1998, Meskill and Swan 1996), one 'medium/high' (Nettelbeck 2000), one 'medium/low' (Wild 1995) and two were deemed to have an overall weighting of 'high' (Morgan 1995, Meskill and Swan 1998).

A range of foci

The studies by Chu (1995), Wild (1995) and Meskill and Swan (1998) all had a primary setting. The first two were concerned with the response of young children to electronic books. Chu's (1995) study was a researcher-manipulated intervention and was characterised by a clear conceptualisation of literature-based literacy within the reader-response tradition (Iser 1978, Rosenblatt 1978). Moreover, it viewed the 'literary experience' as something wider than print-mediated. In terms of the problematic issue of measures, it developed a series of categories (retelling, comparing, judging, inferencing and rationalising) in terms of which active, response-based transactions with literary texts might be tracked. In short, the study provided an interesting and helpful way of conceptualising what literature-based literacy might mean for very young readers.

Wild (1995) worked with a larger sample, but the relevance of his study (at least as reported) was weakened by its being insufficiently conceptualised. For instance, it was unclear whether the interventions designed by the research team were addressing questions of reading comprehension in general or reading as it pertains to what we might call 'literary engagement'. The only clue to the latter was the use of traditional 'literary' categories such as 'plot, characters and events' and an undeveloped (but tantalizing) suggestion that there are particular forms of cognitive attention that a storybook (print) can engender.

Meskill and Swan's researcher-manipulated intervention (1998) was concerned to test the effectiveness of a literature-related software package (*Kid's Space*) they had themselves developed in four elementary classrooms at different levels in two contrasting American schools. These researchers also clearly located their understanding of literature-based literacy within the response-based tradition. The study was characterised by a deliberateness in intervention design, the choice of a range of classrooms and teaching styles, and the use of a wide range of data gathering tools. The study also utilized a range of measures to enable a description and evaluation of the ways in which students (and teachers) made use of the software in question.

The earlier Meskill and Swan study (1996) was rather compromised in its relevance by its dual focus– developing a way of evaluating commercially available literature software packages and having some of these packages trialled in classrooms. However, the study was highly relevant and disciplined in terms of its firm commitment to a model of literature teaching and learning (response-based practices) which the study both described and theorised in relation to its specific ICT focus. Concerned as it was with evaluating available software, its development of assessment criteria and scenarios was a useful example of pedagogical 'envisioning'. This study also developed an understanding of what 'impact' might mean that relates to the idea of symbiosis discussed earlier.

> This article explores the potential of a complementary relationship between the learning and teaching of literature and characteristics specific to multimedia instructional delivery systems. Our research is designed around and is driven by the assumption that the medium potentially represents a powerful means of promoting and enhancing the processes of literary understanding.
>
> (Meskill and Swan 1996: 218)

The study made it clear that complementarity could work two ways. It could enhance aspired-to pedagogical practice or it could construct pedagogical practice in undesirable ways (hence the notion of a 'mismatch') (p. 218–19).

Nettelbeck's (2000) study, based in an independent co-educational school in Melbourne, also had a highly relevant conceptual focus. The researchers in this instance were teachers who appeared to have a common understanding of how literature-related literacy might be described (in terms of a model of constructivist, response-based learning). The study focused on a single, identified, pedagogical intervention, namely, the facilitation of text-based response where students 'contribute to a discussion, present evidence and respect and respond to the views of others' (Nettelbeck 2000: 46). The context had ecological validity in that it was a real school, with real teachers engaged in finding ways of integrating ICTs into an English programme with a thought-out approach to literary study in the wider context of an educational system that had a set of defined outcomes for how it had, in its turn, constructed literary study.

The focus of Morgan (1995) was seen as highly relevant for a different reason, one related to the indeterminacy of the term 'impact' discussed earlier in this chapter. In what we would describe as an 'exploration of relationships', Morgan was concerned to explore the three-way relationship between text (as technologised), reading (including literary response) as a practice and pedagogy. This case study examined the use made of contrasting text-types on a similar theme by three Australian Year 9 English teachers. The focus was on teachers' constructions of literature-related literacies (though it needs to be recognized that Morgan's selection of four texts was not on the basis of 'literariness' as commonly understood). The study as set up allowed conclusions to be drawn in respect of ways in which these constructions *mediated* the 'impact' of ICTs (in this case a CD-ROM) on classroom planning and practice. It effectively provided a methodology for discovering, for example, reasons why the mere provision of ICTs might have absolutely no impact on literature-related literacies as developed in classrooms. It also provided a methodology for discovering how teacher constructions of literate practice mediated the uses to which ICTs might be put and the extent to which they, *in themselves* (as technologies), might determine literate practices.

In Love's study (1998), the focus of what we will call the study's case study narrative was on a student teacher's attempts at integrating ICTs into a classroom environment where students had had very little exposure to them. They had some familiarity with word processing, but no experience of PowerPoint nor the Internet. Despite this limitation, however, there were sections of Love's account where the spotlight did settle on the review question. Specifically:

• An intervention designed to have students compose directly onto the screen which suggests a technology-mediated impact on writing as a material practice and also perhaps on cognition (cf. Haas 1996). There was also a suggestion of impact in terms of writing as a more socialised, collaborative endeavour when focused on a computer screen. However, the focus here was not on the writing of 'literary' texts, but on writing as a more generic category.

- While word processing was used to complete an assessment task oriented to a novel, there was no suggestion that the task itself was altered by the use of the technology. (What could have been hand-written was presented as a word-processed document.) The same applied to Katrina's (the student teacher's) use of PowerPoint.
- There was a suggestive vignette which was not substantially theorised which discussed how formatting tools could be used to 'reconstruct' (our term) a literary text and thereby affect its impact on readers. 'Katrina's students were learning to identity the impact of basic multimedia design features and build a critical language for talking about its impact' (Love 1998: 69).
- It was clear from the study that by making the WWW available to her students' study of the film version of *Little Women*, Katrina was able to teach the text in ways which highlighted the cultural context of its production (a requirement, for example, in critical literacy approaches to literary texts). In this respect, then, it could be seen that the ICT intervention impacted on both pedagogy and the construction of reading literary texts as a practice. Such a construction also raised problems of e-credibility (see Haas and Wearden, in press), an issue identified and also dealt with by Katrina in her classroom practice.

Findings and suggestions

Only two of the studies included in the in-depth review were given an overall 'high' rating. For this reason the findings detailed in this section should be seen as provisional (and often tentative and merely suggestive).

A strong finding was that reading practices (including literature-based ones), technologised practices and pedagogical practices are mediated by discourse. 'Discourse' is not a settled term, but has been usefully described by Fairclough, drawing on the work of Foucault, as 'a practice not just of representing the world, but of signifying the world, constituting and constructing the world in meaning' (Fairclough 1992: 64). A number of these studies confirm ways in which the discourses of teachers have a crucially mediating role in the 'impact' of ICTs on the literate practice of a classroom (including literature-based literacy) (Morgan 1995, Meskill and Swan, 1998, Love 1998).

Meskill and Swan found that none of the elementary teachers who had allowed their software package *Kid's Space* to be trialled in their classrooms viewed technology as something to be integrated into the general classroom programme and all appeared to believe that '... computer-based learning is somehow self-contained' (1998: 361). Findings on the utility of the software package therefore were limited by the dispositions of the teachers and their ability to guide their students in ways that might utilize the various features of the program.

In contrast, Morgan's more specific focus on teachers' subject-ivities enabled the establishment of findings that showed, for example, that 'impact' is mediated in important ways by the manner in which teachers *themselves* construct 'literature-related literacies'. What for Meskill and Swan was an impediment was for Morgan a 'reality check'. It was particularly pertinent because of Morgan's initial disposition to view technologies in a somewhat deterministic light as having the potential to lead users to change their construct-ions of literate practice. 'I wondered ... whether the CD would lead them to redefine the nature of texts and reading more generally' (1995: 9). One of Morgan's own discoveries from the study was that '... electronic text doesn't necessarily change our ways of reading and thinking about reading' (1995: 16). That being the case, electronic text '... won't necessarily change our ways of teaching reading' (1995: 11). That is, technology doesn't necessarily change practice (in significant ways).

A finding confirmed by Meskill and Swan (1996) is that there tends to be a mismatch between commercially available multimedia literature software packages and theories of literature teaching couched in terms of (critical) reader response. However, buoyed by the envisionments of teachers who trialled some of these commercial packages in their own classrooms, Meskill and Swan concluded from their 1998 trial of *Kid's Space* that teacher disposition notwith-standing there was sufficient evidence to conclude that it is possible to design multimedia literature-based software packages that encourage literary response and literary composition. As with their

1996 study, they were working within a response-based paradigm of discourse of literature-based literacy.

Both Chu (1995) and Wild (1995) found that electronic and interactive storybooks can be motivators to reading for young readers in general. Some of the teachers in Meskill and Swan's 1996 study found, on the basis of their own trialling of commercially available software packages, that such books may also motivate reluctant readers and ESL students. Chu's study had a small number of subjects (three boys), who 'showed high interest in reading the computer books'. The experience was 'exciting, meaningful, and, most of all, enjoyable' (1995: 361). Chu also found his subjects generally reduced their hands-on interaction with the computer after the first few books. One might put this beside Wild's finding, with a larger sample over a longer period, that more able readers expressed a preference for traditional reading materials and indicated that electronic storybooks distracted them from 'their enjoyment and their reading rhythm' (Wild 1995: 2). At least for some readers, Wild found, electronic storybooks may be de-motivating after a period of time.

Besides motivation-related findings, Chu (1995) and Wild (1995) also suggested in their studies that electronic and interactive storybooks can facilitate a range of active, 'literary' responses. Chu is very careful to define what is meant by such responses. For Chu, the reading behaviours of the pupils showed them to be active in the reading process and as having their own 'individual, unique' responses (1995: 361).

> The selective retelling and idiosyncratic way of inferencing told us that they were successful sub-creators of their own literary worlds ... They were not merely passive recipients of a techno-logical presentation; instead, they were actively involved in the meaning constructing and responding process.
>
> (Chu 1995: 362)

This active responding included the non-verbal. Wild's study was much less firm on what it meant by literary response. At one point, for example, he surmised that electronic storybooks can help students in the process of forming 'a mental model of the story which they are reading' (1995: 3). But it is not clear how the formation of such 'mental models', and the agency for their formation, fits into an overall view of what it means to read a literary text.

A strong finding of Nettelbeck's (2000) study was that online discussion can give students a new means of formulating and reformulating their thinking in response to literary texts and can give them the opportunity of sharing their thinking with a wider audience. Nettelbeck and his co-teacher-researchers had Kristina Love as their outside evaluator. Her findings included:

- Online discussions are a valid pedagogical tool in respect of the text response outcomes of the VCE English curriculum. 'The mode of on-line discussion offered a means that had been hitherto unavailable for students to formulate and reformulate their thinking about literary texts.'
- Online discussions were successful in encouraging students to 'engage in a reflective activity with someone outside of their normal social groups'.
- 'On-line discussions not only provided all students with an additional mode of expression in text response, but also made available to some students a preferred mode of expression' (Nettelbeck 2000: 48).

Such findings are reflected in an American study by Bain *et al.* (2000), excluded from the review on account of the average age of its senior high school sample. The aim of this study was to evaluate a network-based hypertext discussion tool (HDT) for teaching literature to adolescents. Their results indicated that there were statistically significant improvements in achievement when the HDT was part of the instructional programme, that were not sustained in the reversal condition when the HDT was withdrawn, yet recurred at comparable levels during a second intervention condition (2000: 203).

Finally, a number of studies presented vignettes which were suggestive of impact but which certainly didn't constitute findings, e.g. Love (1998). This article suggests that screen-based writing differs from pen/paper-based writing as a material practice and may have particular cognitive and social effects; that multimedia design features of many software packages offer new possibilities for literary text production and text 'impact'; and that the WWW offers a powerful tool for researching the cultural backgrounds of literary texts but raises issues of e-credibility.

Discourse as mediating impact

Literature-related literacies are a range of competences enabling one to read, interpret and critique literary texts and to engage in the production of such texts. As discussed elsewhere, the impact of a technology (electronic or otherwise) on both social and cognitive aspects of these competences is not a simple one (see Haas 1996). Table 5.2 provides an overview of the studies selected for in-depth review in terms of their ICT focus and the literary activity/ies engaged in. The literary nature of the texts is taken here as a given.

Among other things, Table 5.2 indicates a rather predictable privileging of reading over writing and a significant lack of any studies researching students' responses to literary hypertext. What isn't revealed is the extent to which 'impact' is mediated by discourse. Discursive considerations are crucial, we argue, and we return to these in discussing the possible shape of a future research agenda. While technology mediates textual practice, the discourses which shape teacher dispositions, knowledges and practices are inevitably going to mediate the ways in which technology is integrated in English/literacy classrooms.

Classroom-based interventions were designed by the researchers themselves for three of the studies selected for in-depth review: Chu (1995), Wild (1995) and Meskill and Swan (1998). In respect of the first two, it might be argued that the researchers had control of the discourses in terms of which texts were selected (deemed as literary) and measures (deemed to indicate 'literary' response) determined. In the case of Meskill and Swan (1998), it is clear that a tension existed between the discursive position out of which the researchers

Table 5.2 Studies included in in-depth review showing ICT focus and literary activity subjects engaged in

ICT Focus	Reading	Composing	Investigation
Word processing Desktop publishing	Love (1998)	Love (1998)	
Multimodal software (CD-ROMs, E-books, PowerPoint)	Chu (1995) Love (1998) Morgan (1995) Meskill and Swan (1996) Meskill and Swan (1998) Wild (1995)	Love (1998)	
Email			
Web-based discussion	Nettelbeck (2000)		
Hypertext/WWW			Love (1998)

were operating and the teacher subjects themselves. The call for teacher professional development that the researchers made at the end of their account might be seen as a desire to bring teachers into line in respect of such things as definitions of literary response and the role technology might play in mediating such responses. Indeed, the wording of one of their conclusions is (unintentionally) instructive. 'Effective methods of integrating and valuing on-line work are essential for the software to be used by students as intended' (1998: 365). The nominalization which forms the subject of this sentence renders invisible the actual presence of teachers themselves.

In Nettelbeck's study, the tension between researchers and teachers was eliminated because teachers themselves designed the intervention with their own students (notwithstanding the guidance sought from the external evaluator, Love). These teachers were working within a framework (VCE English) which provided them with a discourse within which an understanding of literary response was implicit. In this sense, literary objectives and measures were not contentious, at least on the surface. The selected ICT intervention was able to be evaluated in a straightforward way regarding its capacity to enable students to meet the stipulated outcomes, e.g. encourage students to engage in a reflective and thinking activity with someone outside their class, normal friendship group and normal comfort zone.

In the studies of Meskill and Swan (1996) and Love (1998), at least in terms of classroom intervention, the researchers took a back seat. Certainly, the former drew on personal growth and reader-response discourses as a basis for their development of evaluation criteria for multimedia software applications for literature. However, for the sketchily reported classroom trials, one must assume that the classroom teachers proceeded via their own discursive lights, but these were not spelled out. Love (1998) also took a back seat beyond the design of a course on technology and English method, which Katrina (the student teacher) participated in prior to her trying out her own ideas in an English classroom. Because the study offers a rich account (and interpretation) of Katrina's experience, readers are able to obtain a sense of the discourses (somewhat eclectic with a leaning towards critical theory) which impact upon the ICT-based interventions this young teacher plans and implements.

Finally, and somewhat in contrast, Morgan's (1995) study in effect made a virtue of proposing an intervention (the use of a CD-ROM) and leaving it to the three teachers who were subjects of this case study as to how they might best make use of it. In contrast with

Meskill and Swan (1998), where in varying degrees the classroom teachers themselves were found wanting, it was Morgan's initial hypothesis (that technologies might have a determining role in leading users to change their constructions of literate practice) that was found wanting by the reading and teaching practices of the teachers. Of all the studies included, Morgan's most clearly articulated the way in which reading practices (including literature-based ones), technologised practices and pedagogical practices are mediated by discourse.

Policy, practice and the research agenda

Meanwhile, in breaking news, a high school in Cambridge, New Zealand, has decided to close its library at the end of the year and replace it with a cybercafe dealing in computers and cappuccino. The principal's description of the library as a 'museum' has prompted a predictable response in local media. An opinion-writer in the local daily newspaper writes that

> Reading skills are the passport to untold pleasures, to people and places and glorious complexities beyond the boundaries of our own imaginations. Reading helps shape our view of the world, makes us think about how we live, introduces us to powerful new philosophies and arguments, makes us laugh and cry ... and keeps us coming back for more.
>
> (Irvine 2003: 9)

In the same paper, an editorial concludes:

> No doubt the cybercafe will be a state-of-the-art showpiece that will enhance student skills in the art of computer-based research. But the ability to occupy oneself by curling up with a good book is also an art that needs fostering from an early age. It should not be schools which make it a dying one.
>
> (*Waikato Times* 2003: 8)

Interestingly, the expression 'curl up with a good book' can also be found in the opinion piece, a reminder, should one need one, that literate practices are embodied. The transformation of the library (as 'museum') into a different kind of space – a cybercafe – underlines the way in which literate practices are situated in a 'technological ecology' involving complexes of people and things serving varying roles and functions (Lemke 1998: 284).

At one point the same editorial shifts its focus from the specific instance to the policy, quoting the New Zealand Ministry of Education's guidelines for New Zealand schools on libraries as stating that 'The school library is a foundation for the school's literacy programmes and a catalyst for the development of lifelong readers' (*Waikato Times* 2003: 8). This line of argument highlights the ways in which literate practices – in this instance a series of decisions on the shape and place of a school's library or 'information centre' – take place in the context of a policy environment. It is to the policy environment as contextualising questions of the impact of ICTs on literature-related literacies that we now turn.

Implications for policy

A policy on school library use is but once instance of a document pertinent to the subject of this chapter. More central are national curriculum statements or profiles, qualifications policies, policies on resourcing, and policies on teacher education (pre-service and in-service). Our concern in this section is to identify a range of factors that we see as needing to be taken into account by policy-makers across a range of areas.

The rationale for the review on which this chapter is based lies in the fact that the study of literature (including literary texts aimed at children and young adult readers) has a traditional place in the English curricula of all English-speaking countries. Although the character of literature as a category is contentious and problematic, there is currently a fair consensus that it is a discrete one. Ultimately, the continuing presence of literature in the intended curriculum of a particular country will be a matter of educational policy. In most but not all constituencies, this continued presence would appear to be secure. However, there is evidence that its nature as a discrete textual category with special status may be under threat from critically theoretical approaches, which would view literary texts as cultural products alongside other texts.

One implication, then, is that curriculum planners need to acknowledge that the term 'literature' is, indeed, problematic. Different discursive positions define 'literature' and 'literature-related literacies' in different ways. Such diversity, we would argue, has the potential to enrich students' understanding of literature and literary study. There is no reason why the problematisation of the term itself cannot be acknowledged in the process of curriculum articulation.

However, it is also clear that the extent to which the term can be productively problematised is constrained by ways in which terms such as 'literature' and 'literary' are framed in curriculum statements. The latter need to be deconstructed as part of any review process in order to identify ways in which they privilege certain constructions of the 'literary' over others. The *National Curriculum for England* (DfEE and QCA 1999), at each of its key stages, partitions English into 'Speaking and Listening', 'Reading' and 'Writing'. At Key Stages 3 and 4, there are extensive references to 'literature' and 'literary' in the 'Reading' strand, where at least 11 of the objectives under 'Understanding texts', 'English literary heritage' and 'Texts from different cultures and traditions' have an explicit literary focus. There is also an extensive prescribed range of texts for 'Literature'. In the 'Writing' strand, there are two objectives under 'Composition' which are explicitly literary, and one statement listing literary texts. In the 'Speaking and Listening' strand at Key Stages 3 and 4, there are 'Drama'-related objectives and a 'Drama'-related statement. An albeit casual reading of this arrangement might draw the conclusion that literature is primarily about reading, with the provision for *some* student writing in traditional literary forms, and that there is a recognizable oral language 'literary' category called 'Drama', i.e. that oral literature is drama.

However 'literature' and 'literary study' are couched in curriculum statements and in centrally produced resources, there needs to be an acknowledgement that textual practices surrounding literary texts are being affected by ICTs and that ICT-based technologies of production are impacting on the character of literary texts themselves (including the production of new forms). Such an acknowledgement also has implications for curriculum planning. If we again take the *National Curriculum for England* (DfEE and QCA 1999) as an example, we can note that its 'Reading' strand at Key Stages 3 and 4 makes reference to ICT-based texts. Curiously, however, the statement uses the term 'ICT-based information texts' exclusively, as if all ICT-based texts are information texts. (What *is* an information text?) What is missing, for example, is any reference to hypertext as a literary form. Literature in this statement is decidedly non-digital.

Acknowledging that ICT-based technologies of production are impacting on the nature of texts themselves has a further implication for curriculum design. Here we can take the national English curriculum in New Zealand as a case in point. This curriculum statement partitions English into three strands: 'Oral Language', 'Written Language' and 'Visual Language' (Ministry of Education 1994). The curriculum statement sits alongside other statements representing the seven areas of learning that the New Zealand national curriculum is divided into. One of these is 'Technology'. It is arguable that in separating 'Technology' out, an opportunity is being lost to have students view all areas of learning as involving literacies that are being shaped in crucial ways by a range of mediating technologies. Supposing these three current major strands were replaced by the following four (with their sub-strands):

- Oral Language: Listening, Speaking
- Printed Language: Close Reading of Printed Text, Producing Printed Text
- Digital Language: Close Reading of Digital Text, Producing Digital Text
- Exploring Language: Wide Reading, Understanding Language, Understanding and Practising the Technologies of Text.

Such a curriculum would embed an entirely different arrangement (and hegemony) of textual media and would foreground the role of technology mediating literacy.

We would also suggest that problems can arise in an intended curriculum if learning outcomes are too narrowly defined (in a behavioural sense). The challenges revealed in the studies previously discussed in clearly articulating outcomes (especially measurable ones) are understandable, given the higher-level thinking skills one would expect to be associated with literary study, however conceptualised. Just as a curriculum statement's partitions and range statements can construct literary textuality in certain ways, so its articulation of learning outcomes can construct the range of literary competences in ways that are problematical (too narrow, too tied to a particular construction of literature-based literacy).

Here are two brief examples. Objective (i) under 'Understanding Texts' in the 'Reading' strand at Key Stages 3 and 4 of *English: The National Curriculum for England* states: 'to distinguish between the attitudes and assumptions of characters and those of the author' (DfEE and QCA 1999: 34). This learning outcome makes certain assumptions about the accessibility of the 'attitudes and assumptions' of an author and even about the ontological status of 'the author'. By way of a second example, the Level 1 achievement objective of the 'Close Reading' sub-strand of *English in the New Zealand*

Curriculum reads: 'Students should respond to language and meanings in texts' (Ministry of Education 1994: 34). In terms of many constructions of literacy, the preposition 'in' is problematical because it locates meaning *in* texts (rather than in some kind of relationship, for example). It may be that an intended curriculum advocating literary study would be better couched in terms of problem-solving or expressive outcomes rather than behavioural ones (Eisner 2002).

Problems in respect of the formulation of behaviourally formulated learning outcomes will inevitably have a flow-on effect where assessment systems are based on these outcomes. In the current context, we would see the following questions about assessment, as formulated by Protherough (1993) as even more pertinent today.

> What is it that counts as learning (and as success) in literature that we propose to measure? For whom and for what purposes is that measuring attempted? What range of measurements is available to us? What is it that we do not or cannot currently measure?
>
> (Protherough 1993: 11, cited in Andrews 2001: 95)

Finally, as a number of the studies included in the in-depth review have indicated, intended outcomes are inevitably mediated by teacher intention (and the discourses that frame those intentions). Policy changes need to be informed by the current practices of teachers as well as set out to change these practices. Indeed, we suggest that it would be wrong-headed for policy-makers to disregard the extent to which literature-related literacy is a contestable concept and textual practice is changing under the impact of ICTs. What is needed is policy that views such 'instability' as fecund, challenging and liberating, and not something to be responded to by pulling up the drawbridge and seeking refuge in traditional formulations and the constraints of narrowly defined learning outcomes. Nor should it be responded to by developing teacher education programmes and resources that reinforce these constraining agendas.

The practice of research and classroom practice

As the preceding discussion has indicated, where literature-based literacy has been carefully conceptualised and a clear understanding of 'impact' articulated (Chu 1995, Meskill and Swan 1998), the process of identifying clear outcomes and performance measures is made easier. Both these research teams were located in the United States and both adopted the reader-response discourse to underpin their studies (Iser 1978, Rosenblatt 1978).

While this particular discourse may enjoy current dominance in the United States, our in-depth review tended to support an impression of reader-response discourses as becoming increasingly contested in other educational settings, especially Australia, where critical literacy, as an enveloping discourse constructing 'literary' study, has become increasingly mainstream (Morgan 1997). Researchers interested in the impact of ICTs on literature-related literacies, then, need to recognize the plurality of discourses that theorise and construct the subject of enquiry. By implication, any study of this topic needs to acknowledge that there are other and competing discourses with the potential to frame literature-based textual practice differently.

Such a situation offers both dangers and opportunities. One danger is the potential for theorists and researchers from competing discourses to talk past each other. Another is a form of polite disparagement which occurs when a particular discourse is labelled as outmoded or outgrown. In a recent example, McIntyre writes:

> Hence, while the heritage and personal growth models of English, underwritten as they are by liberal-humanist concepts of the individual, should never be dismissed as worthless – they have produced teaching that has often been life-changing for students – they prove theoretically defective and politically unpersuasive models for English teaching in schools and universities today.
>
> (McIntyre 2002: 37)

There are dangers when statements such as 'Literacy is a social practice' are transformed from insights into slogans and even mantras. When such a statement becomes read as asserting that 'Literacy is *exclusively* a social practice', then the ground has been established for marginalizing research traditions which focus on the relationship between language/text and mind/cognition (Sadoski 1998, Pinker 1995, Gazzaniga *et al.* 2002, Damasio 2000). Likewise, a privileging of critical theories of literature based in cultural studies and views of the text as socially constructed, has the potential to marginalize, for example, views of the literary text as rooted in competing epistemologies and aesthetics – views such as those represented by evolutionary-based literary theories (Boyd 2001, Carroll 1995).

The opportunity lies in the potential for conversations about literature to be enhanced by the current diversity of approach, for cross-fertilisation to occur, for new questions to be asked. For example, we would see the potential for both cognitive neuroscience and social constructionist approaches to reframe in useful ways a list of research questions cited by Andrews:

- What is the significance of the first response?
- What is the significance of the first unbroken series of responses?
- What has been achieved by this initial response and/or series of responses?
- What is the significance of the subsequent re-entry point?
- What is the significance of subsequent re-readings?
- What has been achieved by the time the reader closes the process of responding privately?
- What is the significance of the follow-up? (Andrews 2001: 87)

In short, we see the current situation as conducive to ensuring that the research agenda is widened.

We also argue a need for conceptual studies that theorise the nexus between ICTs and literacy-centred practices and which project a vision of what a technology-infused classroom might look like (for example, Lankshear and Knobel 1997), especially one in which hypertext is beginning to stretch definitions as to what constitutes a 'literary' text (for example, Snyder 1996). We see real value, for example, in theorised accounts of teaching practice where hypertext is the textual medium for literature. One example is Graham Parr's account of working with hypertext based on his and his colleagues' experience at Methodist Ladies' College in Melbourne (Parr 2001). Another is Wendy Morgan's recent work with pre-service English teacher trainees in Brisbane, where students were 'encouraged and enabled to lay out for exploration their multiple, discursively consti-tuted, positioned selves' using hypertext as the writing medium (Morgan 2002: 6). Such explorations expand the research agenda in a number of ways, for example, by raising questions about the relationship between hypertext as a medium and critical theory (and theories of literature in general), the role of technology in identity formation and the impact of hypertext on the construction of narrative.

As Table 5.2 indicates, there are plenty of gaps indicating where a future research agenda, irrespective of study type, might focus itself. As the nature of literary study becomes affected by approaches based in cultural studies, post-structuralism and critical theory, we would see a growing place for research into the role investigation plays in the study of literary texts in classrooms, something noted in passing in our discussion of Love (1998) in this chapter. There is clearly a place for research into ways in which the new technologies are impacting or can impact on students' *production* of literary forms, either as traditionally conceived or as generated courtesy of the ICT midwife.

As indicated earlier, current curriculum statements give scant recognition to the increasingly multimodal nature of texts in general and literary texts in particular. In the course of our systematic review, we found ourselves intrigued by a descriptive study (and therefore excluded from the in-depth review) by McClay (2002) of 13-year-old Kevin's fantasy writing, where he drew on his experience of fantasy in a number of media (including computer games) to feed his writing and his sense of how he might adapt conventions from one medium into another in effecting generic hybridization. There is clearly enormous scope for research into 'literary' writing and its relationship to different technologies, including ICTs. Certainly, as McClay points out, experimentation such as Kevin's raises important questions about assessment (as discussed in the last section).

There is, of course, room in the research field for various kinds of outcome evaluation, where a particular intervention is being trialled and its effect measured in some way (for example, Bain *et al.* 2000). But there is also room for various kinds of descriptive study (case studies, educational critical studies) that provide rich descriptions and analyses of situations where ICTs are playing a role in literature-centred instruction. Such studies will not be necessarily evaluative (though they can be) and may utilize critical discourse analysis as a way of identifying underlying theoretical positions in respect of the study of literature and pedagogy (for example, Morgan 2001).

It may be, as Donald Leu (2000) points out, that it will be teachers themselves, exploring in their own classrooms hunches and intuitions about the implications for their teaching of the impact of ICTs on a range of literate practices, that provide the strongest lead as to how the future research agenda should be formulated. 'Our understanding,' he writes, 'may be informed more often by individuals who use various technologies on a daily basis and less often by traditional forms of research' (p.761). This focus will lead to individual teachers treating themselves as case studies and reflecting on their own experiments in using ICTs to further programme goals related to literary study.

There is no doubt that the implications for policy-makers indicated earlier have their equivalent in challenges for English teachers and teacher educators. It is clear that ICT is happening, and central to this phenomenon is a radical transformation of text-based practices at all levels of society. Morgan's (1995) study pinpoints the need for an ideal of critically reflective practice to be fostered among teachers. This would involve teachers in conversations where the implications of ICT-mediated textual forms for reading practices and pedagogy are explored. Love's (1998) study shows what can happen when an adventurous young teacher, cued by a relevant teacher education programme, decides to take some risks and think through the implications of ICT for her own English teaching. And Nettelbeck's (2000) study shows what an entire English department can do when it engages in reflective practice and makes a decision to act innovatively in consort.

Afterword

> Good Angel: O, Faustus, lay that damned book aside,
> And gaze not on it, lest it tempt thy soul,
> And heap God's heavy wrath upon thy head!
> Christopher Marlowe, *Dr Faustus*

Well, Faustus heeded not that Good Angel's advice, with dire consequences. One's choice of texts has consequences beyond the acquisition of power. But what about choice of medium? If literature survives a compact with digital technology, what kind of beast (or necessary angel) will it be? In the present 'era of instability', 'characterised by the profound shift in power *from the state and* its conceptions of *the citizen*, to *the market and* its conceptions of *the consumer*'(Kress 2002: 22), what place is there for any kind of canon, for literature as a socially cohesive *taonga* (as the Maori say in New Zealand)?

Does literature require the stability of a medium to survive? Does the digitisation of text and its resultant alterability – something that goes way beyond traditional conceptions of interactivity – also threaten the survival of literature, or literature as we know it? Or does such alterability simply highlight in a material way the co-creative acts that readers have always performed in the reading of literary texts? Answers to questions such as these are waiting in the wings, just a mouse-click away.

Studies included in the map and synthesis

Studies included for in-depth review are marked with asterisks

Bigum, C., Durrant, C., Green, B., Honan, E., Lankshear, C., Morgan, W., Murray, J., Snyder, I. and Wild, M. (1997) *Digital Rhetorics: Literacies and Technologies in Education – Current Practices and Future Directions* (Executive Summary and Volumes 1, 2 and 3), Canberra: Department of Employment, Education, Training and Youth Affairs.

*Chu, M. (1995) 'Reader response to interactive computer books: examining literary responses in a non-traditional reading setting', *Reading Research and Instruction*, 34: 352–66.

*Love, K. (1998) 'Old cyborgs, young cyborgs (and those in between)', *English in Australia*, 121: 63–75.

McClay, J. (2002) 'Hidden "treasure": new genres, new media and the teaching of writing', *English in Education*, 36: 46–55.

McKeon, C. (2001) 'E-mail as a motivating literacy event for one struggling reader: Donna's case', *Reading Research and Instruction*, 40: 185–202.

McKeon, C. and Burkey, L. (1998) 'A literature-based e-mail collaborative', in Sturtevant E. and Dugan J. (eds) *Literacy and Community: The Twentieth Yearbook: A Peer Reviewed Publication of the College Reading Association 1998*, Carrollton, GA: College Reading Association.

*Meskill, C. and Swan, K. (1996) 'Roles for multimedia in the response-based literature classroom', *Journal of Educational Computing Research*, 15: 217–39.

*Meskill, C. and Swan, K. (1998) 'Response-based multimedia and the culture of the classroom: a pilot study of *Kid's Space* in four elementary classrooms', *Journal of Educational Computing Research*, 18: 339–67.

Moore, M. and Karabenick, S. (1992) 'The effects of computer communications on the reading and writing performance of fifth-grade students', *Computers in Human Behavior*, 8: 27–38.

*Morgan, W. (1995) 'Safe harbours or open seas: English classrooms in an age of electronic text', *English in Australia*, 111: 9–16.

*Nettelbeck, D. (2000) 'Using information technology to enrich the learning experiences of secondary English students', *Literacy Learning: The Middle Years*, 8: 40–9.

*Wild, M. (1995) 'Using CD-Rom storybooks to encourage reading development', *Item 5 of Set: Research Information for Teachers, 2*, Canberra: Australian Council for Educational Research.

References

Andrews, R. (2001) *Teaching and Learning English: A Guide to Recent Research and its Applications*, London: Continuum.

Andrews, R., Burn, A., Leach, J., Locke, T., Low, G. and Torgerson, C. (2002) 'A systematic review of the impact of networked ICT on 5–16-year-olds' literacy in English' (EPPI-Centre Review), *Research Evidence in Education Library*, 1, London: EPPI-Centre, Social Science Research Unit, Institution of Education.

Bain, A., Huss, P. and Kwong, H. (2000) 'The evaluation of a hypertext discussion tool for teaching English literature to secondary school students', *Journal of Educational Computing Research*, 23: 203–16.

Boyd, B. (2001) 'The origin of stories: Horton hears a who', *Philosophy and Literature*, 25: 197–214.

Carroll, J. (1995) *Evolution and Literary Theory*, Columbia, MO: University of Missouri Press.

Cope, B. and Kalantzis, M. (eds) (2000) *Multiliteracies: Literacy Learning and the Design of Social Futures*, London: Routledge.

Curriculum Corporation (1994) *English – A Curriculum Profile for Australian Schools*, Carlton, Vic.: Curriculum Corporation.

Damasio, A. (2000) *The Feeling of What Happens: Body, Emotion and the Making of Consciousness*, London: Vintage.

DfEE and QCA (1999) *English: The National Curriculum for England*, London: Department for Education and Employment/Qualifications and Curriculum Authority.

Durrant, C. and Hargreaves, S. (1995) 'Literacy online: the use of computers in the secondary classroom', *English in Australia*, 111: 37–48.

Eagleton, T. (1983) *Literary Theory: An Introduction*, Oxford: Basil Blackwell.

Eisner, E.W. (2002) *The Educational Imagination: On the Design and Evaluation of School Programs*, Upper Saddle River, NJ: Merrill Prentice Hall.

Fairclough, N. (1992) *Discourse and Social Change*, Cambridge: Polity Press.

Gazzaniga, M.S., Ivry, R.B. and Mangun, G.R. (2002) *Cognitive Neuroscience: The Biology of the Mind*, New York: Norton.

Green, B. and Bigum, C. (1996) 'Hypermedia or media hype? New technologies and the future of literacy education', in G. Bull and M. Anstey (eds) *The Literacy Lexicon*, Sydney: Prentice Hall.

Guillory, J. (1995) 'Canon', in F. Lentricchia and T. McLaughlin (eds) *Critical Terms for Literary Study*, Chicago: University of Chicago Press.

Haas, C. (1996) *Writing Technology: Studies on the Materiality of Literacy*, Mahwah, NJ: Lawrence Erlbaum Associates.

Haas, C. and Wearden, S. (in press) 'E-credibility: building common ground in web environments', *L1 – Educational Studies in Language and Literature*, 3.

Halliday, J. (2001) 'Information and communication technology in the secondary school: a study of integration in the English curriculum', *English in Aotearoa*, 45: 29–36.

Ham, V. (2001) 'Putting computers in their place – ten years on', *English in Aotearoa*, 45: 6–13.

IRA and NCTE (1996) *Standards for the English Language Arts*, Newark, Del./Urbana, IL: International Reading Association/National Council of Teachers of English.

Irvine, D. (2003) 'A few choice words, before the library goes', *Waikato Times*, 22 March: 9.

Iser, W. (1978) *The Act of Reading: A Theory of Aesthetic Response*, Baltimore: Johns Hopkins University Press.

Jody, M. and Saccardi, M. (1998) *Using Computers to Teach Literature: A Teacher's Guide*, Urbana, IL: National Council of Teachers of English.

Kress, G. (2002) 'English for an era of instability: aesthetics, ethics, creativity and "design"', *English in Australia*, 134: 15–23.

Lankshear, C. and Knobel, M. (1997) 'Literacies, texts and difference in the electronic age', in C. Lankshear, J. Gee, M. Knobel and C. Searle (eds) *Changing Literacies*, Buckingham: Open University Press.

Lemke, J. (1998) 'Metamedia literacy: transforming meanings and media', in D. Reinking, M. McKenna, L. Labbo and R. Kieffer (eds) *Handbook of Literacy and Technology: Transformations in a Post-typographic World*, Mahwah, NJ: Lawrence Erlbaum Associates.

Leu, D.J.J. (2000) 'Literacy and technology: deictic consequences for literacy education in an information age'. in M.L. Kamil, P.B. Mosenthal, P.D. Pearson and R. Barr (eds) *Handbook of Reading Research*, Vol. 3, Mahwah, NJ: Lawrence Erlbaum Associates.

Locke, T. and Andrews, R. (2003) 'A systematic review of the impact of ICT on literature-related literacies in English 5–16', in *Research Evidence in Education Library, Version 2*, London: EPPI-Centre, Social Science Research Unit, Institution of Education.

McIntyre, M. (2002) '(Dis)inheriting English', *English in Australia*, 134: 33–43.

Ministry of Education (1994) *English in the New Zealand Curriculum*, Wellington: Learning Media.

Morgan, W. (1997) *Critical Literacy in the Classroom: The Art of the Possible*, London: Routledge.

Morgan, W. (2001) 'Critical Literacy Teachers: uptake of new technologies', in C. Durrant and C. Beavis (eds) *P(ICT)ures of English: Teachers, Learners and Technology*, Kent Town, SA: Wakefield Press.

Morgan, W. (2002, December) ' "Here be monsters": emergent discourses of hybrid identity in students' hypertextual constructions', paper presented at the Australian Association for Research in Education Conference, Brisbane, Australia.

Parr, G. (2001) 'If in a literary hypertext a traveller ... preparing for travel', in C. Durrant and C. Beavis (eds) *P(ICT)ures of English: Teachers, Learners and Technology*, Kent Town, SA: Wakefield Press.

Pinker, S. (1995) *The Language Instinct: The New Science of Language and Mind*, London: Penguin.

Protherough, R. (1993) 'More absurd than in other subjects? Assessing English literature', *English in Education*, 27: 10–18.

Reinking, D., McKenna, M., Labbo, L. and Kieffer, R. (eds) (1998) *Handbook of Literacy and Technology: Transformations in a Post-typographic World*, Mahwah, NJ: Lawrence Erlbaum Associates.

Rosenblatt, L. (1978) *The Reader, the Text, the Poem: The Transactional Theory of the Literary Work*, Carbondale, IL: Southern Illinois University Press.

Sadoski, M. (1998) 'Mental imagery in reading: a sampler of some significant studies', online. Available http://www.readingonline.org/research/Sadoski.html (accessed 31 March 2003).

Scholes, R. (1985) *Textual Power: Literary Theory and the Teaching of English*, New Haven: Yale University Press.

Snyder, I. (1996) 'Towards computer mediated literacy in the secondary school', in P. Clarkson and R. Toomey (eds) *Computing Across the Secondary Curriculum: A Review of Research*, Geelong, Vic.: Deakin University Printery: The National Professional Development Project Computers Across the Secondary Curriculum Reference Group.

Waikato Times (2003) 'Schools need their libraries', *Waikato Times*, 22 March: 8.

West, A. (1994) 'The centrality of literature', in S. Brindley (ed.) *Teaching English*, London: Routledge.

Chapter 6

ICT and moving image literacy in English

Andrew Burn and Jenny Leach

This chapter will review research studies of work on the moving image in English, where such work involves ICT. In keeping with the rest of this book, and the systematic review on which it is based (Burn and Leach 2003), this review deals with a kind of literacy. Where such a conception is unexceptional in the context of language, it is less obvious, even contentious, as a way of thinking about film, video, television or animation as forms of communication. We will begin, then, by considering the idea of a literacy of the moving image, which has a tangled and complex history.

As Buckingham shows, in a comprehensive and useful account of 'media literacy' (Buckingham 2003), the idea that to watch television or film is like a literacy is essentially to use an analogy with language. This has three main implications. First, at a 'micro' level, media texts can be analysed in detail as if they have the kinds of clear structures which language has – in particular, grammatical structures. Second, as with language, media literacy can be seen as a wider set of interpretive competences, or as a form of critical literacy. Third, media literacy can be seen as socially embedded, dependent, as is language, on social contexts for its meanings.

As Buckingham points out, these analogies are often useful for those who make them at a polemical level, which can take different forms. Proponents of media education (such as the authors of this chapter!) can use the literacy analogy to assert the value and status of media texts in the curriculum. Politicians can use it as a handle for policy initiatives aimed at protecting citizens from the dangers of the mass media by equipping them with skills of critical analysis. Indeed, it is this emphasis which forms the core of government promotions of 'media literacy' in many countries, including the UK, which has recently allocated responsibility for media literacy to its new media regulator, OFCOM.

The notion of media literacy easily shades into other kinds of 'literacy' when it is considered in association with ICT. In particular, the notion of multiliteracies (Cope and Kalantzis 2000), which sees practices of textual interpretation and production as moving across and between media, or multimedia; and 'digital literacies' (Buckingham 2003), in which the digital transformation of all communicative forms changes the nature of the literacies needed to understand and produce them.

A more recent development is the idea of 'multimodal literacies' (Jewitt and Kress 2003). This notion proceeds from social semiotic theory, which seeks to establish broad principles of communication across different semiotic systems. The theory of multimodality proposes that in most acts of communication, different modes are employed, and also different media. Because these modes and media work together, they are integrated in particular ways, so that contemporary producers and audiences of texts become able not only to read individual modes (writing, visual design, music), but also to 'read' them in integrated forms. The subject of this chapter, the moving image, is a good example of such a multimodal form. Burn and Parker (2003) outline some principles of a multimodal theory of the moving image. They term it the 'kineikonic mode' (literally, 'moving image'), and suggest that it operates as a combinatorial mode which assembles and integrates other modes (speech, image, gesture, music) through its own 'grammar' of filming and editing.

While the multimodal approach tends to concentrate on micro-level aspects of media literacy, other influential perspectives in the field of media education take a broader view of media literacy and digital literacy. In these accounts (e.g. Buckingham and Sefton-Green 1994; Buckingham 1996; Buckingham *et al.* 1999), the most important aspects of media literacies are the ways in which young people engage with a range of popular media, both as consumers and producers, as active participants in contemporary cultures. They will typically use media forms and technologies to explore their social worlds, to represent themselves and their preoccupations, and to gain satisfying and pleasurable experiences related to conceptions of creativity, identity transformation, and social allegiance. Though this approach, based in cultural studies and audience research traditions, sits alongside the more linguistic-derived perspectives described above, the two approaches in many ways complement each other, and are, indeed, often evoked together in some of the research studies included in this review.

A final, important point about all of these literacies is that they theorise the production of texts as well as the interpretation of them. This may seem too obvious to need saying in the context of English, where reading and writing are so obviously two sides of the literacy coin. However, the history of media and moving image education is quite different. For one thing, it emerged from academic disciplines such as sociology and literary theory, concerned entirely with interpreting texts rather than producing them. For another, the technological limits on production has effectively prevented all but a very few from 'writing' the moving image, until the recent arrival of affordable digital technologies for video editing. At the time of writing, such facilities, though rapidly expanding, are still only available to a minority of schools. The first mass access will arrive as schools upgrade their PCs (still the dominant platform) to the new Windows XP operating system, containing the simple and free editing software, Microsoft Moviemaker.

Before clarifying how this review will use the idea of moving image literacy, it is important to look at the problems with the literacy analogy. First, the use of an analogy with print literacy is problematic. It makes language the governing metaphor, implying both that language has a kind of primary status as a mode of communication, and that other modes in some ways behave like it, rather than (as we believe) that communicative modes may operate certain common semiotic principles. Second, it suggests that the analogy is consistent, when in fact the various communicative modes in question may be as marked in their differences as their similarities. Therefore, the closer the analogy is drawn, the more it starts to break down. Third, the analogy may move in the opposite direction, becoming no more than a vague metaphor invoking worthy ideas of something which, like apple pie and books, is invariably good for you. And fourth, as we have seen, the notion of 'media literacy' has much wider currency than a more specific focus on the moving image. Can a more narrow focus on the moving image be distinguished from the more general notion of media literacy?

In view of these problems, we need to explain why this review focuses on 'moving image literacy'.

First, to address the problem of the language analogy. We accept that the analogy with language breaks down; in fact, a multimodal view of the moving image would absolutely resist the idea that language should be a determining model, and would look instead for general principles which are common to different signifying modes, and at the same time look for specific characteristics of each mode. However, references to linguistics can be productive, even provocative. The idea of the linguist Halliday that language has three overarching functions (to represent, to enable interaction between those who communicate, and to organise texts) has been adapted by proponents of multimodality theory in various ways (Kress and van Leeuwen 1996; Lemke 2002). Similarly, the idea of modality in language (how language expresses degrees of certainty) has been adapted as a more general semiotic principle to throw light on the old problem of realism in the moving image, in visual design, and in music (Hodge and Tripp 1986; Kress and van Leeuwen 1996; van Leeuwen 1999). A final point to make is that the branch of socio-linguistics developed by Halliday and others, systemic-functional linguistics (Halliday 1978, 1985), has been particularly influential on conceptions of language in English teaching, especially in the UK, Australia and New Zealand. It seems possible, then, that a theory of moving image literacy which draws on the same tradition might make sense to English teachers; and might provide a basis for students to explore processes and structures of signification across the different media they encounter in English lessons, including language and the moving image (think how often they are presented with a book and a film or TV adaptation during the same course, for instance).

Second, while more general conceptions of media literacy, embracing a range of cultural practices and competences, are valuable in considering the field of media education (Buckingham 2003; Kirwan *et al.* 2003), there is equally a value in the more precise focus on a medium-specific literacy. The moving image is a specific medium of this kind, built around practices of filming and editing which, since their inception, have been seen by practitioners and theorists as a kind of language, from the pioneering work of the early Soviet directors, especially Sergei Eisenstein, through the structuralist theorists of the 1970s, such as Christian Metz, to the interpretive frameworks of contemporary writers such as Bordwell and Thompson, whose books have become standard text-books of film theory, running to many editions. This substantial tradition of theory has led to a relatively settled idea that the moving image has its own kind of language, even its own kind of grammar. However, we would distance ourselves from the exclusive association with cinema evoked by these names; and, to some extent, by the BFI's notion of cine-literacy. The moving image has been at least as important in its broadcast incarnation as television in the second half of the twentieth century; and at the beginning of the twenty-first century, it is finding new places in computer games, in multimedia formats, and in internet-based distribution.

Third, we would echo Buckingham's point, endorsed by a recent research study of media literacy in the UK (Kirwan *et al*. 2003), that any meaningful use of the 'literacy' analogy suggests writing as well as reading. Moving image audiences, and media audiences in general, have been positioned largely as 'readers' and consumers through the twentieth century, so that the notion of 'media literacy' in many countries has meant learning how to critically read the media.

However, the recent advent of affordable digital technologies for video editing have enabled a growth in the 'writing' of the moving image by school pupils. Accounts of such work included in this chapter describe pupils' work with digital video specifically as a form of literacy, involving cultural knowledge of film and television, an understanding of the textual conventions of the moving image, and the ability both to interpret these and to deploy them in the making of moving image texts. Again, then, a medium-specific focus on these practices should allow, in principle, detailed research work on digital filming and editing as a distinctive and relatively settled form of communication and expression.

Nevertheless, any such focus on the medium can only be provisional. While some of the studies reviewed here do indeed explore broadly similar practices in schools, such as the use of video editing software, others look at computer animation and computer games, which both undeniably involve the moving image, but which are produced and engaged with quite differently by the young people in the studies.

With this in mind, our working definition of 'moving image literacy' is intended to be tentative, provisional, and built on an awareness of the ways in which audiovisual media in the contemporary landscape of media cultures can overlap and converge, as well as in many cases retain a distinctive form.

The definition of moving image literacy adopted for the purpose of this review will be:

• cultural awareness and knowledge of moving image texts

- the ability to interpret systematic patterns of meaning in such texts
- the ability to design and produce moving image texts.

Policy and practice background

The uses of ICT in the context of moving image media in areas of the curriculum related to English are diverse. The emergent contexts can be described as:

- attention to moving image media, in particular recently-available digital video editing and computer animation software
- attention to multimedia texts which incorporate moving image elements, including web-based texts (Lachs 2001)
- attention to computer games, in which a dominant communicative mode is moving image, in the form of animation.

The relation between these kinds of textual engagement and ICT has shifted as the digital technologies needed to produce such texts have become available and affordable for schools: in particular, DV (Digital Video) editing software and hardware, and digital animation software. Though government assumptions about the digital curriculum in the UK might focus on changed forms of content delivery, many practitioners are focusing by contrast on enabling students to produce their own texts, shifting the emphasis from information delivery to questions of representation, self-representation, and digital literacy (Buckingham 2001; *et al.* 1999).

At the same time, mandatory curricula in different countries include requirements to teach children how to communicate in relation to visual or audiovisual media. In the National Curriculum for England and Wales, study of the moving image is mandatory, though it is located in the Reading section of the curriculum, so that interpretation, but not production, of the moving image is what is required. Similarly, in Australia, Beavis (1999) notes the breadth of text embraced by the English curriculum of the state of Victoria, including 'literary, mass media and everyday texts'. Though this is not restricted to reading, the emphasis is still on critical analysis rather than production. Indeed, the expanse of digital literacies practised by teenagers outside school shrink to pen-and-paper tests set by the Victoria curriculum, notes Doecke (2000). The English curriculum for New Zealand moves further than the UK or Victoria, including a strand called Visual Language which has equal status with Oral Language and Written Language. However, it falls short of requiring the production of visual texts, breaking the strand down instead into 'viewing and presenting'. In the Canadian state of Ontario, the English secondary curriculum is constructed as four strands, the fourth of which is Media Studies. Uniquely, this requires that students both 'learn to understand and interpret media works', and that they should 'learn about the media through the process of creating their own media works, using a range of technologies to do so'. However, there is no statutory requirement to include the moving image in such production; indeed, the examples given of what students might create are, disappointingly, restricted to book jackets, songs and sample webpages.

In the UK, the BFI has been persistently active in lobbying for the inclusion of moving image media in the curriculum (FEWG 1999), and in researching and promoting the use of moving image making technologies in the classroom. This interest is reflected in this review, in that four of the studies considered have a link with the BFI's research and development work.

Also in the UK, the notion of media literacy has emerged as a specific responsibility of the government, devolved to the newly-created media regulator, OFCOM. The definition of 'media literacy' in OFCOM's brief is wide, and includes reference to media production; but its emphasis is clearly on protecting citizens from the dangers of the media by developing critical skills.

The use of ICT in these contexts has emerged quite recently as the subject of empirical inquiry. Until recently, research was largely confined to small qualitative case studies, as the EPPI English Review Group's study so far reveals. However, larger projects are beginning to emerge, such as a recent experiment introducing digital video equipment into 50 schools by the UK government agency BECTa (British Educational Communications and Technology Agency) (BECTa 2002). Although this study was published too late to be included in the systematic review, its findings extend the evidence base for the understanding of the nature of moving image literacy, its relation to digital filming and editing technologies, and how this relation in turn impacts on notions of creativity in the classroom, what kinds of pedagogy are appropriate, and what kinds of learning styles can be addressed in this context. These perspectives will be considered in the course of this chapter.

Review question

The review question was: 'What is the impact of ICT on the learning of literacies associated with moving image texts in English?'

The notion of moving image literacy has been addressed above. It remains to clarify what is meant by ICT in this context; and what is meant by 'English'.

For the purposes of the search for studies during the review, and the mapping of the field, no specific definition of ICT was used; rather, it was left to the studies to announce, define and report on the relevant technologies. In fact, these emerged as digital video editing technologies and computer games. Clearly, there is little impact on the viewing and interpretation of the moving image to be found in digital technologies – it makes little difference whether a film is viewed from an analogue or a digital video source (at any rate, we have found no research studies of the kinds of difference this might make). As far as reading the moving image goes, the only studies thrown up by our search were ones which explored computer games, where, of course, the whole notion of 'reading' and 'interpretation' is, first of all, necessarily digital; and is, second, transformed into something quite different by the interactive nature of the medium, as well as its character as play, a quite different cultural activity from reading.

Finally, it is necessary to locate the review in the specific context of English 5–16 as it relates to moving image literacy. The reason why the impact of ICT on moving image texts should be studied in the context of English specifically is partly related to curriculum policy, and partly to the history of work on media texts in English. In the first case, the study of the moving image, or of media more generally, is, as we have seen, typically situated within the English curricula in Australia, Canada, New Zealand and the UK. In the second case, the history of work in the moving image is closely implicated with the history of English teaching. Even specialist media studies are often taught by English teachers. For these reasons, this review included studies which are set in the contexts of 'English and media education, or their broad equivalents'.

The studies: some general characteristics

The research studies included in the review were found by using the keyword 'moving image' along with the generic keywords of our overall review. This should have produced any studies found by our search strategy which were related to ICT, to English 5–16, and to the moving image. Thirteen studies were found, though four were later excluded: one because it had no reference to ICT; one because it was mostly about the still image; one because it referred only marginally to a movie project; and one because it was more generally about digital literacies, with no real focus on the moving image.

The nine remaining studies were found to have some notable features, which will be briefly considered here before a more detailed account of their content and findings.

First, most of the studies were UK-based, though one UK study was published in an Australian journal (Burn 2000), and the two studies of computer games were from Australia (Mackereth and Anderson 2000) and the US (McClay 2002). This might suggest a greater research attention to the use of digital video in English and media education in the UK; certainly, such research has been actively promoted in recent years, particularly by the BFI and BECTa.

Second, there were more studies focusing on older children and on secondary schools. One possible reason for this is that editing equipment, though it can now be acquired free in some circumstances, was expensive only a few years ago, and thus, at least in the UK, bought initially by secondary schools with bigger budgets than primary schools. Another reason might be that there is more curriculum time to experiment with such work in secondary schools, as students work towards increasingly specialised courses. A third reason might be that there is no established model of progression in respect of moving image literacies, which might begin with the basic building blocks of communication as language literacy does in early years education.

Third, a glance at the authorship of the studies found and included shows that there is overlapping authorship. Four of the nine studies were either authored or co-authored by Burn; and three authored or co-authored by Parker. In the case of the first author, this sustained interest is attributable to the author's work in a specialist media school in the UK, committed to innovative work in the media arts. In the second case, the author is Research Officer with the BFI, and represents a continuing interest of this UK institution in researching moving image production.

It should be noted at this point that one of these authors is also a co-author of this chapter, and the review on which it draws, raising the question of possible bias. The response given to this problem in the review has been to demonstrate steps taken to ensure objectivity. None of the studies found here was found or keyworded by this author – they were all either found by the electronic database searches, or by hand searches by other members of the review group (Andrews and Locke). The method of extracting data and judging quality in this systematic review involves the rigorous application of an electronic system, guarding further against bias. All the reviews were doubly evaluated by the two authors of this chapter; and one (Burn and Reed 1999) by an impartial member of the EPPI team at the London Institute of Education, Diana Elbourne. Finally, the review was independently peer-reviewed.

Fourth, a weakness of the review is that it missed some important studies in this field, which will be considered in this chapter, either because they were not found by the review's search strategy, or because they were published too late to be included. Three of these (Beavis 2001; Sefton-Green and Parker 1999; and Reid *et al.* 2002) will be considered along with the reviewed studies in this chapter, making twelve studies in all.

The studies: a summary

A brief summary of the twelve studies will give an indication of what aspects of the moving image and ICT they address.

The three studies additional to those included in the review are summarised first.

- Beavis (2001) reports on a school-based research project in Australia, looking at what kinds of literacy are in evidence in Year 8 students' work on computer games, including how their writing might demonstrate aspects of such literacies.
- Sefton-Green and Parker (1999) report on the use of computer animation 'edutainment' software by primary school children in the UK.
- Reid *et al.* (2002) is an evaluation project by the BFI in the UK for BECTa, assessing a large intervention project in which 50 schools (primary, secondary and special) were given an i-mac and camera to experiment with digital filming and editing.
- Burn and Reed (1999) explore the work of four able 16-year-old girls making a trailer for *Psycho* as a piece of coursework for a Media Studies exam in the UK, using the digital editing software Media 100.

- Burn (2000) is in many ways a companion piece to the first study, exploring the same project a year later, but this time with two underachieving boys.
- Burn *et al.* (2001) report on a government-funded research study by a group of UK teachers in collaboration with the BFI and Cambridge University. The group develops a conceptual framework for digital editing and tests it against observations of their own pupils.
- Burn and Parker (2001) explore a primary school computer animation project in the UK, developing a social semiotic model of moving image production.
- Mackereth and Anderson (2000) studied access to and use of computer games by a cohort of 15–17-year-old girls in an Australian high school; and followed this up with a qualitative study of a smaller sample of girls to determine their perceptions of and attitudes to games.
- McClay (2002) studied the narrative writing of a 13-year-old Canadian boy, to explore influences which his experiences of computer games might have had on the generic form and other aspects of his writing.
- O'Brien *et al.* (2001) analyse the multimedia productions of students with special literacy and social needs in an American high school, looking at how conceptions of literacy needed to be broad, both semiotically and culturally, to account for these students' achievements. This study is the one most loosely related to the moving image, but it was included as there was a moving image component in the multimedia compositions, and it raised the interesting question of how the moving image might combine with other media, and what questions about literacies this raised.
- Parker (1999) reports on a research collaboration between the BFI and King's College London in the UK, looking at how moving image work might improve print literacy. In this article, he looks specifically at two classes of primary school children, and how the quality of writing in one of them is affected by using computer animation while studying a class reader.
- Parker (2002) presents an overview of BFI research, including two studies which include computer animation.

What did they find?

Four strongly-marked patterns emerge.

First, several of the studies find a connection between media literacy and the cultural experience and preoccupations of young people, suggesting that curriculum content which recognizes this factor is more likely to motivate high quality work, to locate learners as determiners of their own meanings, and to be aware of ways in which the developing social identities of young people are implicated with their media cultures. So O'Brien *et al.*, for instance, document how the most effective multimedia production by young people with literacy problems incorporated moving image sequences of favourite rock stars, interpreted and manipulated within a multimedia text. Similarly, Burn finds that the pleasure of the horror genre, even in the context of an 'old' horror film, *Psycho*, becomes integral to the literacy required of two low-achieving boys to make a moving image text, influencing how they choose images of the monster, Norman Bates, and how they select a music track with the right kind of mood and pace. In the context of computer games, McClay finds that the experience of games like the *Final Fantasy* franchise have specific influences on the narrative structure, point of view, and character-construction of a 13-year-old boy's fantasy writing. It is worth noting that these findings are not simply the (quite common) claim that rooting literacy work in students' cultural experience is motivating, though they are also that. These points are quite specific instances of how cultural experience and the media discourses in which young people routinely engage provide the very semiotic raw material for their own work, as well as modelling the kinds of structures they build in their own video, multimedia or writing.

However, prior cultural experience is not always found to be beneficial. Mackereth and Anderson's quantified findings about less time spent by girls on computer consoles, coupled with their perception of games as a predominantly male activity, is set against the qualitative finding that the sample of girls are both competent at playing the selected games, and that they do not conform to stereotype in their diverse preferences for game genres. Here, the suggestion is that curricular incorporation of a literacy normally based outside the school can redress a cultural imbalance (an argument promoted elsewhere in the literature about girls and games in education; see Orr-Vered 1998).

Second, several studies find that the incorporation of moving image media in curriculum programmes led to gains in literacy, broadly defined. In some cases (Parker 1999; Parker 2002; McClay), this meant specific gains in print literacy as a result of the experience of, respectively, making computer animations and playing computer games. Parker's study makes a close analysis of children's descriptive and empathetic writing about a Roald Dahl story, finding aspects of point-of-view and visualisation attributable to the children's experience of designing a computer animation of the story. McClay finds that the writing of her subject follows the episodic structure of action adventure and role-playing games, that it omits visual description of character (already accomplished in drawings influenced by these games), and that it moves beyond the characterisation offered by the games, constructing histories and motivations for the characters. Some aspects of these findings are questioned by this review. First, Parker (1999) does not exclude the possibility of other explanations, in particular the novelty for the experimental group of working with a new approach and new equipment. Second, McClay does not analyse the computer games alongside the writing it is claimed is influenced by them. Third, as we have seen, both studies work with limited samples. However, both sets of findings are suggestive if not conclusive.

Beavis, like McClay, also finds certain gains in print literacy related to the experiences of computer games both within and beyond the classroom. Part of her analysis looks at the literate practices required of these students to play *Heroes of Might and Magic* and *Beyond Time* – such practices as reading instructions both on and off screen, understanding and engaging with narrative structures and fantasy genres, interpreting and using iconic signification and moving image sequence, such as the cut scenes presenting backstories. She also goes on to analyse how the writing of selected students can demonstrate critical distance, in reviews of the games, but can also develop complex approximations to the experience of playing.

Elsewhere, gains are related to moving image literacy, and in particular, the literacies required to produce the moving image. Burn and Reed find that the process of digital production allows for the internalization of abstract notions of genre, narrative and audience which are then realized in the composition of the students' own video sequence, a trailer for *Psycho*. In the course of the article, they show how specific signifying practices articulating these understandings can be found in the choice of specific images, in the use of intertitles in which language is juxtaposed with image, and in the use of music tracks to depict mood and to structure pace and rhythm. In relation to all of this, they find that metalinguistic scaffolding helped students of high ability to conceptualise and write about their work.

Other findings related specifically to literacy are those related to particular aspects of visual composition. The importance of spatial-visual communication is noted in McClay, who observes that drawings based on computer game characters take the place of descriptive writing. Similarly, Burn and Parker find that in the computer animation project under investigation, children construct spatial elements – the synchronic aspect of the text – before they construct temporal elements – the diachronic – because the software (The Complete Animator) demands this, and because animation necessarily follows this sequence (you have to draw or model something in space before you can animate it in time). There are a number of implications here for how such skills can be taught in sequence, and how quite abstract characteristics of animation can, and must be, grasped by quite young children (10–11-year-olds in this case). This finding connects with Parker and Sefton-Green's finding that the younger children in their study, also using The Complete Animator (along with other packages), were not able autonomously to understand how frame-by-frame animation produced movement; they tended to grasp the more obvious idea of the whole scene, rather than understanding the durative nature of the frame. There are two implications here – one is to do with pedagogy (the children in the Burn and Parker study were explicitly taught how to animate by a specialist teacher and artist-in-residence); and one is to do with the clarity and accessibility of the software. Parker and Sefton-Green draw the conclusion that better-designed softwares need to be developed.

Though most of the studies produce some findings as evidence of the development of moving image literacy through production, it is less easy to discern the specific impact of digital technologies. The studies sometimes do not sufficiently separate out this factor, by asking, for instance, how many of the gains observed could have been achieved with analogue technologies. Specific reference to digital formats are made in the findings of six of the studies.

Reid *et al.* look at specific features of digital video in one section of their findings. They identify four advantages of the digital medium exemplified by work documented in the study of schools using I-movie with digital camcorders. These were that the digital medium provided: continuous feedback, allowing students to reflect as they worked; iterative opportunities, so that editing could be frequently revised; opportunities for dynamic presentation of work through LCD (liquid crystal display) screens, data projectors and so on; and possibilities for integration of DV with other media, examples from the project being web images, music technologies, and electronic text.

Parker and Sefton-Green find that editing promoted 'cine-literacy', but that the digital 'edutainment' softwares explored in this study also constrained what was possible by limiting functionality. This finding is extended into the conclusion that better quality, accessible editing software is needed for this age group.

Burn finds that the process of audiovisual composition is observably a form of literacy, involving a variety of forms of assembly of image and music sequences, and that this process is enabled by the digital format. (In this study, the reviewers pointed out a lack of clarity over how the data was collected, rendering the findings less authoritative.)

Burn and Reed find that digital media blur the distinction between theory and practice, analysis and production. It is not clear, however, on what evidence this particular finding is based.

Burn and Parker find that digital production is characteristically provisional – that the undoing and redoing of work is a specific affordance not to be found in analogue technologies. (Here, the reviewers agreed with the findings and conclusions of the study.)

Beavis argues that the nature of literacy is changed by digital technologies, and that the literacies required by computer games, as well as the cultures in which they are embedded, need to be taken account of by schools.

Third, four of the studies report findings which relate to the collaborative nature of media production. Parker and Sefton-Green observe how the collaborative work of the children used the computer as a co-worker, in a 'choric', improvisatory process akin to children's drama. Burn and Parker report that an important aspect of the animation-making they describe was the sharing of digital images in a networked image bank. Reid *et al.* report on the different models of collaborative production observed across this project. These ranged from group production to more individual styles of editing, where students made their own edited video, but exchanged ideas and experiences in ways structured by the teacher.

In Burn *et al.*, all three of the action research studies report positive findings about the collaborative nature of the work, and the social roles adopted by pupils as part of the editing process. In respect of the last instance, the collaborative nature of media production work is a well-known phenomenon, raising well-known questions (e.g. Buckingham *et al.* 1995; Buckingham *et al.* 1999). It is not clear that new light is shed on these questions by Burn *et al.*

Fourth, seven of the studies report findings indicative of motivational aspects of working with moving image media, while one (Mackereth and Anderson) finds a negative effect in the case of girls and computer games; that is, that girls are less motivated to play games than boys, even when they have equal access to consoles. The seven studies reporting positive effects mention the motivating effect of digital video editing widely reported by the teachers in Reid *et al.*; the social and aesthetic pleasures of editing (Burn *et al.*); the link between school literacies and the 'rich textual worlds in their out-of-school lives' (Beavis); the improvement of motivation by moving image production in the context of print literacy development (Parker 2002); the greater duration of reading and writing for students with special needs when working with multimedia (O'Brien *et al.*); the increased sense of self-worth in two low-attaining boys (Burn); and increased self-esteem among four able girls (Burn and Reed). However, in some of these cases it is difficult, if not impossible, to separate out the effect of media production in general from the specific effect of the digital medium.

What theoretical models of moving image literacy did the studies develop?

There are a number of consistent threads running through the theoretical models proposed by many of these studies, which is unsurprising given that there is overlapping authorship in eight of them. One of the most consistent themes is the argument for a wider conception of literacy beyond print, which can include visual and other communicative modes. This argument is rooted mainly in the work of Kress and van Leeuwen (1996), and in associated work by the New London Group (e.g. Cope and Kalantzis 2000) and by others in the general field of social semiotic approaches to language and other media (Halliday 1985; Hodge and Tripp 1986). These references are made by eight of the studies.

The evidence here is that, in order to approach the practices of moving image interpretation and production in schools, researchers have needed to find an approach to communication which will cast light on how the moving image is understood by learners. This approach is promoted by these studies for various reasons. First, it includes a theory of visual grammar (Kress and van Leeuwen 1996), from which a 'grammar' of the moving image can begin to be developed. This is the explicit concern of Burn and Parker (2001).

Second, this approach makes an explicit association between literacy and the moving image, in particular because the social semiotic approach is developed partly from systemic-functional linguistics, which is influential in the understanding of literacy, especially in the UK, Australia and New Zealand. Third, this approach places emphasis on the social nature of communicative practices. All these studies view literacy from a socio-cultural perspective, as the keywording demonstrates. They are, then, either influenced by the arguments of variants of this sociolinguistic tradition, or they are located in other research traditions which accommodate easily such an approach.

The latter suggestion is borne out by the other most consistent set of references, which is to cultural studies models of media education, in particular those developed by Buckingham and Sefton-Green (Buckingham *et al.* 1995; Buckingham 1996; Buckingham and Sefton-Green 1994). These references are invoked in nine of the studies, and indicate an emphasis on the cultural contexts of moving image media and computer games. Particular aspects of this emphasis include the nature of popular culture and how this can be accommodated by school curricula and conceptions of literacy; the emergence of new technologies which allow children to become producers of moving image and multimedia texts for the first time; and the link between media experience and the development of social identities.

In terms of actual models of learning, some specific suggestions are made. Parker and Sefton-Green suggest that we need to develop notions of how literacies associated with visual and moving image media can be developed into models of progression, and how collaborative learning can be developed, but also how computer-based editing allows individual media production for the first time in schools. Burn and Parker (2001) propose a series of processes characteristic of the use by children of different software packages to produce animation. These processes include ways in which the flexibility of the media allow for the audiovisual equivalent of redrafting in writing, though more emphasis is placed on how the existing available semiotic resources and tools are shaped by the cultural interests and communicative needs of the children.

Burn *et al.* propose a conceptual framework arising from an action research project led by the BFI. Here, the processes of digital video editing are categorized under those which relate to social roles, those which relate to creativity, and those which relate to literacies and communicative practices. The research of the teachers largely confirmed the model; though it was judged in the conclusions to the article to be weak in its specificity about the kinds of literacy process involved, and in its attention to the pleasure of editing, and how this related not simply to motivation, but to the relation of the students to the film being edited (*The Matrix*), and to popular cinema more generally.

McClay proposes, much more tentatively, a process whereby the experience of computer games informs the fantasy writing of a young boy. The proposal is that the influence of games results in more fluid, episodic narratives, and new genres of writing which literacy educators need to become aware of. There is little evidence on which the proposal can generalize, since this is a case study of one boy; and the study applies no analysis to the games as texts, so part of the claim rests only on interview evidence or on assumption. However, the hypothesis that games-influenced writing displays characteristics of a new kind of narrative form of which schools need to be aware is interesting, and deserving of further research. It is compromised by the claim that the boy's writing deepens the computer narratives by investing the characters with history. This claim would be considerably weakened by an analysis of the games cited, one of which is the *Final Fantasy* series which in fact spends considerable effort in constructing character histories through backstories conveyed through video and text. Arguably the issue here is more to do with the expectation of psychological depth, prized within both the traditions of Western drama and the novel, but completely untypical of oral narrative (Ong 2002) and computer games, which one commentator has compared to Homeric narrative in their use of characters in whom psychological depth is simply not the point (Murray 1997). In any case, to analyse effects in a child's writing of computer game experience without analysing the properties of the game texts which are assumed to be transmitted to the writing is a weakness of the analytical methodology of the study, pointing to interesting possibilities for future approaches.

Parker (1999, 2002) proposes a model in which the development of moving image literacy can be fruitfully linked with the development of print literacy. This is tested by a controlled experiment (Parker 1999) in which children who have worked on the animation of a story as well as reading it are shown to have progressed further in the quality of their writing than children in a comparable group without the animation experience. Specific effects demonstrated relate to understandings of narrative, quality of descriptive writing, and quality of empathetic writing. This project was part of a larger research project on the effects of the moving image on literacy, a collaboration between King's College London and the BFI. The interest of the project, rather than focusing on the nature of narrative writing, as in McClay's study, was on how moving image media might be of value in the context of literacy teaching in the UK, and, specifically, how it might improve the quality of writing in observable, even quantifiable, ways.

Finally, the BFI evaluation of the BECTa DV pilot project raises a wide range of questions about learning and digital video: the nature of collaborative learning; the technological requirements needed; the models of moving image literacy at play; the pedagogy needed to bring such work to fruition.

Taken together, there is a strong sense across these studies that a literacy in moving image media should have certain characteristics. It should be systematically understood on the one hand as a communicative practice, in which the details of semiotic work can be addressed by educators; and on the other hand, as a practice which is rooted in the cultural experience of children across a wide range of media. It should be a literacy which includes both the interpretation and analysis of moving image media, and the production of such media using the digital technologies now available. And it should be a literacy recognized by formal education, a point most strikingly made by Mackereth and Anderson, who site their exploration of girls and computer games in a high school, although games form no part of the formal curriculum.

A gap opens up, however, between the studies concerned with the making of the moving image and the three papers about computer games. Although all three of these are concerned very much with active notions of literacy, it is not clear conceptually how such 'literacy' relates to the proposals to study and produce the moving image in schools which are typical of the other papers. There is a link, however, between McClay's focus on the improvement in writing caused by the influence of games and Parker's focus on a similar effect in respect of animation. Both explain their findings in relation to an expanded awareness of visually-based narratives in their subjects. Similarly, Beavis indicates clearly how the recognition of games in English can lead to both the development of medium specific literacies and to gains in students' abilities to deploy multimodal principles of narrative, point-of-view, and generic convention.

Though she does not relate these specifically to the moving image, it is easy to see how such a connection could be made.

What are the strengths and weaknesses of the studies?

The main weakness of these studies, taken together, is the sample sizes. Apart from the first part of Mackereth and Anderson's study, which is a quantitative survey for contextual information across a whole year cohort in a high school, all the other sample groups range between one child (McClay) and 60 children (the experimental and control groups in Parker 1999). Even in the larger groups (Mackereth and Anderson; Parker), the studies are located in a single school, so it is difficult to claim results typical across diverse socioeconomic or ethnic ranges. The studies themselves are typically cautious about their findings, calling them tentative, preliminary, suggestive, and not making claims that they are typical in any way of a given population. The only studies judged to be of 'high' quality in providing evidence to answer their own questions were those of Mackereth and Anderson, which combined quantitative findings from a whole year group with observation and interview data from a group of six girls, thus providing a robust account of girls' engagement with computer games; and Burn *et al.*, which provided a conceptual unity for a diverse action research project by relating the research process to a clear conceptual framework.

The only study which is larger – which must be, in fact, the largest research study so far into the moving image and ICT in schools – is Reid *et al.* Here, the breadth of evidence makes some of the findings more convincing than they can be in the smaller studies.

The stronger points of the smaller qualitative studies, of course, are in the depth of analysis. Here, the attention to detailed analysis related to the conceptual frameworks of the respective studies resulted in the 'high' quality assessment of the teachers' action research work in Burn *et al.* (2001), and in Parker (1999) and Burn and Reed (1999). These studies provide rich accounts of children's descriptive and narrative writing as influenced by animation, of the collaborative decision-making of digital editing, and of a culturally-informed semiotics of moving image production.

Similarly, Beavis' attention to the details of how children interpret icons, deploy understandings of generic and narrative conventions, and adapt the affective and subjective experience of a computer game to the resources of narrative writing, lend authority to the development of a theory of multiliteracy.

There is unevenness of method, however, in some of the studies. McClay analyses the writing of a teenage boy to show the influence of computer game images, narratives and structures, but does not analyse the games themselves, so that claims for effect are based solely on interview evidence where there could have been a textual comparison which could have made an innovatory contribution to this area of research. Similarly, Burn analyses the video production of two boys, but uses no interview data, which could have deepened the analysis and made the study more robust.

The studies with the same or overlapping authorship share conceptual approaches. In these cases, though the samples are small in each study, the aggregation of data strengthens the case for the findings. So, for instance, the study of animation cited in Parker (2002) complements the evidence in Parker (1999) and Burn and Parker (2001), to show that the production of computer animations by primary school children in the UK promotes understandings of narrative texts. However, in each of these studies, the ability of the research design and method to rule out other explanations of the data was judged by the reviewers to be 'a little'; so where the studies complement each other's data and findings, they also replicate each other's weaknesses in this respect.

Similarly, Burn and Reed (1999) and Burn (2000) complement each other by adopting similar theoretical bases and by studying different groups in broadly similar ways, so that the limitations of the sample in terms of quantity, gender and academic attainment is to some extent compensated for. However, the two studies still add up to a sample of six, and that within the same socioeconomic setting; so this is still a very limited study. Also, again, in the case of the second of these two studies, the design and method is unable to rule out other explanations. In the first case, however, a triangulation design which analyses data from classroom observation, interview, video text and pupils' writing provides more robust data and more demonstrably valid analysis.

Finally, in spite of the richness of the analysis in many of the studies, there is often a failure in the conceptual design to distinguish sufficiently clearly between key variables. Though claims are made for the benefits of digital technologies, some of the studies do not sufficiently distinguish between the impact of media production in general and the impact of digital media in particular. This particular lack of clarity makes it difficult, on the basis of this evidence, to answer the present review question with confidence.

Altogether, the quality of the studies included in the review emerges as 'medium' across all studies apart from two. In general, this is because the sample limitations are often compensated for by the quality of qualitative analysis, which produces strongly suggestive outcomes if not conclusive ones. In the case of the two studies judged to be 'low' overall (Mackereth and Anderson; O'Brien *et al.*), this is not necessarily because of the intrinsic quality of the study (which in the first case was 'high'), but because the focus was less helpful in answering the review question. In the case of these two studies, the theoretical models they adopted formed part of the pattern which helped to answer the review question; and Mackereth and Anderson also demonstrated engagements with computer games by girls which were convincingly argued as evidence for an expanded notion of literacy.

Implications: what does it mean?

Policy

Implications for educational policy fall into two main areas.

First, the case that pupils' interpretation of the moving image and understanding of it can only fully be regarded as a 'literacy' if they also have opportunities to produce moving image texts, has implications for literacy policies produced by government education departments. In the UK, for instance, the National Curriculum for English includes the moving image, but only in the Reading section of the curriculum. The emphasis on production in these studies make a case for it to be regarded as a form of 'writing' also.

At the same time, the studies suggest that moving image making in schools is a literacy with wider implications beyond the English curriculum, and should be addressed also within the Arts, and within models of ICT curricula, whether discrete or distributed across other subject domains. This implication, though not strongly represented in the smaller case studies, is reinforced by the findings of the BECTa DV pilot (Reid *et al.* 2002).

Second, the studies do not make specific cases for the purchase of specialised equipment for schools. This question, again, would be more clearly revealed by the findings of the BECTa report, which, while it makes a case for high levels of access to digital editing software, does so in the context of Apple's I-movie, which is either very cheap or free, depending on circumstances. At the present time, following the release of Windows XP, it is also clear that editing software is incorporated as standard in this operating system, in the form of Microsoft Moviemaker (available in version 2 as a free download). The question, then, rather than one of financial outlay, becomes one of curriculum time, appropriate pedagogies, and interpretations of literacy. Similarly, the perception of computer games as both literate practices and as objects worthy of analysis and study in schools is a question of curriculum design rather than of cost.

Practice

The draft version of the review report was discussed with a member of the Advisory Group representing potential users of the report in the English and Media teaching community, James Durran (Parkside Community College, Cambridge). His comments were as follows:

- The report will be helpful on occasions in which he has to justify moving image work in the classroom as a form of literacy work; it will provide a synthesis of theoretical approaches to cite on these occasions. The example he gave was an animation project with primary schools, the outcomes of which he has often been required to present (and which forms the subject of one of the included studies: Burn and Parker 2001).
- The report will be useful to cite in his work with trainee teachers at the Cambridge University School of Education, where his work with postgraduate student teachers involves practical experiences of media production with children, but also the need to underpin this with theoretical explanation and analysis.
- The report will be helpful to him in his analysis of his own practice. He pointed out that theory and practice should not be divided between researcher and practitioner, but that practitioners should research and theorise their own work (in fact, as an action researcher, he has contributed to one of the studies included in the review, Burn *et al.* 2001).
- As a disseminator of good practice in a wide variety of contexts (initial teacher education, continuing professional development work with teachers, Best Practice Research Scholarships), he would find the report useful.

- On the specific subject of the studies relating to computer games, he commented that this is an area he recognizes as an influential part of popular culture which should be included in the teaching of literacy. Any research evidence about how games might be conceived of as a literacy, or how they might be incorporated into teaching programmes, would be welcome.

It is worth considering further how these implications for practice might have a more general impact on the teacher community. It is already the case that moving image technologies in the UK are beginning to be explored by teachers through voluntary training and in-service provision (provided, for instance, by the National Association for the Teaching of English, by the BFI, by the English and Media Centre in London, and by Film Education, amongst others).

However, all of this relies on the enthusiasm of relatively small sub-sets of the English teaching community; and it seems fair to suppose that the position is similar in the other Anglophone countries. The obvious implication, not from this review, but from further research, should it confirm the tentative findings of this study, would be the incorporation of digital moving image production in the initial training of teachers.

Research

The implication of this review of research in moving image literacies and ICT is that more research is needed, of specific kinds. First, the general character of these studies as small, qualitative case studies needs to be complemented both by more in-depth qualitative analyses of children's moving image work, but also by larger studies, combining qualitative and quantitative methods. Mackereth and Anderson's study shows, for example, how a quantitative survey can produce important contextual data for a large sample, to be combined with smaller qualitative studies of process and outcome.

Second, further research needs to clearly distinguish the impact of digital formats in particular, and not allow this to become confused with the impact of media production work in general, or with other, motivational, factors.

Third, the comments of the practitioner-adviser point to a strength of some of the UK-based work, which is action-research-based collaborations between specialist agencies, academics, and practising teachers. If these kinds of detailed case-study work can be extended, for instance into longitudinal studies (the ones in this review are mostly cross-sectional), and if they can be systematically coordinated to produce generalisable findings, then this model, already supported by the UK's education ministry, should be valuable and effective in impacting on practice.

The studies reviewed

Beavis, C. (2001) 'Digital cultures, digital literacies', in Durrant, C. and Beavis, C. (eds) *P(ICT)ures of English: Teachers, Learners and Technology*, Norwood, SA: AATE and Wakefield Press.

Burn, A. (2000) 'Repackaging the slasher movie: digital unwriting of film in the classroom', *English in Australia*, 127–8: 24–34.

Burn, A. and Parker, D. (2001) 'Making your mark: digital inscription, animation, and a new visual semiotic', *Education, Communication and Information*, 1: 155–79.

Burn, A. and Reed, K. (1999) 'Digi-teens: media literacies and digital technologies in the secondary classroom', *English in Education*, 33: 5–20.

Burn, A., Brindley, S., Durran, J., Kelsall, C. and Sweetlove, J. (2001) ' "The rush of images": a research report into digital editing and the moving image', *English in Education*, 35: 34–47.

Mackereth, M. and Anderson, J. (2000) 'Computers, video games, and literacy: what do girls think?', *The Australian Journal of Language and Literacy*, 23: 184–95.

McClay, J.K. (2002) 'Hidden "treasure": new genres, new media and the teaching of writing', *English in Education*, 36: 46–55.

O'Brien, D.G., Springs. R. and Stith, D. (2001) 'Engaging at-risk high school students: literacy learning in a high school literacy lab', in E.B. Moje and D.G. O'Brien (eds) *Constructions of Literacy: Studies of Teaching and Learning in and out of Secondary Schools*, Mahwah, NJ: Lawrence Erlbaum Associates.

Parker, D. (1999) 'You've read the book, now make the film: moving image media, print literacy and narrative', *English in Education*, 33: 24–35.

Parker, D. (2002) 'Show us a story: an overview of recent research and resource development work at the British Film Institute', *English in Education*, 36: 38–45.

Reid, M., Parker, D. and Burn A. (2002) *Evaluation Report of the BECTa Digital Video Pilot Project*. British Educational Communications and Technology Agency, http://www.becta.org.uk/research/reports/digitalvideo/index.html.

Sefton-Green, J. and Parker, D. (1999) *Edit-Play*, London: British Film Institute.

Bibliography

Beavis, C. (1999) 'Literacy, English and computer games', paper presented at The Power of Language, International Federation for the Teaching of English Seventh Conference, July 1999, University of Warwick.

BECTa (2002) *Computer Games in Education Project Report*. BECTa website (http://forum.ngfl.gov.uk/Images/vtc/Games_and_education/Games Reportfinal.rtf), Coventry: British Educational Communications and Technology Agency.

Bigum, C., Durrant, C., Green, B., Honan, E., Lankshear, C., Morgan, W., Murray, J., Snyder, I. and Wild, M. (1997) *Digital Rhetorics: Literacies and Technologies in Education – Current Practices and Future Directions* (Executive Summary and Volumes 1, 2 and 3), Canberra: Department of Employment, Education, Training and Youth Affairs.

Buckingham, D. (1996) *Moving Images: Understanding Children's Emotional Responses to Television*, Manchester: Manchester University Press.

Buckingham, D. (2001) 'New media literacies: informal learning, digital technologies and education', in D. Buckingham and A. McFarlane (eds) *A Digitally-Driven Curriculum?*, London: Institute for Public Policy Research.

Buckingham, D. (2003) *Media Education: Literacy, Learning and Contemporary Culture*, Cambridge: Polity Press.

Buckingham, D., Grahame, J. and Sefton-Green, J. (1995) *Making Media – Practical Production in Media Education*, London: English & Media Centre.

Buckingham, D., Harvey, I. and Sefton-Green, J. (1999) 'The difference is digital? Digital technology and student media production', *Convergence* 5: 10–20.

Buckingham, D. and Sefton-Green, J. (1994) *Cultural Studies Goes to School: Reading and Teaching Popular Culture*, London: Taylor & Francis.

Burn, A. and Leach, J. (2003) *A Systematic Review of the Impact of ICT on the Learning of Literacies Associated with Moving Image Texts in English, 5–16 (EPPI-Centre Review, version 1)*, Research Evidence in Education Library, London: EPPI-Centre, Social Science Research Unit, Institute of Education.

Burn, A. and Parker, D. (2003) 'Tiger's big plan: multimodality and the moving image', in C. Jewitt and G. Kress (eds) *Multimodal Literacy*, New York: Peter Lang.

Cope, B. and Kalantzis, M. (2000) (eds) *Multiliteracies: Literacy Learning and the Design of Social Futures*, Melbourne: Macmillan.

Cunningham, H. (1997) 'Moral kombat and computer game girls', in D. Buckingham and C. Bazalgette (1999) *In Front of the Children*, London: British Film Institute.

Doecke, B. (2000) 'Yet I still want to teach', *English in Australia*, 127–8.

Film Education Working Group (FEWG) (1999) *Making Movies Matter*, London: British Film Institute.

Halliday, M.A.K. (1978) *Language as Social Semiotic*, London: Edward Arnold.

Halliday, M.A.K. (1985) *An Introduction to Functional Grammar*, London: Arnold.

Hodge, R. and Kress, G. (1988) *Social Semiotics*, Cambridge: Polity.

Hodge, B. and Tripp, D. (1986) *Children and Television: A Semiotic Approach*, Cambridge: Polity.

Jenkins, H. (1998) 'Complete freedom of movement: video games as gendered play spaces', in J. Cassell and H. Jenkins (eds) *From Barbie to Mortal Kombat: Gender and Computer Games*, Cambridge, MA: MIT Press.

Jewitt, C. (2002) 'The move from page to screen: the multimodal reshaping of school English', *Visual Communication*, 2(2).

Jewitt, C. and Kress, G. (2003) *Multimodal Literacy*, New York: Peter Lang.

Kirwan, J., Learmonth, J. and Sayer, M. (2003) *Mapping Media Literacy*, London: British Film Institute.

Kress, G. and van Leeuwen, T. (1996) *Reading Images: The Grammar of Visual Design*, London: Routledge.

Kress, G. and van Leeuwen, T. (2001) *Multimodal Discourses*, London: Arnold.

Lachs, V. (2001) *A Teacher's Guide to Multimedia*, London: Routledge Falmer.

Lemke, J. (2002) 'Travels in hypermodality', *Visual Communication*, 1: 299–325.

Murray, J. (1997) *Hamlet on the Holodeck: The Future of Narrative in Cyberspace*, Cambridge MA: MIT Press.

Ong, W. (2002) *Orality and Literacy: The Technologizing of the Word*, London: Routledge.

Orr-Vered, K. (1998) 'Blue group boys play incredible machine, girls play hopscotch: social discourse and gendered play at the computer', in J. Sefton-Green (ed.) *Digital Diversions: Youth Culture in the Age of Multimedia*, London: UCL Press.

Raney, K. (1997) *Visual Literacy: Issues and Debates; A Report on the Research Project 'Framing Visual and Verbal Experience'*, London: Middlesex University, School of Lifelong Learning and Education (Reports and Evaluations series).

Sefton-Green, J. (1995) 'New models for old? English goes multimedia', in D. Buckingham, J. Grahame and J. Sefton-Green (eds) *Making Media – Practical Production in Media Education*, London: English & Media Centre.

van Leeuwen, T. (1999) *Speech, Music, Sound*, London: Macmillan.

Vincent, J. (2001) 'The role of visually rich technology in facilitating children's writing', *Journal of Computer Assisted Learning*, 17: 242–50.

Chapter 7

Methodological issues

Rebecca Rees and Diana Elbourne

Introduction

In this chapter we begin by exploring the needs for research evidence to inform policy, practice and future research, and introduce the role of systematic reviews. Having described this approach, we then consider some controversies which have been generated. We go on to detail the methods used in the work of the Evidence for Policy and Practice Information and Coordinating Centre (EPPI-Centre), and finally the implementation of these methods in the particular systematic review which is the basis of this book – the impact of ICT on 5–16-year-olds' literacy in English.

The role and nature of systematic reviews

The issue of the need for evidence to inform policy and practice is currently very topical, but it is not new. The difficulties for practitioners and policy-makers of accessing research have been outlined for some time (Light and Pillemer 1984). There have been debates around how, and even if, research can influence policy and practice (e.g. Weiss 1979); however, it seems relatively uncontroversial that those making policy and practice decisions require accessible research evidence (Davies 2000; Hammersley 2001). For this, syntheses of existing research are required. Systematic reviewing, or systematic research synthesis is one approach to synthesising existing research.

Most of the current activity within evidence-informed policy and practice aims to review primary research to aggregate and then summarize what is known. It conceptualizes research as potentially cumulative and involves the use and reporting of procedures to increase objectivity and minimize bias.

This approach to research synthesis is not universal, however. Most studies that identify themselves as reviews (including 'expert' reviews) will not have aimed to be systematic in their methods. Indeed these, more traditional, reviews have been criticized for not providing the methodological detail needed if readers are to understand how conclusions were reached (e.g. Oliver *et al.* 1999). Glass and colleagues commented:

> the conception of research review and integration that prevails in the social and behavioural sciences is one in which the activity is viewed as a matter of largely private judgement, individual creativity, and personal style. Indeed, it is and ought to be all of these to some degree; but if it is nothing but these, it is curiously inconsistent with the activity (viz., scientific research) it purports to illuminate.
>
> (Glass *et al.* 1981: 14)

There are many ways to take a more systematic approach to research synthesis but they all share a common basic principle: an explicit methodology. The main stages of a systematic review include setting the question, comprehensive searching, using explicit criteria to include and exclude studies, extracting data from and quality assessing studies, synthesis and drawing conclusions. These stages are detailed further later on in this chapter. The reporting of each stage is key: only when the details of a review's methods are clear does critical appraisal of the review itself, replication and updating become a possibility.

Several broad types of systematic review can be recognized. One particular type (as exemplified by the work of the Cochrane Collaboration (http://www.cochrane.org) in the field of health care and its sister organisation the Campbell Collaboration in education, social welfare, and crime and justice (http://www.campbellcollab oration.org)) assesses the effects of different interventions and relies largely on studies that use experimental methods, mainly randomized controlled trials (RCTs). The rationale is that only such designs can ensure that the groups being compared are similar in terms of pre-existing predictive factors (both known and unknown). Because allocation to these groups is random, differences between the groups are due only to statistical chance. Commonly these reviews use the statistical technique of meta-analysis to summarize the effects from more than one trial.

One recent overview analyses a range of philosophical and technical issues related to research synthesis, focusing particularly on critiques from the field of educational research (Gough and Elbourne 2002). This overview contrasts systematic research synthesis, which has been labelled as positivist by some critics (e.g. Hammersley 2001), with interpretative qualitative synthesis. The latter approach starts from an understanding that certain types of research are so contextually dependent and interpretive that cumulative synthesis makes little sense. As some have pointed out (e.g. Popay *et al.* 1998), studies do not always aim primarily to produce valid and generalizable results. A frequently cited text on this form of approach talks of the value of syntheses that develop 'new interpretative constructions' rather than generalizations (Noblitt and Hare 1988: 23).

Gough and Elbourne conclude that many of the critiques of systematic research synthesis are based upon misunderstandings or on examples of inappropriate or poor application of its methods. Some have based arguments, for example, on the idea that research synthesis is necessarily based around questions of effectiveness. Their concern is then that a focus on research synthesis will direct educational research away from other questions important for educational policy and practice (Hammersley 2001; Evans and Benefield 2001). There is undoubtedly a predominance, notably within the Cochrane Collaboration, of reviews that ask questions of effectiveness. However, the principles of explicit synthesis methods can and have been applied to a variety of research questions. Systematic reviews have recently addressed, for example, people's views on factors influencing various health states and behaviours (Harden *et al.* 2001; Rees *et al.* 2001; Shepherd *et al.* 2001) and experiences of diabetes and diabetes care (Campbell *et al.* 2003).

The systematic review approach has also been criticized for ignoring 'qualitative' research, and yet qualitative research has acted as the primary source of data for systematic reviews. The three reviews of factors influencing health states and behaviours cited above (Harden *et al.* 2001; Rees *et al.* 2001; Shepherd *et al.* 2001) are examples where some of the studies reviewed could be considered qualitative in that they scrutinized small samples in considerable detail so as to provide rich conceptual understanding and develop exploratory themes.

Systematic research synthesis, like any set of tools, can be used carelessly or inappropriately. As Gough and Elbourne point out, the simplistic use of statistical meta-analysis has also been criticized, notably by Slavin (1984). Slavin argued that decisions about including studies in a review were frequently being made primarily on the basis of study design, without the quality of the implementation of that design being taken into account. He suggested that it was preferable to consider 'best evidence' which included consideration both of the appropriateness of the design, but also the quality of the execution of that design.

Systematic review authors have also been criticized, for example, for over-concentration on statistical significance rather than the practical relevance of the findings (Davies 2000). As with all research, the readers' role as contextual interpreter is crucial. For example, readers may have different views from reviewers as to whether individual study populations or settings are similar enough to be grouped together and will need to appraise whether the people or places examined by the review have relevance for any specific policy or practice problem (Cook *et al.* 1992).

In practice, much of the original work on systematic approaches to research synthesis was conducted in the area of education in the USA (Glass *et al.* 1981). Since then, systems and methods for sustainable systematic research reviews have been established, notably by the international Cochrane Collaboration. Until recently, there has been no equivalent in education in the UK. Rather, there have been criticisms of the quality of research evidence and its accessibility (Hillage *et al.* 1998). More recently, a number of initiatives have been established by the Department for Education and Skills (DfES) (England and Wales). In addition to setting up a forum for educational research, National Educational Research Forum (NERF), in 2000 these initiatives included funding a programme of support for research synthesis in education at the Evidence for Policy and Practice Information and Coordinating Centre (EPPI-Centre), part of the Social Science Research Unit (SSRU) at the University of London's Institute of Education.

The EPPI-Centre and EPPI systematic reviews

The EPPI-Centre works with the following vision of evidence-informed policy and practice in education:

- high quality systematic reviews of research accessible to people making policy, practice and personal decisions
- collaboration that develops systematic review methodology and social research generally, and helps ensure the use of review findings
- a process for seeking, assessing and synthesising research across health, education, welfare and other public policy sectors that is open to scrutiny and criticism
- a process that values and takes steps to encourage participation, at all stages, by people with diverse perspectives
- reviews that build on the expertise and knowledge of these diverse perspectives
- a sustainable infrastructure for supporting the preparation of reviews and advancing research methodology.

One of the key products of this work is an electronic library of high quality systematic reviews of research in education that aims to be accessible to all potential users of research evidence. The Research Evidence in Education Library (REEL), is a searchable, user-friendly database on the World Wide Web (http://eppi.ioe.ac.uk). The reviews on REEL are conducted and updated by Review Groups which, in turn, are supported by the EPPI-Centre. In each of the first three years of its work, the centre has registered a new set of four or more of these Review Groups. The English Review Group, whose work forms the basis of this book, was part of a 'first wave' registered during the initiative's first year. The groups currently registered with the centre are described in Figure 7.1. The EPPI-Centre also conducts and supports a number of non-DfES reviews. Work in education is complemented by two other streams of work at the EPPI-Centre. Systematic reviews of health promotion and public health and projects to develop the evidence base in these fields are conducted within a Health Promotion stream, funded by the Department of Health. A third stream of work is exploring, through systematic and primary research, the perspectives and participation of people using services.

Review Groups participate in workshops run by the EPPI-Centre and work collaboratively with centre staff at key stages during their reviews. Each registered group is expected to complete a new review every 12 months and to update their reviews when appropriate. Also to be found on REEL are user perspectives on the reviews, the detailed 'data extractions' created by Review Groups when they

FIRST WAVE (First registered in 2000–1)
Assessment and Learning Research Synthesis Group
English Review Group
Inclusive Education Review Group
School Leadership Review Group

SECOND WAVE (First registered in 2001–2)
Continuing Professional Development Review Group
Early Years Review Group
Modern Languages Review Group
Thinking Skills Review Group

THIRD WAVE (First registered in 2002–3)
Art and Design Education Review Group
Citizenship Review Group
Science Review Group
Transitions Review Group

Figure 7.1 Registered EPPI-Centre DfES Review Groups. A number of these Review Groups have received funding from other organisations for their work. These organisations include the Nuffield Foundation, the Economic and Social Research Council, the Teaching and Learning Research Programme, the National Union of Teachers, and the Higher Education Funding Council for England.

interrogate individual research studies during a review, a register of studies spanning the Review Groups' topic areas, educational materials about systematic reviews and review tools.

Review Groups also commit themselves on registration with the EPPI-Centre to the active involvement of a range of research user constituencies in review decision-making. Groups need to specify publicly who has participated in decisions about the review's scope. It is expected that teachers and others with perspectives drawn from expertise outside academia, including parents, policy-makers and students, will have an input from the earliest stages of a review. Several Review Groups have taken steps to involve practising school teachers, for instance, as reviewers of studies, but further work is needed to identify good practice in supporting such activity.

Although funded by the DfES, the Groups are also encouraged to take an international perspective. This can arise in two main ways. First, there is no *a priori* restriction on the countries from which the studies for the reviews can be drawn, although resource constraints mean there may be pragmatic difficulties about access to non-English language material. The other way in which an international perspective may be felt is the inclusion of overseas members in the Review Groups. Currently there are members in 13 countries worldwide.

Key stages in an EPPI-Centre systematic review

Like any piece of research, a systematic review applies research methods in order to produce valid and reliable findings. A look at some of the key stages of an EPPI-Centre systematic review can help illustrate the EPPI-Centre's approach both to these methods and to ways in which they can be made explicit.

Deciding on the review's scope and approach

The most fundamental stage in any review is the definition of the review's research question. The question drives the remainder of the review. While other approaches to research synthesis have been designed to support reviews of studies of intervention effectiveness, the EPPI-Centre's systems have been designed so that reviews can address a wider range of questions. For example, because different research questions require the use of different study designs, the core questions asked of all studies at the in-depth stage of an EPPI-Centre review (described further below) include questions designed to help reviewers assess the implementation of a wide range of study types.

Once a research question is selected, reviewers work on establishing a protocol. In a review protocol reviewers describe their methods in detail, prior to their conducting the review. The protocol describes, for example, how searches are to be conducted, the criteria with which studies are to be included or excluded from the review, ways in which the quality of individual studies are to be appraised and the methods for synthesising study findings. It is argued that, if such methods are defined explicitly at the review start, reviewers are less likely to be influenced by, for example, their knowledge of study authors or by study findings as these become apparent. EPPI-Centre review protocols are peer refereed and are then published on REEL early on in the review, meaning that anyone with access to the Web can feed into the process at a stage at which they can potentially influence how the review is done.

Another important aspect of a review's protocol is a plan for assuring the quality of the review. EPPI Review Groups work jointly with staff from the EPPI-Centre on samples of studies at key decision-making stages in the review, notably at the point of applying inclusion and exclusion criteria, when coding studies so as to produce a descriptive map (see below), and when data extracting and quality appraising studies in-depth. Additional quality assurance work within the Review Group is also recommended.

Identifying relevant studies

After developing the protocol, reviewers search for primary studies which address the review's research question. The ideal is to find as much as possible of this research. This is important if the review's conclusions are not to be over-influenced by studies which are simply the easiest to find. Methodological research from health care indicates that research is more likely to be published if results are statistically significant (e.g. Dickersin 1997). It is as yet unclear how great an impact different search strategies might have on estimates of effects in education, although it is likely that different sources (e.g. a range of databases combined with hand searching through journals and tracking of citations) need to be used if relevant studies are not to be missed. Detailing the search process is, again, vital.

Following the searching stage of the review, the set of criteria for including or excluding studies established in the protocol is applied to each study to aid decisions as to whether they should remain in or be omitted from the review. EPPI Review Groups formulate criteria around the concepts they consider most pertinent to their review question. Groups have tended to include a wide range of study types in their reviews. If different study types are included at early stages of the review process, the suitability of each study type for answering the review's question needs to be addressed. Fitness of study type for purpose is built into the review's synthesis stage in EPPI reviews for this reason, as is discussed later.

Describing the studies found

EPPI Review Groups are encouraged to undertake their reviews in two phases, an initial descriptive 'mapping' of the literature, followed by an 'in-depth' review. The mapping is defined by a relatively broad research question, the in-depth review by a tighter refinement of the same question – both of which are pre-specified to differing degrees in the review's protocol. In contrast with the review's in-depth stage, which aims to synthesise the findings of studies and contextualize these in considerable depth, the mapping stage describes the types of research studies that have been done – and by implication, the areas where there are gaps.

A core set of codes (known as mapping keywords), covering study type and country, the learner population, setting and aspect of education under study, is applied to all studies mapped, making for consistency between the maps of different Review Groups. These are supplemented by review-specific codes. 'Descriptive maps' of these codes within EPPI reviews have ranged from relatively simple presentations of the numbers of studies of a topic conducted in different countries, to more complete descriptions of the size of the literature involving different sub-sections of the population of interest, or different manifestations of an intervention under review. As a guide to the research base for a topic, the mapping can be a useful product in itself. In terms of a review, the mapping can help to frame or inform a priority-setting exercise to determine areas to review in-depth. Highly specific searches can also be run on REEL using both the core and review-specific codes. The study type keywords also allow the creation of a register of randomized controlled trials and controlled trials.

While the map aims to describe systematically the scope of research addressing a given question, the more fundamental purpose of a review is the abstraction from primary studies of findings and their context, so that these can be synthesised. For data extraction purposes, EPPI Review Groups use a detailed set of over 100 coded core questions, each with a set of categorical answers, known as 'review guidelines'. As the EPPI-Centre approach is not restricted to one type of research question or study type, these guidelines are flexible enough be used for a very wide range of types of study. All the studies that are included in an EPPI-Centre review's in-depth stage have to be data extracted and quality appraised independently by two reviewers who then meet to reach a consensus, a third reviewer resolving disputes if necessary.

The review guidelines, and the keyword codes applied at the review's mapping stage are held electronically in a specialized database called EPPI-Reviewer. Reviewers use a web browser to access specially designed software to create their responses to the guidelines for each of the studies in their in-depth review. The software allows for additional detail to be recorded for most responses. It can also automatically compare the categorical answers of two reviewers so as to speed the consensus process. The complete data extractions for all the studies reviewed in-depth are published on REEL at the same time as groups publish the written reports of their reviews.

Assessing study quality and synthesising

The guidelines are also used to gauge explicitly the weight of evidence an individual study brings to the review. The methodological quality of each study (A) is reviewed in terms of how well it was executed in terms of its own study question. There is a variety of criteria for assessing methodological quality and they may differ according to the different types of study although some basic criteria are suggested in the guidelines. In addition, each study is assessed for how much weight of evidence it provides for the specific review in terms of (B) the appropriateness of research design for the review question, and (C) the relevance of the study for the review question. Finally, on the basis of judgements about (A), (B) and (C), an overall weight (D) is ascribed to each study. The weight of evidence assessments are taken into consideration in the syntheses.

These syntheses are of two main types, both based on the original conceptual framework for the review. For qualitative data the information from the individual studies is summarized in narrative form and tables, predominately using words. Alternatively, or in addition, if the data are of suitable quantitative form, the information can be brought together as part of a statistical meta-analysis.

A meta-analysis essentially adds a number of studies together using a statistical method that gives the greatest weight to the studies with the smallest standard errors, which usually means the largest studies. The formulae for the meta-analysis statistics are shown in Appendix 3. A further challenge currently being addressed by staff at the EPPI-Centre is the synthesis of material from studies that ask different kinds of research question (e.g. Harden et al. 2001; Rees et al. 2001; Shepherd et al. 2001).

One source of bias for systematic reviews arises due to the way in which studies are or are not published. If studies showing a positive (beneficial) effect are more likely to be published than negative or inconclusive studies, this will give a biased estimate of effect. One method of determining the existence of this 'publication bias' is to draw a funnel plot. This plots the effect size of a study (on the x-axis) against its sample size (on the y-axis). Very small studies will have a high probability of showing an inconclusive effect even if the intervention is effective, just as they will have a raised probability of showing a positive effect if the intervention is ineffective. If there is no publication bias, small studies should be scattered along the x-axis, with the larger trials being situated closer to the true estimate of effect (as they are less subject to variability).

Refereeing and beyond

When a review is completed, and the draft report written, it is sent, like the review protocols, for peer refereeing. These referees bring in perspectives from policy, practice and academic backgrounds. One or two-page summaries are also written from these and other perspectives and these eventually appear with the revised review on REEL.

The review report and the 'perspectives' are underpinned by the keywording codes and detailed data extractions for studies from the reviews which are also available on REEL. This level of accessibility and transparency is set up to encourage amendment in the light of constructive criticism or new research becoming available – no EPPI review is the last word. This is illustrated below by the English Review Group's series of reviews, as this series includes not just a map and five reviews at a particular point in time, but an updating of a map and a review from one year to the next.

Methods for the review: what is the impact of ICT on 5–16-year-olds' literacy in English?'

This section lays out the background to the review and then presents the review stages outlined above in considerable detail, to prevent the need for repetition in other chapters of this book.

Review development and participation

As is discussed in Chapter 1, the development of this review was underpinned both by a theoretical framework and by policy and practice concerns. At the protocol development stage and throughout the review a range of different potential research users influenced the review's scope by virtue of the make-up of the review's advisory group. This included serving secondary and primary schoolteachers, an advisory primary literacy expert and an acting parent governor, as well as individuals with primarily academic positions. Most members were parents of school-age children. This group determined the topics for the review. It also commented on the draft protocol and on the map of studies, in particular advising on which sub-areas of ICT and literacy were most appropriate for in-depth review. At the end of the two-year review period, a group of students, teachers, LEA advisory teachers, parents, researchers and governors attended a colloquium to discuss the final draft of the report and assist with planning for its dissemination.

The review was conducted over a two-year period. In the first year, the research literature was mapped out and one in-depth review, concentrating on networked ICT, was published (Andrews *et al.* 2002). In the second year, this map and the first in-depth review were updated, and four further in-depth reviews completed.

Identifying relevant studies

Searching was initiated in May 2001 and was limited to research written in the English language. The search terms were based on:

- Condition/outcome: literacy near English; literacies near English; reading English; writing English; learning near English; teaching near English; dyslexia near English; (read or reading) near (learn* or teach*); learn* near (writing or write or spell or spelling); teach* near (writing or write or spell or spelling); reading disability.
- Intervention technology: ICT; information and communication technology*; CAL; CAI; networked technology*; computer*; mobile phones; multimodal communication technologies; IT; digital media; internet; multimedia; CD-ROM; hypertext; interface* and software.
- Population: child or children; infants; teenagers; pupils; adolescents.

The following eight electronic databases were searched: PsycINFO, ERIC (Educational Resources Information Center), BEI (British Education Index), SSCI (Social Science Citation Index), the Cochrane Library, SIGLE (System for Information on Grey Literature in Europe), Dissertation Abstracts, and C2–SPECTR (The Campbell Collaboration's Social, Psychological, Educational and Criminological Trials Register). Searches looked for studies by combining sets of terms for English literacy processes and outcomes (e.g. 'literacy near English', 'learning near spelling', 'dyslexia near English'), ICT intervention (e.g. 'ICT', 'computer', 'mobile phones') and children or young people (e.g. 'child', 'children', 'infants', 'pupils'). A combination of controlled term and free-text (abstract and title) searches were used for ERIC, BEI and PsycINFO. All other databases were searched using free-text terms only.

Six members of the review team and the advisory group hand searched the following 12 key journals in the fields of literacy and ICT: *English in Education* (RA); *Australian Journal of Language and Literacy* (TL); *Education, Communication and Information* (RA); *Changing English* (AB); *Dyslexia* (MS); *Journal of Educational Computing Research* (CT); *Research in the Teaching of English* (RA); *Literacy Learning: Secondary Thoughts* (TL); *English in Australia* (TL); *English in Aotearoa* (TL); *Reading and Writing* (PH); *and Education Media International* (TL). Where editions were available, the indexes of these journals for the years 1990 – 2001 were scanned using the inclusion and exclusion criteria for the mapping study described below. All papers identified as potentially relevant were screened by four members of the review team on the basis of the abstracts and, where necessary, a reading of the full paper. Potentially relevant documents were identified from relevant websites and publication lists and screened as described above for journals. A similar searching process was carried out on the bibliographies of all relevant systematic reviews, and potentially relevant studies were also identified on an ad hoc basis on reading full reports. Members of the Review Group were also invited to identify potentially relevant studies from their knowledge of the field. Full details of the searching are available in Appendix A of the first review (Andrews *et al.* 2002).

To be included in the mapping study, a paper had to be about the impact of ICT on literacy learning in English and focus on study populations of children and young people aged between 5 and 16. In addition, papers were only included if they were one of the following study types: systematic reviews; evaluations of the processes or outcomes associated with an intervention; or evaluations of something other than an intervention, e.g. a needs assessment.

Papers were excluded if they met any of the following criteria:

- Exclusion on scope: not ICT or literacy; not children aged 5–16, or main focus not children aged 5–16; not about the impact of ICT on literacy learning and/or teaching, or vice versa.
- Exclusion on study type: editorials, commentaries, book reviews; policy documents; prevalence or incidence of ICT in literacy learning; non-systematic reviews; non-evaluated interventions; surveys examining a range of curricular activities; resources;

bibliography; theoretical paper; methodology paper; non-evaluated non-interventions; dissertation abstracts, unless randomized controlled trials (RCTs).
- Exclusion on setting in which study was carried out: settings in which a language other than English is being used as a primary medium for literacy learning, i.e. include ESL and EAL, exclude EFL.
- Exclusion on publication status: if published before 1990 or if report contains only the preliminary findings of as yet otherwise unpublished research.

Screening on the basis of these criteria was first done on titles and/or abstracts alone. One reviewer screened all the citations found through electronic database searching, and 90 per cent of these (those retrieved from the PsycINFO, ERIC and BEI databases) were also screened independently by a second reviewer. Any disagreements were discussed and resolved. For purposes of quality assurance, a further screening exercise of a 5 per cent random sample was undertaken independently by two members of the review team and a 2.5 per cent random sample by a further two. Scores of inter-rater reliability were calculated using the Cohen's Kappa.

The electronic searches were updated in August 2002 on PsycINFO, ERIC, BEI, SSCI, SIGLE, C2-SPECTR and Dissertation Abstracts. In addition, members of the review team and advisory body who hand searched key journals in the field for the 2001–2 review undertook hand searching of the same journals for the period July 2001–Oct. 2002 in order to identify any other potentially relevant studies not retrieved through the updated electronic searches. These were screened by a member of the review team initially using titles and abstracts, and all potentially relevant studies were then sent for and screened to assess whether they met the inclusion criteria which were the same as in the previous round with the exception of a change for the study type to: 'an exploration of relationships, an evaluation, or a systematic review'. For pragmatic reasons, the database for 2002 was closed on 30 November 2002. Any studies received after that time will be included in the next update.

Describing the studies found

As described already, an initial mapping of the literature was followed by several in-depth reviews. These are described in turn, with details of updating presented where appropriate.

The descriptive mapping

At the start of the descriptive mapping full reports were obtained and first classified according to a standardized 'core' keywording system developed by the EPPI-Centre (EPPI-Centre 2001a). This classifies studies in terms of the type of study; the country where the study was carried out; the educational focus of the study; and the study population. For outcome evaluations, studies were also keyworded in terms of the intervention provider and the type of intervention. In addition, studies were then classified according to an additional standardized keywording system, developed for the purposes of the review (review-specific keywords). The strategy classifies studies in terms of literacy, learning and ICT focus of the study, type of information technology intervention and outcomes reported.

In addition, the principal aspect of literacy focused upon by the study was categorized into 'psychological' or 'social and/or cultural/critical', where:

- Psychological aspects or representations of literacy are those which focus principally on internal dimensions: cognitive advances, mental processing, literacy as expressed via thought, internal dialogue, and individual expression. The underlying conception of literacy is one which sees it as the development of individual skills and capabilities.
- Social and/or cultural/critical aspects or representations are those which are not only socially embedded – most classroom practices or interactions with a computer are – but which inform literacy with an interactive, social dimension, whether that interaction is between student and student, student and teacher, or student and different audience. The underlying conception of literacy is one which sees it as the development of social skills and capabilities.

All members of the Review Group completed a pre-keywording moderation exercise involving four papers to standardize keywording procedures. Thereafter, the English Review Group coordinator double-keyworded 5 per cent of the total number of included papers; and three members of the review team (including one from the EPPI-Centre) double-keyworded 2.5 per cent of the total number of included papers. In a post-keywording moderation exercise, all members of the project team plus a representative from the EPPI-Centre double-keyworded two included papers, one of which was discussed at the meeting. Between the first and second year of the review, the EPPI-Centre's guidelines for core keywording had been amended, particularly simplifying the type of study into descriptive, exploration of relationships, and evaluation (either naturally occurring or researcher-manipulated) (EPPI-Centre 2002a). In addition, the Review Group's own review-specific keywords on literacy, learning and ICT focus were streamlined. All studies in the map were re-keyworded using both new sets of guidelines. For the purposes of quality assurance two members of the review team and one member of the EPPI-Centre independently screened a random sample of 10 per cent of the studies in the updated database. After double screening, the inter-rater reliability scores were calculated using the Cohen's Kappa. For the purposes of quality appraisal a random sample of papers was double re-keyworded by two members of the EPPI-Centre.

The in-depth review stage

The five in-depth reviews were characterized by the following additional inclusion/exclusion criteria:

- Studies for the in-depth review entitled 'What is the impact of networked ICT on 5–16-year-olds' literacy in English?' were those characterized on the map by the review-specific keyword 'networked'.
- Studies for the in-depth review entitled 'What is the effectiveness of ICT on 5–16-year-olds' literacy in English?' were those characterized on the map by the keyword 'randomized controlled trial'. (Cluster randomized trials were only included if each arm contained more than two clusters, and if there was no unit of analysis error.) Additionally, the trials had to have an appropriate non-ICT control group; include a literacy based intervention (reading, writing or spelling); include at least one quantified literacy outcome measure (reading, writing, or

spelling test or curriculum-based assessment); and include sufficient data in order that reviewers could calculate effect sizes (either means of post-tests or mean gain scores with numbers and standard deviations in both intervention and control groups or means and numbers and either a precise p value or t value).

- Studies for the in-depth review entitled *'What is the impact of ICT on 5–16-year-olds' literature-related literacies in English?'* were those characterized on the map by the keyword 'literacy'. The additional inclusion criteria were: any intervention which involves the utilisation of ICTs in some way in teaching/learning contexts where the object of study is literature and which analyses in some way the impact of one or more ICTs on the development of literature-related competences (and vice versa); and which focuses on the development of literature-related literacies in both home and school settings.

- Studies for the in-depth review entitled *'What is the impact of ICT on literacy learning in English of learners between 5–16 for whom English is a second or additional language?'* were those characterized on the map by the review-specific keywords 'ESL' or 'EAL'. To be included, studies would have to be based on a clear body of empirical data, which the authors had collected in a systematic way, and retained for examination and analysis. Studies which had no obvious data, or which were based on very subjective and/or inconsistent field coding would not be included. Similarly, case studies which examined just one student or unit would not be included if they were purely descriptive. If an intervention was involved (and analysed), however, then the study would be included. Studies had to report on progress (process, product or both) of ESL learners; the language of instruction must be English (or primarily English); the language of the wider community (or a large part of it) must be English; and English must be the (or an) official language.

- Studies for the in-depth review entitled *'What is the impact of ICT on the learning of literacies associated with moving image texts in English, 5–16?'* were those characterized on the map by the review-specific keyword 'moving image'. The literacies could be within the context of English and media education, or their broad equivalent subject domains.

Data extraction of the included studies was undertaken independently by two reviewers, using standardized sets of guidelines. The set applied to the studies contained in the review 'What is the impact of networked ICT on 5–16-year-olds' literacy in English?' (EPPI-Centre 2001b) was further developed during 2002 and a modified set of guidelines (EPPI-Centre 2002b) was therefore applied during the remaining four in-depth reviews.

Where relevant, quantitative information was calculated using a standard measure of effect for the range of literacy outcomes in the included trials (effect size). An effect size is a standardized measure that allows studies using different outcome measures to be compared using the same metric (i.e. the mean difference between groups divided by a pooled standard deviation). In order to present these effect sizes the most appropriate literacy outcome measures at immediate post-test were selected. If a 'total' reading, writing or spelling test was used in addition to a variety of subtests, the 'total' test was selected. If a number of 'total' tests were used the outcome selected was the one felt to have the most important educational significance. Where there were two outcomes of equal importance both effect sizes were calculated for the syntheses.

The guidelines were also used to gauge the weight of evidence an individual study brought to the review as described above. The weight of evidence assessments were then taken into consideration in both the narrative syntheses and the meta-analyses.

Two reviewers independently extracted data and assessed the weight of evidence for each study and then compared their results. Differences were discussed and resolved. A sample of studies was also data extracted and quality assessed by members of the EPPI-Centre, and any differences were discussed and resolved.

Synthesis

A narrative synthesis of the included trials was undertaken using the conceptual framework described in Chapter 1. Where appropriate, a statistical synthesis of outcomes (meta-analysis) was also used. Some of the studies were pooled in a series of meta-analyses that investigated effectiveness in different aspects of ICT and literacy. To investigate whether or not there was any publication bias in research in the effectiveness of ICT on literacy learning a funnel plot was drawn.

Concluding remarks

As this chapter has shown, systematic reviews provide one way of bringing together accumulating evidence in an explicit manner. The extended examples in this book taken from the first reviews of the EPPI-Centre's English Review Group reveal one model of this approach. The approach to research synthesis used by this and other Review Groups has been the subject of criticism, mainly by educational researchers in the UK, in the early years of the EPPI-Centre. As the overview at the start of this chapter points out, many appear to have been based on misunderstandings of systematic review methods or are criticisms more of poor application of these methods, rather than of the methods themselves; however, many challenges remain.

Some challenges are methodological and relate to the nature of the questions which can be addressed by systematic reviews, and the type of study design and data which can be included. In addition there are few agreed criteria for judging the methodological quality of primary studies across a range of study types. There is insufficient infrastructure currently in terms of training, sustainability and, of course, people and other resources, to support all the reviews that might be useful. There is a need to explore ways of making user involvement real and valuable, both to improve the reviews and to facilitate their influence on practice and policy. Timing is important as the policy need is always for quick answers. Reviews of research are likely to be quicker than primary research, but they are not instant, unless there are existing and up to date reviews in an openly accessible library of such reviews.

As an indication of the level of active interest in systematic reviews in education in the UK, Figure 7.2 shows the geographical locations of members of current EPPI Review Groups. Worldwide links through the Campbell Collaboration and other international organisations should help to create a climate in which systematic reviews can take their appropriate place within the world in which research, practice and policy interact.

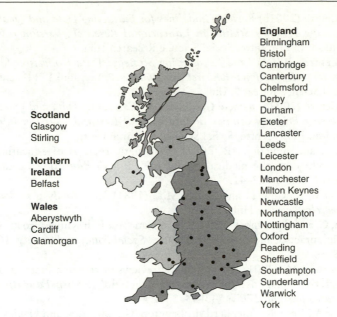

England
Birmingham
Bristol
Cambridge
Canterbury
Chelmsford
Derby
Durham
Exeter
Lancaster
Leeds
Leicester
London
Manchester
Milton Keynes
Newcastle
Northampton
Nottingham
Oxford
Reading
Sheffield
Southampton
Sunderland
Warwick
York

Scotland
Glasgow
Stirling

**Northern
Ireland**
Belfast

Wales
Aberystwyth
Cardiff
Glamorgan

Figure 7.2 Bases for members of EPPI Review Groups

References

Andrews, R., Burn, A., Leach, J., Locke, T., Low, G. and Torgerson, C. (2002) 'A systematic review of the impact of networked ICT on 5–16-year-olds' literacy in English (EPPI-Centre Review), *Research Evidence in Education Library*, 1, London: EPPI-Centre, Social Science Research Unit, Institute of Education.

Campbell, R., Pound, P., Pope, C., Britten, N., Pill, R., Morgan, M. and Donovan, J. (2003) 'Evaluating meta-ethnography: a synthesis of qualitative research on lay experiences of diabetes and diabetes care', *Social Science and Medicine*, 56(4): 671–84.

Cook, T.D., Cooper, H., Cordray, D.S., Hartmann, H., Light, R.J., Louis, T.A. and Mosteller, F. (1992) *Meta-Analysis for Explanation*, New York: Russell Sage.

Davies, P. (2000) 'The relevance of systematic reviews to educational policy and practice', *Oxford Review of Education*, 26(3 and 4): 365–78.

Dickersin, K. (1997) 'How important is publication bias? A synthesis of available data', *AIDS Education and Prevention*, 9: 15–21.

EPPI-Centre (2001a) *Core Keywording Strategy: Data Collection for a Register of Educational Research, Version 0.9.4*, London: EPPI-Centre, Social Science Research Unit.

EPPI-Centre (2001b) *Review Guidelines for Extracting Data and Quality Assessing Primary Studies in Educational Research, Version 0.9.4*, London: EPPI-Centre, Social Science Research Unit.

EPPI-Centre (2002a) *Core Keywording Strategy: Data Collection for a Register of Educational Research, Version 0.9.5*, London: EPPI-Centre, Social Science Research Unit.

EPPI-Centre (2002b) *Review Guidelines for Extracting Data and Quality Assessing Primary Studies in Educational Research, Version 0.9.5*, London: EPPI-Centre, Social Science Research Unit.

Evans, J. and Benefield, P. (2001) 'Systematic reviews of educational research: does the medical model fit?', *British Education Research Journal*, 27(5): 527–41.

Glass, G.V., McGaw, B. and Smith, M.L. (1981) *Meta-Analysis in Social Research*, Beverley Hills: Sage.

Gough, G. and Elbourne, D. (2002) 'Systematic research synthesis to inform policy, practice and democratic debate', *Social Policy and Society*, 1(3): 225–36.

Hammersley, M. (2001) 'On systematic reviews of research literatures: a "narrative" response to Evans and Benefield', *British Educational Research Journal*, 27(5): 543–54.

Harden, A., Rees, R., Shepherd, J., Brunton, G., Oliver, S. and Oakley, A. (2001) *Young People and Mental Health: A Systematic Review of Research on Barriers and Facilitators*, London: EPPI-Centre, Social Science Research Unit.

Hillage, J., Pearson, R., Anderson, A. and Tamkin, P. (1998) *Excellence in Research in Schools*, London: Department for Education and Employment/Institute of Employment Studies.

Light, R.J. and Pillemer, D. (1984) *Summing Up. The Science of Reviewing Research*, Cambridge: Harvard University Press.

Noblitt, G.W. and Hare, D.W. (1988) *Meta-Ethnography: Synthesizing Qualitative Studies*, Beverley Hills: Sage.

Oliver, S., Peersman, G., Harden, A. and Oakley, A. (1999) 'Discrepancies in findings from effectiveness reviews: the case of health promotion for older people', *Health Education Journal*, 58: 78–90.

Popay, J., Rogers, A. and Williams, G. (1998) 'Rationale and standards for the systematic review of qualitative literature in health services research', *Qualitative Health Research*, 8(3): 341–51.

Rees, R., Harden, A., Shepherd, J., Brunton, G., Oliver, S. and Oakley, A. (2001) *Young People and Physical Activity: A Systematic Review of Research on Barriers and Facilitators*, London: EPPI-Centre, Social Science Research Unit.

Shepherd, J., Harden, A., Rees, R., Brunton, G., Garcia, J., Oliver, S. and Oakley, A. (2001) *Young People and Healthy Eating: A Systematic Review of Research on Barriers and Facilitators*, London: EPPI-Centre, Social Science Research Unit.

Slavin, R.E. (1984) 'Meta-analysis in education: how has it been used?', *Educational Researcher*, 13(8): 6–15.

Weiss, C.H. (1979) 'The many meanings of research utilization', *Public Administration Review*, 39: 426–31.

Chapter 8

Conclusion

Richard Andrews

In this brief concluding chapter, I summarise the results of the five in-depth reviews; explore their implications for policy, practice and further research; and come to some tentative conclusions about the field. To remind readers, the overall research question that the five reviews were attempting to answer was 'What is the impact of ICT on literacy learning in English, 5–16?'

The five in-depth reviews

The effectiveness of ICT interventions on literacy learning

Within the analysis of the effectiveness of different types of ICT interventions on a range of literacy outcomes, results were mixed. In the cases of word processing and speech synthesis, there was positive benefit. Specifically, in the case of word processing, there was a large positive benefit in writing quality (which was statistically significant) in one outcome study and a modest benefit in writing quality (which was not statistically significant) in another. As far as speech synthesis is concerned, only one of the 12 RCTs evaluated for the analysis of effectiveness focused on this aspect of the impact of ICT on literacy learning; it showed a large positive effect for the intervention which was statistically significant.

The one study that looked at the effectiveness of networked ICT noted a positive effect size in its two main outcomes, but neither of these effect sizes was statistically significant. It is impossible to say from this study whether the effect of networked ICT was positive or negative. Similarly, the evidence for the effectiveness of computer-mediated texts was equivocal.

For computer-assisted instruction (CAI) interventions, however, the data overall suggest a negative effect on literacy outcomes. Two of the eight studies showed a statistically harmful effect, while a further three noted a non-statistically significant harmful effect. None of the three remaining studies, all of which showed a positive effect, was statistically significant. A notable exception to the overall pattern of outcomes on studies of CAI interventions is in the effect on spelling, where a pooled meta-analysis of studies showed a small, but non-significant, benefit of CAI on spelling outcomes. Three further studies on CAI and reading were not sufficiently homogeneous to come to an overall conclusion as to their effectiveness; whereas two studies on word processing indicated an overall positive effect on writing quality after meta-analysis of their results.

Of two meta-analyses of studies investigating the impact of computer-mediated texts on comprehension, one suggested that there was a small, but statistically insignificant, gain for the control group (i.e. the group without ICT intervention) and the other suggested a small positive gain for the experimental group (with borderline statistical significance). Results are therefore inconclusive in this regard.

Overall the studies identified in the review were of 'medium' or 'high' quality, but the sample sizes were small, ranging from 20 participants to 120 participants. Small trials are likely to miss important effect sizes (either positive or negative) of ICT on literacy outcomes. In addition all the included RCTs were US-based. The generalisability to a UK or other settings is therefore questionable. The sample of pupils in seven out of the 12 included trials consisted wholly or partly of pupils experiencing learning disabilities or difficulties or specific learning disabilities. Again this limits the potential generalisability of the results.

Key conclusions from this particular review are that:

- policy-makers should refrain from any further investment in ICT for literacy until at least one large and rigorously-designed randomised trial has shown it to be effective in increasing literacy outcomes
- teachers should be aware that there is no evidence that non-ICT methods of instruction and non-ICT resources are inferior to the use of ICT to promote literacy learning
- a series of large, rigorously-designed RCTs to evaluate ICT and literacy learning across all age ranges from 5 to 16 is required.

Moving image literacies

There is a lack of empirically-based studies of moving image literacies, most of the existing studies concentrating on the exploration of relationships in the field. What evidence there is suggests benefits of digital formats in moving image production; though this evidence cannot, at present, be considered conclusive.

Three of the nine studies that were used in the in-depth review suggest a beneficial impact on print literacy (specifically writing) of engagement with digital moving image media (computer animation production and computer game-play).

A larger number of studies (not all within the systematic review) found confirmation of theoretical models of moving image literacies, based in several cases on social semiotic models of multimodal communication. These studies can be regarded as contributing to an understanding of the nature of multimodal literacies; they operate largely inductively, by generating theoretical patterning from the data they analyse. As such, they offer useful ways to understand learning processes related to the moving image. One of the most consistent themes running through the papers studied in the in-depth review is the argument for a wider conception of literacy beyond print, which can include visual and other communicative modes.

Taken together, there is a strong sense across these studies that a literacy in moving image media should have certain characteristics. It should be on the one hand systematically understood as a communicative practice in which the details of semiotic work can be addressed by educators; and on the other hand, as a practice which is rooted in the cultural experiences of children across a wide range of media.

The empirical studies, however, often fail to distinguish sufficiently between media production and digital media production. It is therefore difficult to form a general picture of the benefits of digital formats on the basis of these studies. What can be said is that the motivational power of digital moving image was suggested, though again it is impossible to rule out other explanations for the increased motivation of pupils, or to gauge the lasting motivational effect of digital media on the development of print-based or moving image literacies.

In short, the findings to date permit only very limited conclusions. Because of limited sample sizes (despite the quality of qualitative analysis) the results can be seen as suggestive and as contributing towards further clarification of the theoretical landscape, rather than as evidence of positive impact of moving image media on (wide and narrow conceptions of) literacy, or vice versa.

Implications for policy, practice and research are that:

- moving image literacy needs to be seen in terms of 'writing' as well as 'reading'
- moving image literacy is not confined to English in schools, but needs to be seen as addressed within the arts and models of ICT curricula
- rather than considerations of financial outlay on equipment, issues of curriculum time and design, appropriate pedagogies and interpretations of literacy are more important
- training in digital moving image production should be incorporated into the initial and continuing professional development of teachers
- existing small-scale qualitative studies need to be complemented by more in-depth qualitative analysis of children's moving image work and also by larger studies, combining qualitative and quantitative outcome methods
- further research is needed to distinguish between the impact of digital formats on the one hand and media production work on the other, separating both of these from motivational factors
- there should be further development of teacher-based research through the DfES' Best Practice Research Scholarships scheme (or equivalent, and in other countries), extending the scheme to embrace longitudinal as well as cross-sectional studies.

The impact of ICT on literature-related literacies

A common strand in the research reviewed on literature-related literacies is that rather than measuring the impact of ICT on the learning of literature-related literacies, it has tended to point to the conclusion that it is teachers who matter more than the technology. 'Impact' is mediated by teachers in the classroom, and specifically by the discourses that teachers and students create in the classroom and school context. The ideology, values and practices of the teachers mediating the learning experience are more significant than the impact of the technology *per se*.

A number of studies reviewed focused on the social interaction that can be fostered in an environment that integrates ICT and suggested positive ways in which ICT can foster collaborative meaning making *around* texts. Within a largely reader-response theory of reading literature, this social dimension afforded by ICT was more evident than any change in cognitive aspects of textual response brought about by ICT. In other words, ICT changes the relationship between teacher and student more than it changes the way in which students respond to literary texts.

Although motivation to read and respond to literary texts is largely increased by the intervention of ICT, there is a suggestion that extended duration of exposure to a technology can affect motivation negatively; and that there may be a connection between de-motivation and cognitive aspects of what happens when readers engage with digital texts structured in certain ways.

Implications for policy, practice and further research are that:

- there needs to be a recognition from policy-makers that despite the seemingly secure place of literary studies in the school curriculum, textual practices surrounding literary texts are being affected by ICT and that ICT-based technologies are impacting on the character of literary texts themselves (including the generation of new genres)
- the impact of ICT on literature-related literacies is of more significance for teacher roles than directly in its impact on student responses to literature. Policy changes need to be aware of this
- teachers need to address the relationship between ICT-mediated textual forms, pedagogies and reading practices/ideologies
- more research is needed in mapping the conceptual field of literary studies in relation to ICT, e.g. in hypertext, talking books
- more outcome evaluations are needed in which particular interventions are trialled; but there is also a need for more in-depth case studies or critical evaluations of the practice of using ICT to teach literary awareness
- further classroom-based studies, with teachers as researchers, are needed; and with a more generous time-span than has been the case in most teacher-based research.

The ESL/EAL review

Eight studies were included in the in-depth review: four at primary level and four at secondary. Three studies were considered to have a 'medium' weight of evidence for the review and the remainder were 'low'. The reasons for this varied from uncertainty about classification, to methodological and analysis problems. The primary result was that it was impossible to find a clear impact pattern. There was some evidence that word processing could under some conditions improve writing and editing quality. There was a general trend towards students finding computer assisted sessions enjoyable and helpful and teachers reported their role changing towards being facilitators. There were some suggestions that integration into regular class procedures and activities, a high-support user-friendly environment and the use of collaborative work with the goal of a concrete end-product aids learning and motivation, but the evidence was not clear-cut or conclusive.

It was found that the research reviewed focused largely on low level literacy skills as opposed to the higher order discoursal skills; the implication is that teacher intervention is important for the learning of these higher skills. Equally, it emerged as a consistent factor (but not always represented in the research approach) that integrating ICT into a learning environment, rather than hiving it off into a separate space, was helpful in ensuring its impact on learning.

In sum, the studies in the review suggest that, where the task is appropriate to students' needs and their language and intellectual level, CALL materials are as useful for teaching ESL as they are for teaching English mother tongue students.

Implications for policy, practice and research are that:

- introduction and development of ICT-based ESL/EAL programmes should be on the basis of careful consideration of the intended role of the computers and software
- where the ICT equipment has a specific and unique role, and where that is clear and observed by practitioners, then it can have a beneficial impact on improving literacy, especially writing skills
- development of ESL/EAL using ICT requires systematic evaluation so that policy-makers obtain essential information on what is effective
- ICT can help create more motivated ESL/EAL learners
- it is not clear what ICT has to offer ESL/EAL learners as distinct from other learner groups (SEN, EFL, at-risk learners)
- there is evidence that suggests the use of ICT in the classroom changes the role of the teacher towards the role of being a facilitator of learning
- the level of sophistication which ESL/EAL software can bring to literacy tasks is often low, such as with word-level operations

and proof-reading; greater use of ICT's potential in text manipulation and other higher order literacy skills is needed
* appropriate training for staff using ICT as a teaching medium with ESL/EAL is necessary
* a number of research studies is needed to address the research question, taking due care to record, monitor and investigate learners' ethnicity and existing level of proficiency in English; the learning processes that particular items of ESL/EAL software engender; the relationship between these processes and the learning/teaching processes of the mainstream classroom and the culture at large; learning gains and attitude changes; and ICT-based outcomes in relation to those of other forms of delivery.

The updated networked ICT review

In 2001/2, an in-depth review on the impact of networked inform-ation and communication technologies on literacy learning in English for 5–16-year-olds was undertaken as part of a larger systematic review of the impact of ICT on literacy development. From searches in a number of internationally recognised databases and in a number of journals by hand, 1,867 post-1990 studies were identified that were of possible relevance to the larger review. Of these, 188 were selected on the basis of a 'protocol' or plan of work, which included exclusion and inclusion criteria. Of the 188 studies relevant to the larger review, 16 pertained to the topic of the impact of networked ICT on literacy learning. These 16 studies were data-extracted and provided the basis for an in-depth review. Overall, eight of the studies in the in-depth review provided no firm basis for accepting their findings and therefore could have little bearing on the answering of the main research question for the in-depth review. Of the remaining eight, two provided theoretical and practical insights into widening conceptions of literacy; five suggested increased motivation and/or confidence in pupils as a result of ICT use with regard to literacy development; and one saw empowerment and ownership as an important factor to bear in mind in an increasingly diverse digital world. Methodological issues were discussed, and a map for future research was drawn.

In the 2002/3 update of the in-depth review on networked ICT and literacy, a further eight studies were included and analysed. These began to shed a different light overall on the research in the field, suggesting that case studies were – for the moment – the most illuminating type of study in this fast-changing field. In total, after the update, eight studies explored relationships in the field (mostly case studies), two analysed naturalistic interventions and the remaining fourteen analysed researcher interventions. The case studies were the most illuminating because they attempted to account for the complex and related factors at play in the role of networked ICT in the literacy classroom; and also suggested ways in which further research in the field might progress, both substantially (in the asking of key questions) and methodologically (in how such questions might be answered).

Implications for policy, practice and research, such as they can be formulated in this particular field, are:

- indications of the motivational impact of networked ICT need to be looked at over a period of time to ensure that the motivation is not merely short-term
- studies of hybrid, multimedia practices need themselves to be hybrid and possibly multimodal
- case studies cannot in themselves be generalized to a large population and need to be complemented by larger-scale studies which test some of the hypotheses that have emerged
- research *about* networked ICT and literacy may never catch up with practice; it may therefore need to consider whether it is better placed contributing to research and development in the field
- teachers are at least as, if not more, important as technologies in the mediation of learning for young people.

Implications

The implications of the five in-depth reviews are here grouped in terms of policy, practice and future research.

Policy

- policy-makers should refrain from any further investment in ICT for literacy until at least one large and rigorously-designed randomised trial has shown it to be effective in increasing literacy outcomes

- moving image literacy needs to be seen in terms of 'writing' as well as 'reading'
- moving image literacy is not confined to English in schools, but needs to be seen as addressed within the arts and models of ICT curricula
- rather than considerations of financial outlay on equipment, issues of curriculum time and design, appropriate pedagogies and interpretations of literacy are more important
- there needs to be a recognition from policy-makers that despite the seemingly secure place of literary studies in the school curriculum, textual practices surrounding literary texts are being affected by ICT and that ICT-based technologies are impacting on the character of literary texts themselves (including the generation of new genres)
- the impact of ICT on literature-related literacies is of more significance for teacher roles than directly on student responses to literature. Policy changes need to be aware of this
- introduction and development of ICT-based ESL/EAL programmes should be on the basis of careful consideration of the intended role of the computers and software
- where the ICT equipment has a specific and unique role, and where that is clear and observed by practitioners, then it can have a beneficial impact on improving literacy, especially writing skills
- development of ESL/EAL using ICT requires systematic evaluation so that policy-makers obtain essential information on what is effective.

Practice

- teachers should be aware that there is no evidence that non-ICT methods of instruction and non-ICT resources are inferior to the use of ICT to promote literacy learning
- training in digital moving image production should be incorporated into the initial and continuing professional development of teachers
- teachers need to address the relationship between ICT-mediated textual forms, pedagogies and reading practices/ideologies
- ICT can help create more motivated ESL/EAL learners
- it is not clear what ICT has to offer ESL/EAL learners as distinct from other learner groups (SEN, EFL, at-risk learners)

- there is evidence that suggests the use of ICT in the classroom changes the role of the teacher towards the role of being a facilitator of learning
- the level of sophistication which ESL/EAL software can bring to literacy tasks is often low, such as with word-level operations and proof-reading; greater use of ICT's potential in text manipulation and other higher order literacy skills is needed
- appropriate training for staff using ICT as a teaching medium with ESL/EAL is necessary
- teachers are at least as, if not more, important as technologies in the mediation of learning for young people.

Research

- a series of large, rigorously-designed RCTs to evaluate ICT and literacy learning across all age ranges from 5 to 16 is required
- existing small-scale qualitative studies need to be complemented by more in-depth qualitative analysis of children's moving image work and also by larger studies, combining qualitative and quantitative outcome methods
- further research is needed to distinguish between the impact of digital formats on the one hand and media production work on the other, separating both of these from motivational factors
- there should be further development of teacher-based research through the DfES' Best Practice Research Scholarships scheme (or equivalent, and in other countries), extending the scheme to embrace longitudinal as well as cross-sectional studies
- more research is needed in mapping the conceptual field of literary studies in relation to ICT, e.g. in hypertext, talking books
- more outcome evaluations are needed in which particular interventions are trialled; but there is also a need for more in-depth case studies or critical evaluations of the practice of using ICT to teach literary awareness
- further classroom-based studies, with teachers as researchers, are needed; and with a more generous time-span than has been the case in most teacher-based research
- a number of research studies is needed to address the research question, taking due care to record, monitor and investigate learners' ethnicity and existing level of proficiency in English; the learning processes that particular items of ESL/EAL software engender; the relationship between these processes and the

learning/teaching processes of the mainstream classroom and the culture at large; learning gains and attitude changes; and ICT-based outcomes in relation to those of other forms of delivery

- indications of the motivational impact of networked ICT need to be looked at over a period of time to ensure that the motivation is not merely short-term
- studies of hybrid, multimedia practices need themselves to be hybrid and possibly multimodal
- case studies cannot in themselves be generalized to a large population and need to be complemented by larger-scale studies which test some of the hypotheses that have emerged
- research *about* networked ICT and literacy may never catch up with practice; it may therefore need to consider whether it is better placed contributing to research and development in the field.

Conclusions

Taking into account the present in-depth reviews and the previous one on the impact of networked ICT on literacy learning for 5–16-year-olds (Andrews *et al.* 2002), which has been updated for inclusion in this book, what can be said in answer to the overall research question, 'What is the impact of ICT on literacy learning in English, 5–16?'

First, the question is a complex one because its four key terms – impact, ICT, literacy and learning – are neither stable nor simple entities. We have tried to define these as best we can in order to carry out the research and bring more conceptual clarity to the field. We are clearer about the first three than we are about the fourth, as we have yet to carry out an investigation of the learning and teaching models implied by the studies we have examined.

Such complexity leads naturally to the second conclusion, *viz* that there is no single answer to the overall research question, other than 'mixed'. Specific answers to the sub-questions are more helpful in determining the positive and negative impact of ICT on literacy learning. If we were to draw out the main conclusions from the two-year study and from the five in-depth reviews reported here, they would be that:

- word processing and speech synthesis functions of ICT suggest the most positive applications to literacy learning to date
- CAI and CALL applications tend to operate at the lower levels of literacy within a narrow (psycholinguistic) model of language development, whereas (inversely) moving image research tends to focus on higher order compositional skills in sociocultural contexts
- there is a need for ICT to address the higher orders of literacy and literacy development
- many of the studies of the impact of ICT on literacy tend to be on learners with special educational needs rather than on the majority of learners in schools
- there is no evidence that non-ICT methods and non-ICT resources are inferior to ICT-based approaches in learning outcomes
- the motivation to engage with literacy practices is often intense at the beginning of mediation via ICT, but then tails off
- more theoretical work is needed to chart the landscape of relationship between narrow conceptions of literacy and broader conceptions, including moving image literacies and other ICT-informed literacies – such advances may well come from more and better in-depth qualitative studies
- more large-scale research studies are needed, including the use of RCTs to determine effect
- there is a need for longitudinal studies of the use of ICT in the classroom in relation to literacy development
- the teacher's role is changing with the increasing presence of ICT within the classroom and school; this change from teacher to mediator/facilitator needs to be considered by policy-makers, practitioners themselves and by researchers
- teachers and the discourses they shape within the classroom are more important than the ICT that accompanies literacy learning.

Two further points may be made by way of conclusion: first, that the future of research in the area of ICT's impact on literacy learning in schools must have teachers at the centre of the process, otherwise research is in danger of setting up frameworks and methods that do not apply to the classroom. Second, the caveat we made in the introduction on the impact of networked ICT on literacy learning still stands: our project has concentrated on the impact of ICT on literacy development rather than on the wider picture of the symbiotic relationship between ICT and literacy/

literacy development. We think there has been virtue in concentrating on this aspect of the field in that we are much clearer about the advantages and limitations of ICT and its relationship with literacy/literacies than we were at the beginning of the project. But the larger, more difficult questions of how to research symbiosis remain.

English Review Group working document

Systematic review on 'The impact of ICT on 5–16-year-olds' literacy in English'.
Screening studies for inclusion in 'Mapping' section of review.
Exclusion criteria: to be included, a study must NOT fall into any one of the following categories.

If a study is to be excluded, record reason by using appropriate exclusion code (One, Two, Three, Four, or Five)

Exclusion on scope

One   Not ICT or literacy:
- *Definition of ICT:* ICT stands for 'information and communication technologies', networked technologies with a multimodal interface, ie. networked and stand-alone computers, mobile phones with the capacity for a range of types of communication, and other technologies which allow multimodal and interactive communication.
- *Definition of literacy:* Literacy can be defined narrowly, as the ability to understand and create written language. It is, however, frequently defined in two broader senses, and both are included in the present study. Firstly, the scope can be expanded so that written language becomes written language and graphical or pictorial representation. Secondly, the skill can be treated as social, rather than psychological; in this view literacy is the ability to operate a series of social or cultural representations. Since sets of expectations and norms differ depending on the situation, the social view of literacy entails a number of different 'literacies'.

Two   Not children aged 5–16, or main focus not children aged 5–16

Three Not about the impact of ICT on literacy learning and/or teaching, or vice versa
- *Definition of the impact of ICT on literacy:* Impact will be defined as the result on end-users (here children between 5 and 16) of an intervention aimed at improving the teaching or learning of

literacy. It may also be the result of a non-intervention activity which could reasonably be expected to increase or decrease literacy. Either can be considered as 'literacy-related activities'. Entailment: A research study which focuses on teachers' or learners' perspectives, opinions or strategies, may be considered to deal with the impact of ICT on literacy as long as it refers to a specific literacy-related activity.

Exclusion on study type

Four
(a)   Editorials, commentaries, book reviews
(b)   Policy documents
(c)   Prevalence or incidence of ICT in literacy learning
(d)   Non-systematic reviews
(e)   Non-evaluated interventions
(f)   Surveys examining a range of curricular activities
(g)   Resources
(h)   Bibliography
(i)   Theoretical paper
(j)   Methodology paper
(k)   Non-evaluated non-interventions[1]
(l)   Dissertation abstracts (unless RCTs)

Exclusion on setting in which study was carried out

Five   Settings in which a language other than English is being used as a primary medium for literacy learning, i.e. include ESL and EAL, exclude EFL.

Acknowledgements

This document was developed from the EPPI-Centre Working Document on Inclusion Criteria for Mapping. Training and support are acknowledged.

Note

1   A non-evaluated non-intervention would typically describe a naturally occurring phenomenon, rather than evaluating it. So an ethnographic case-study of a classroom, or a learning site of some other kind, could fall into this category if it didn't attempt to evaluate processes or outcomes. Of course, all description is a kind of evaluation (as it will be based on selection according to certain principles); but if those principles aren't articulated, then it is hard to judge the work as research.

EPPI-Centre educational keywording sheet

1. **Identification of report**
   Citation
   Contact
   Handsearch
   Unknown
   Electronic database
   (please specify) ....

2. **Status**
   Published
   In press
   Unpublished

3. **Linked reports**
   Is this report linked to one or more other reports in such a way that they also report the same study?

   Not Linked
   Linked (please provide bibliographical details and/or unique identifier)
   ....
   ....

4. **Language** (please specify)

5. **In which country/countries was the study carried out?** (please specify)
   ....
   ....

6. **What is/are the topic focus/foci of the study?**
   Assessment
   Classroom management
   Curriculum*
   Equal opportunities
   Methodology
   Organisation and management
   Policy
   Teacher careers

Teaching and learning
Other (please specify)
....

*6a. **Curriculum**
Art
Business Studies
Citizenship
Cross-curricular
Design & Technology
Environment
General
Geography
Hidden
History
ICT
Literacy – first language
Literacy – further languages
Literature
Maths
Music
PSE
Phys. Ed.
Religious Ed.
Science
Vocational
Other (please specify) ....

7.   **Programme name** (please specify)
....
....

8.   **What is/are the population focus/foci of the study?**
Learners*
Senior management
Teaching staff
Non-teaching staff
Other education practitioners
Government
Local education authority officers
Parents
Governors
Other (please specify) ....

*8a. **Age of learners** (years)
0-4
5-10
11-16
17-20
21 and over

*8b. Sex of learners
   Female only
   Male only
   Mixed sex

9. **What is/are the educational setting(s) of the study?**
   Community centre
   Correctional institution
   Government department
   Higher education institution
   Home
   Independent school
   Local education authority
   Nursery school
   Post-compulsory education institution
   Primary school
   Pupil referral unit
   Residential school
   Secondary school
   Special needs school
   Workplace
   Other educational setting (please specify) ....

10. **Which type(s) of study does/do this report describe?**
   A. Description
   B. Exploration of relationships
   C. Evaluation
      a. naturally occurring
      b. researcher-manipulated
   D. Development of methodology
   E. Review
      a. Systematic review
      b. Other review

Please state here if keywords have not been applied from any particular
category (1–10) and the reason why (e.g. no information provided in the
text)
....
....
....

11. **Focus of the report** (tick all that apply)

literacy	learning	ICT
genre	assessment	CAI/CAL
literacies	dyslexia	hypertext
literature	learning difficulties	moving image
multimodality	learning disabilities	multimedia
reading	motivation	word processing
spelling	teaching	
writing	ESL/EAL	
	audience	
	comprehension	

12. **Type(s) of intervention or non-intervention** (tick <u>all</u> that apply)
   computer – stand alone (software)
   computer – networked (e-mail)
   computer – networked (internet)
   mobile phone
   other technology (please specify) ....

13. **What principal aspect(s) of literacy is the study focused on increasing?**
   (tick <u>all</u> that apply)

13a. – psychological aspects or representations
   – social representations and/or cultural/critical representations

13b. – writing print and graphical or pictorial representations
   – reading print and graphical or pictorial representations

14. **Which outcomes are reported?** (tick <u>all</u> that apply)
   test results – reading
   – writing
   – spelling
   examination results
   motivation/engagement
   self-esteem/attitude
   quality of writing
   increased awareness of process
   quality of reading
   quality of response to multimedia

15. **If study type in question 10 is C.b. (researcher-manipulated), is it**

   A. RCT
   B. Trial
   C. Other

KEYWORDER .... DATE ....

A systematic review of the impact of ICT on 5–16-year-olds' literacy in English

Appendix 3

Examining heterogeneity in meta-analysis

The following formulae are based on the chapter 'Statistical methods for examining heterogeneity and combining results from several studies in meta-analysis' by Deeks *et al*.

Calculating Hedges' *g*

First, Cohen's *d* is calculated from the means, standard deviations and sample sizes entered into outcome records.

$$d = \frac{\overline{X}_1 - \overline{X}_2}{s}$$

Where:

$\overline{X}_1$ = mean of intervention group

$\overline{X}_2$ = mean of comparison or control group

$$s = \sqrt{\frac{(n_1 - 1)SD_1^2 + (n_2 - 1)SD_2^2}{n_1 + n_2 - 2}}$$

Where:
n_1 = sample size for group 1
n_2 = sample size for group 2
SD_1 = standard deviation group 1
SD_2 = standard deviation group 2

g_c, Hedges' *g*, is then calculated by correcting *d* for sample size using the formula:

$$g_c = g\left(1 - \frac{3}{4N - 9}\right)$$

Where: n_1 = sample size of group 1,
n_2 = sample size of group 2
and
$N = n_1 + n_2$

and the standard error of g_c is calculated:

$$SE = \sqrt{\frac{n_1 + n_2}{n_1 n_2} + \frac{(g_c)^2}{2(n_1 + n_2)}}$$

Formulae for combining studies using the inverse variance method

Each study is weighted according to the formula

$$w_i = \frac{1}{SE(\Theta_i)^2}$$

where Θ_i is the effect size of the study and SE is its standard error
The combined effect Θ_{iv} is calculated:

$$\Theta_{iv} = \frac{\sum w_i \Theta_i}{\sum w_i}$$

and its standard error:

$$SE(\Theta_{iv}) = \frac{1}{\sqrt{\sum w^i}}$$

The heterogeneity statistic, Q, is calculated using the formula below. Since it is distributed as a chi-square, a p-value is obtained with $k-1$ degrees of freedom where k is the number of effect sizes being combined.

$$Q = \sum w_i (\Theta_i - \Theta_{iv})^2$$

95% confidence intervals for individual and overall effects are calculated using the formula:

$$\Theta \pm (1.96^* SE(\Theta))$$

The test statistic (z) for overall effect is:

$$z = \frac{\Theta}{SE(\Theta)}$$

Reference

Deeks, J.S., Altman, D.G. and Bradburn, M.J. (2001) 'Statistical methods for examining heterogeneity and combining results from several studies in meta-analysis', in M. Egger, G. Davey Smith and D. Altman (eds) (2001) *Systematic Reviews in Health Care*, London: BMJ Publishing Group.

Glossary

Assessment The measurement of learning performance, either 'summative' (at the end of a process of learning) or 'formative' (during the process of learning).

Audience This term can refer to an audience of one, as in a single respondent or listener, or to an audience of inestimable size via the Internet.

CAI/CAL 'Computer-assisted instruction' and 'computer-assisted learning'. The former tends to be associated with self-supporting computer programs which replace the teacher, rather than complementing him/her.

Comprehension Understood by psychologists as a key activity in learning to read, and complementing 'decoding' of printed text. Understood by English teachers as a now outmoded form of textual analysis and appreciation in which a series of questions is asked about a text to elicit understanding.

Dyslexia Difficulty with learning to read or spell, arising from problems with grapho-phonemic equivalence.

ESL/EAL 'English as a Second Language' (as opposed to English as a Foreign Language) refers to the language as learnt and taught by people for whom English is not a first language or mother tongue, but is acquired (often with much teaching help) as a second language with distinct functions in society. 'English as an Additional Language' is now the preferred term, as it implies that English may be learnt not only as a second language, but as a third or fourth language in a culture.

Genre Basically, a type or category of text. In the Australian tradition, it means 'text-type'. In the North American sociological tradition, it means identifiable patterns of 'social action' grounded in texts.

Hypertext   Computer-readable text which allows for extensive cross-referencing, particularly 'vertically', i.e. it is possible to conceive of and present text in vertical layers rather than conventionally, in a horizontal plane.

ICT   ICT is taken to include stand-alone computers, networked technologies with a multimodal interface, mobile phones with the capacity for a range of types of communication, and other technologies which allow multimodal and interactive communication.

Learning   The transformation from one state of personal knowledge to another.

Learning difficulties   These are difficulties with learning encountered by any children or young people at any age, and are associated with a variety of barriers to learning that may be temporary and which may be overcome by teaching strategies, appropriate curricula, etc.

Learning disabilities   These are more profound and developed difficulties with learning encountered by children and young people at any age, and are associated with a variety of barriers to learning that are usually more permanent.

Literacies   Literacy can be defined narrowly, as the ability to understand and create written language. It is, however, frequently defined in two broader senses, and both are included in the present review. First, the scope can be expanded so that written language becomes written language and graphical or pictorial representation. Second, the skill can be treated as social, rather than psychological; in this view, literacy is the ability to operate a series of social or cultural representations. Both these expansions of the narrow term 'literacy' can be termed 'literacies'.

Literacy   The ability to read and write.

Literature   Fictional, dramatic or poetic texts.

Motivation   The impulse and/or desire to learn.

Moving image   Film, video, animation.

Multimedia   The use of more than one medium of communication to convey information. Whereas multimodality refers to the combination of more than one mode of communication (e.g. the verbal and visual), multimedia is a more technical term referring to a range of media which can convey such modes of communication.

Multimodality   The use of more than one mode of communication to convey 'information'. All texts, in a sense, are multimodal in that printed writing is both visual and verbal. Multimodality is usually reserved for the combination of word and image and/or sound conveyed via the computer screen.

Reading   The act of bringing meaning to print.

Spelling   Orthographic representation of phonemes, morphemes and words.

Teaching   Teacher-centred strategies for encouraging, eliciting and developing learning in pupils and students.

Word processing   The composition of verbal language on screen, usually on computer and in substantial form – as opposed to 'texting'.

Index